CONSTRUCTION MATERIALS
FOR
ARCHITECTS
AND DESIGNERS

CONSTRUCTION MATERIALS FOR FOR ARCHITECTS AND DESIGNERS

Terry L. Patterson, AIA

College of Architecture
University of Oklahoma

PRENTICE HALL
Englewood Cliffs, New Jersey 07632

Library of Congress Cataloging-in-Publication Data

Patterson, Terry L.
 Construction materials for architects and designers / Terry L.
 Patterson.

  Includes index.
  ISBN 0-13-168345-4
  1. Building materials. I. Title.
TA403.P315 1989
691—dc20   89-3972
                                                               CIP

Editorial/production supervision and
  interior design: Marcia Krefetz/Fred Dahl
Manufacturing buyer: Dave Dickey

Note: The material in this book may be subject
to local codes and regulations. Check with
local building officials when planning your
project.

 © 1990 by Prentice-Hall, Inc.
A Division of Simon & Schuster
Englewood Cliffs, New Jersey 07632

Printed in the United States of America
10 9 8 7 6 5 4 3 2 1

ISBN 0-13-168345-4

Prentice-Hall International (UK) Limited, *London*
Prentice-Hall of Australia Pty. Limited, *Sydney*
Prentice-Hall Canada Inc., *Toronto*
Prentice-Hall Hispanoamericana, S.A., *Mexico*
Prentice-Hall of India Private Limited, *New Delhi*
Prentice-Hall of Japan, Inc., *Tokyo*
Simon & Schuster Asia Pte. Ltd., *Singapore*
Editora Prentice-Hall do Brasil, Ltda., *Rio de Janeiro*

To my wife, Jennie

CONTENTS

4: WOOD IN ARCHITECTURE 50

5: PROPERTIES OF MASONRY 72

6: ASSEMBLIES IN MASONRY 83

7: MASONRY IN ARCHITECTURE 112

13: CONCRETE IN ARCHITECTURE   237

14: CONCLUSION   263

APPENDICES

GLOSSARY   294

INDEX   296

PREFACE

Acknowledging the nature of building materials in architectural design is a concept often praised but rarely applied as a consistent and methodical practice. Although the architecture of Frank Lloyd Wright includes occasional violations, it has a general sense of harmony with the essence of its materials. Patterns suggesting purposeful intent with regard to the nature of materials are lacking in contemporary architecture. Equally rare are discussions of methodology and criticism of material expression.

The haphazard record of attention to materials expression in architecture and literature suggests two possibilities. First, it is likely that the philosophical aspects of materials are not important to many designers. It is also possible that many do not understand the nature of building materials. This work is addressed to both groups.

This book describes the nature of wood, masonry, steel, and concrete with both philosophical and technical reasoning. The materials are examined with regard to the properties of their substances and the characteristics of their assemblies in construction. The visual impact of building form and detailing that complements or violates the nature of the materials is examined. The expression of these materials in historic and contemporary architecture is analyzed. Conclusions are drawn regarding the expressive effect of material applications. Checklists are provided for the analysis of materials expression in architecture.

The book promotes neither compatibility nor incompatibility between the nature of materials and their expression. It is intended to help the designer exercise control over this relationship and thus increase the general effectiveness of the design.

TLP
Norman, Oklahoma

CONSTRUCTION MATERIALS
FOR
ARCHITECTS
AND DESIGNERS

Chapter 1

INTRODUCTION

If building materials are to be examined as an element of architectural expression, it is prudent first to clarify the realm in which the role is played. Structures without artistic intent are excluded. Material considerations beyond the practical are superfluous in purely utilitarian buildings. Conversely, reasoning beyond the purely utilitarian is warranted for materials contributing to an artistic statement. It is architecture as both an art and science where the principles described here have meaning. Building materials are not alone in this arena. A number of considerations influence design expression.

DESIGN GENERATORS

Traditionally, creative people have acknowledged something outside themselves as the inspiration for their creations. A blank sheet of paper can be discouraging if faced without a motivating force. A goal gives the creative process direction and purpose. Limits and guidelines focus the mind and assist in control of the progress. For the genius, this is an intuitive process. For others, a methodology is useful.

Since architecture is scientific as well as artistic, design guidelines rooted in order seem more appropriate than those that are arbitrary. Deriving the guidelines from recognized systems of order lends a sense of purpose and, therefore, credibility to them. The following considerations with their associated systems of rules are among the major forces influencing architectural design.

Welfare.   Architects are licensed to protect health, safety, and welfare in the production of architecture. This design influence differs from many motivators in that, although subject to interpretation, it is not optional. Law, by way of building codes and ordinances, is the vehicle for implementing this need. For example, ordinances derived to provide natural light and ventilation require that buildings be set back specified distances from property lines. In

Figure 1–1 The buildings with stepped forms comply with code requirements designed to provide light and ventilation to the lower floors of adjacent buildings. The stepped buildings have been shaped by the need to protect health and welfare.

New York and other large cities where the distance varies with height, stepped building forms have been the result (Fig. 1–1). Codes affect building plans and facades through egress requirements that correspond to the need for fire protection. Fire escapes and stair towers often participate in a building's image. Considerations of personal welfare in terms of architectural expression are subtle but apparent.

Function.   The functions of many buildings may be identified by their form. The size of spaces and the nature of glazing often vary with function. Compare apartments (repetitive small rooms) to churches (large central space). Compare auto showrooms (transparent walls) to art museums (opaque walls). Occasionally, buildings are purposefully designed to reflect the varied functions within (Fig. 1–2). The intensity of function's influence on building form is subject to the designer's judgment.

Figure 1–2 The functions of International House in Philadelphia are expressed in the facade. Restaurants and shops are on the ground floor. Directly above are offices. The next three levels are apartments. The sixth floor consists entirely of offices. The upper eight floors are dorm rooms. Architect: Bower and Fradley.

Figure 1-3 The covering of the column webs with mirrors was possible because of a generous budget for the Price House in Bartlesville, Oklahoma. Architect: Bruce Goff.

Cost. The budget can visibly affect expression in architecture. Size, variety of forms, quality of materials, and sophistication of detail are some of the conditions affected (Fig. 1-3). Although costs may rarely be ignored, the architect usually may choose which aspects will be developed or sacrificed in meeting a budget. A limited budget differs from most design generators in that it is generally seen as being a negative rather than a positive influence.

Site. Deriving inspiration for expression from the site has been cyclical in its popularity. Wright promoted respect for the site. International School architects did not. Certainly, some sites offer more inspiration than others (Fig. 1-4). While the trend is to respect the site, sensitivity and desire continue to monitor the intensity of this design motivator.

Figure 1-4 The extraordinary site for the Chapel of St.-Michel d'Aiguilhe, Le Puy, France, limits the perimeter of the building and encourages a response to the verticality of the land form.

Figure 1–5 The likelihood of high water during hurricane season forced this school in Plaquimines Parish, Louisiana, to a position high above grade. It is an example of the environment affecting a building design.

Environment.   Attention to environmental conditions was once more of a choice than now. Energy shortages of the 1970s heightened interest in environmental forces, which in some locales, have a lasting influence through energy codes. Since such forces as the sun and wind are not applied symmetrically, their influence on architectural form can be clear. The difference in the treatment of glass on the south facade compared to the north, for example, is a readily apparent response to the sun. Earth sheltering in response to air temperature lowers a building's profile. Hurricane-driven rain can have the opposite effect (Fig. 1–5).

Context.   The frequency of architectural designs that respond to the characteristics of surrounding buildings has varied in recent history (Fig. 1–6). The primitive vernacular, where buildings are similar because they respond

Figure 1–6 This San Francisco condominium responds to its context with a new interpretation of the traditional bay window. Architect: Donald MacDonald.

to the same local influences, and the International Style, where the same building may occur anywhere in the world, illustrate the extremes of attention to context. Currently, respect for context is considered a legitimate influence on architectural design. It is generally a matter of choice except where established patterns of size and position encourage conformity through zoning laws and in historic districts where ordinances dictate style, such as in Sante Fe, New Orleans, and Boston.

Artistic Vocabulary.   Unity, proportion, rhythm, balance, contrast, harmony, and other artistic principles are the traditional vocabulary of the designer. These principles have been the most consistently applied design influences, although interpretations have varied with era and designer. Although ignoring artistic principles does not result in punitive, economic, or other measurable penalties, artistic failure may be the consequence.

Fashion.   While few designers will admit to following the current fashion, many will recognize this tendency in others. Without the willingness of designers to emulate current popular forms we would have had no Gothic, Victorian, International, Post Modern, or other styles. A name for unique forms and detailing is coined only after repetition. Designers are free to ignore or follow fashion. To deny verbally but to follow in practice is common.

Concept.   Design goals and a plan for their achievement are the components of a concept. The concept includes decisions regarding the roles of all form generators. It might also include a nearly arbitrary theme that has the role of inspiring and providing direction. John Johansen has identified the nature of an electronic component as the inspiration for some of his buildings (Fig. 1–7). Animals, plants, or more abstract themes might fulfill such a role. Justification of an arbitrary concept may be difficult. Once committed to an arbitrary concept, however, subsequent decisions seem purposeful. The achievement of unity is facilitated by following a concept, even an arbitrary one.

Figure 1–7   John Johansen used the nature of electronic circuitry as inspiration for the design of the Oklahoma Theater Center. The form is clearly affected by the concept.

Figure 1–8 The brick towers of the Richards Medical Research Building on the University of Pennsylvania campus by Louis Kahn illustrate the impact of technology on building form. They house vertical services, including fresh-air intake and exhaust ducts.

Technology. The issue of technology has practical and philosophical sides. Structural limitations have affected the nature of buildings throughout history. With advancing structural technology providing increased numbers of options, the visual effect of structure has, to some degree, become a matter of choice. This leads to the philosophical side. To emphasize or subdue the effect of technology on architectural expression is a decision each designer makes based on, among other things, personal philosophy (Fig. 1–8). Other technological components that may be emphasized or subdued include mechanical and plumbing systems, lighting, acoustics, vertical transportation, and building materials.

Materials are one of several generators of architectural expression that may be ignored or embraced. Discussion in subsequent chapters illustrates their potential.

EXPRESSION

If a material's "personality" is revealed in its use, the expression is in the nature of the material. If the installation gives a false impression of the material's properties, the expression violates its nature. Accommodating or violating the nature of a material has visual impact, in part, due to expectations. Compatible expressions lend a sense of order and harmony to the image. Purposeful violations may create visual tension, a legitimate component of visual expression. Haphazard violations are likely to dilute the visual order. They signify a loss of control over the work.

The expressive effect of materials is apparent when comparing two constructions that are identical in every respect except materials. Such a comparison can be made between two entry foyers of Herrenchiemsee Castle in Germany (Fig. 1–9). The symmetrical building was to have had identical entries. One remains unfinished. The brick of the unfinished space gives a sense of serenity and unity. The other foyer is lively and opulent. The difference in the feelings projected by the two spaces is due entirely to the visual impact of the materials.

Expectations.   People are generally aware of common materials and their traditional uses through observation of the physical environment. Artists sometimes tamper with expectations of the public when they produce known forms in the "wrong" materials. Viewers' reactions to giant ice cream bars made of stuffed fabric, for example, are evidence that common attitudes about certain materials exist but have been denied in the sculptures. More significantly, these works suggest that materials are a medium of communication that can result in an emotional response.

Expectation juggling can also be found in buildings. Although window glass and neon tubes are inappropriate for a basketball backboard and hoop, they occur in this form over an entry to a residence by BumpZoid (Fig. 1–10). The role of materials in the visual twist is significant. They inspire images of rebounding basketballs and broken glass.

For the most part, the backboard window addresses structural expectations. Nonstructural properties of materials manifest themselves in the detailing of surfaces, edges, corners, and other details.

Figure 1–9   These two foyers of Herrenchiemsee Castle in Germany are identical except for their materials. The differences in feelings projected by the spaces can only be due to the differences in materials.

Figure 1–10 The glass blackboard with a neon hoop serves as a window and porch light for a garage/study. Although backboards may be found on garages, the materials do not meet expectations for the image. (Printed with permission of the architect, BumpZoid Ben Benedict and Carl Pucci, Architects.) Photo by BumpZoid.

The relationship of details to overall expression can be seen in a branch of graphic art where efficiency and clarity of expression are the key to success. Cartoonists' manipulations of facial features are a standard technique for communicating ideas. The expression of the whole (the face) is derived from the collective expression of the parts (eyes, eyebrows, mouth). Editorial cartoonists identify a few unique characteristics of a face and exaggerate them (Fig. 1–11). The exaggeration is an easily identified symbol. Recognition of the idea is facilitated. The same can be true of building details and their effect on architectural expression. An exaggerated response to a material property can add clarity to the visual impact of a detail, component, or building.

Peters

Figure 1–11 Exaggeration of unique characteristics is the key to producing a recognizable caricature. Editorial cartoonist Mike Peters has exaggerated hair and upper lip to create a likeness of Ronald Reagan. (Courtesy of Mike Peters/Dayton Daily News.)

Personalities. The facial features of a cartoon project a different message with each unique combination of traits. Similarly, each material may have a unique visual statement derived from its combination of traits. The concept is not new. Some authors go so far as to speak of materials as if they had personalities. Susan Doubilet referred to the materials in the Italian Trade Center as "sumptuous, punk, decadent, sensuous, elegant, delicate, provocative, and sublime."[1] John Burchard suggested that ". . . we have to learn to combine what we have and to minimize their antagonisms."[2] Ayn Rand summarized the concept in statements of her mythical hero, Howard Roark. Upon being dismissed from architecture school, Roark told his dean, "Here are my rules: what can be done with one substance must never be done with another. No two materials are like."[3]

A philosophy of design based on building materials must grow from the differences in their personalities. While it is true that certain materials have similarities, it is useful to dwell on their differences to magnify sensitivity. The personality or nature of a material includes the properties of its substance and the characteristics of its assemblies in construction.

Philosophy. The role of a material in architectural expression depends on the relationship between its nature and its use. Assuming that design goals include controlling all vehicles of expression, it follows that the expression of materials should be controlled. The premise embraces designing in a way that is both *purposefully compatible* with and *purposefully in opposition* to the nature of a material. It rejects accidental harmony or contrast. Accidents result in random expression which leaves part of the visual impact out of the designer's control. To express the nature of a material is a way to create harmony in design. To oppose a material's nature creates visual tension. Either may be useful and appropriate for the designer's goals. Since the number of options to express harmony are fewer and more easily defined than those that express discord, discussion will focus on the former. For the most part, the ways to violate the nature of each material will be left to the creativity of the designer.

PROPERTIES

The technical properties of materials are too numerous to be considered separately for expressive purposes. They are grouped under a few general categories to make the system less cumbersome. The penalty for this simplification is the loss of precision in certain terms. For this study, material properties are divided into the following categories:

Form
Strength
Durability
Workability

Form. The shapes that are considered to represent the spirit of a particular material are those that result from the primary manufacturing process, are made of a single piece, and are structural. These are referred to as *primary forms.* All other product shapes are called *secondary forms.* Secondary forms general-

[1]Susan Doubilet, "Mind over materials," *Progressive Architecture,* 62 (August 1981), pp. 95–99.

[2]John Burchard, *Bernini Is Dead? Architecture and the Social Purpose* (New York: McGraw-Hill, Inc., 1976), p. 97.

[3]Ayn Rand, *The Fountainhead* (Indianapolis, Ind.: The Bobbs-Merrill Company, Inc., 1943), p. 18.

ly result from a second manufacturing process or special adjustments to the standard primary manufacturing process. They are often made from or with primary forms. They may be laminated. They may have nonstructural functions such as cladding or decoration. Forms are described by their geometry, attitude (straightness), and refinement.

Forms fall into one of three basic geometries; linear, planar, or blocklike (Fig. 1–12). *Linear* forms are those with one dimension significantly larger than the other two. *Planar* forms have two dimensions significantly larger than the third. *Blocklike* forms have three dimensions without significant differences between them. The length of a linear form may be 100 times its next larger dimension, whereas the length of a blocklike form may be five times its thickness. The need for simplicity prevents the identification of specific ratios that separate the geometries. Intuitive judgment must be used to determine whether a product seems more like a line, plane, or block.

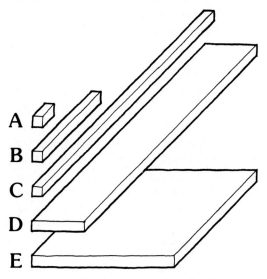

Figure 1–12 The form of A is blocklike. C is linear. E is planar (assuming that it is large enough to be a structural plane). The forms of B and D are borderline cases.

A material's relative level of *refinement* is judged. This includes the precision and visual mass of the primary form, its ability to form thin, closely spaced, precise elements in construction, and the longevity of the precision. Refinement depends on several aspects, including manufacturing, strength, and durability. Refinement is not a measure of value. A low level of refinement does not signify low value. It is simply a description of a physical characteristic. Like all quantitative characteristics, refinement is expressed most clearly at its extremes. The rusticity of a material can be exaggerated as a way to express its low level of refinement. The delicacy and precision of a material may be emphasized to express its high level of refinement. Medium levels of refinement may not be exaggerated and therefore have limited potential for expression. The strategy for expressing medium refinement is simply to avoid expressing a high or low level.

Strength.   The *strength* property responsible for the greatest difference in materials expression within this group is the ability to resist tension. The expression of bending strength can also be used to distinguish between materials—but not as clearly as pure tension. Bending is the most violated strength property. It is popular to span or give the appearance of spanning long distances in all materials. Strong materials can span long as well as short distances. Weak materials are limited to the latter. Short spans do not express the potential of strong materials. They confuse the images of strong and weak materials. The expression of strength can clarify the image of a material if the spans of strong materials are exaggerated, the spans of weak materials are minimized, and the spans of medium-strength materials are maintained between the extremes.

Since all materials can resist compression, its potential to distinguish between materials is limited. Reasoning is provided in subsequent chapters for establishing a policy of expression that makes compression less common. Such a policy boosts the ability of compression to clarify material differences. The ability to resist shear has less of an effect on structural image than tension and compression because conditions in architecture often challenge limits of bending before shear. Although deflection often governs beam sizes, it does not offer expressive opportunities that are significantly different from those of bending. Tension, bending, and compression are adequate to distinguish between the strength expressions of materials. Shear, torsion, stiffness, and other structural properties are not addressed individually.

Durability. This term is used with some imprecision. Traditionally in concrete work it means the ability to resist the freeze–thaw cycle. In many materials it is commonly thought to relate to wear and tear. Here *durability* is defined as resistance to all nonstructural destructive forces in exterior applications. Included are the freeze–thaw cycle, corrosion, decay, insect attack, and other types of weathering and deterioration. Expressing high durability (i.e., contact with the earth) is fairly common for the durable materials. The commonness of certain details prevents their being expressive. Exaggerated contact with the earth or exposure to deteriorating elements is necessary to express high durability. Low durability can be expressed by exaggerating the methods that protect the material.

The fire protection of steel usually results in its covering with other materials. While protecting wood offers limited visual opportunities, wood is generally excluded where fire is a threat. The high resistance of masonry and concrete has no expressive outlet. The noncombustibility of these materials cannot be demonstrated by their continued contact with fire. Consequently, the expressive ramifications of fire safety in materials is addressed to a limited degree.

Workability. The degree of ease with which a significant change may be made to the primary form is *workability* (Fig. 1–13). As used here, workability should not be confused with the traditional term used to describe the consistency of plastic concrete. The issue here is the changeability of product form after completion of the manufacturing process. Plastic concrete does not reach that point until it hardens. Materials requiring only simple tools and skills to

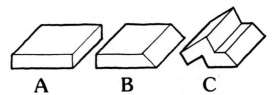

Figure 1–13 The form of A is cut to produce the form in B. It is then bent to produce the form in C. C expresses a higher degree of working than B because the form differs more from the original.

achieve extensive changes in form have high workability. By definition, workability is in opposition to the primary form of a material. To express workability is to subdue primary form characteristics. To express lack of workability is to express primary form. It is possible to express both primary form and workability with compromises to each. Ultimately, the balance of expression between the two is subject to the judgment of the designer.

ASSEMBLIES

Materials may be assembled into building components so as to express or ignore the properties of form, strength, durability, and workability. If attention is drawn to these characteristics, the work is taking advantage of the material's properties to create a visual impact. If in the application it appears that a material has a property that it does not have, the use violates the nature of the material. If the use is in the nature of the material and is also standard practice, the visual contribution is subdued because of its commonness. If a configuration is so common that it is not noticed, it is not expressive. Expression is more than simply exposure. Exaggeration is one tactic to enhance the expressiveness (noticeability) of standard assemblies.

It is useful to limit the number of assembly categories for simplicity. The components of buildings are divided into the following four groups:

> Structures
> Connections
> Surfaces
> Edges

Structures.   This category includes individual components such as beams, columns, trusses, and arches and entire systems of vertical and horizontal support. Form and strength of materials translate into configuration and size of structure. They are the major characteristics determining the nature of a structural system.

Although some materials can form all the structural systems, the goal of seeking uniqueness encourages the assignment of certain systems to certain materials. A purely tensile system would be representative of the material with the highest tensile strength. A compressive system would be representative of the material that can resist only compressive stress. A cantilever would be in the nature of a material that can resist bending stresses. An arch would naturally be associated with a compressive material.

The expression of material form is easily accomplished if the structure is exposed to view. This condition is not recommended for all buildings or even for most buildings, as it would make the built environment monotonous. There are other ways of expressing, revealing, or at least hinting at the configuration of a structure that is partially or completely hidden (Fig. 1–14). Configuration of the windows and cladding can reveal information about the size and shape of the structure underneath. Overall building form can illustrate the general shape of a system, especially for a one-story building. A common form for buildings with floors suspended from above omits the lower floor to show that no compressive support exists at the perimeter. The degree of subtlety with which information about the structure is revealed is a function of the designer's judgment.

Size can be a vehicle for expression for materials at the strength extremes. The span potentials of the weakest and strongest materials are significantly

Figure 1–14 Much can be understood about this structure without its components being exposed to view. The overall shape and configuration of the cladding are revealing.

different. Very large spans are expressive of great strength. Very short spans can be expressive of low strength, especially where numerous columns result. Many closely spaced columns will draw attention to the fact that the beams spanning them are short.

Workability may be expressed in the individual members or in the configuration of the structure. Framing with a shape requiring numerous cuts of individual members expresses workability even if the cuts themselves are not visible. Durability may be expressed in the surfaces and edges of the structural members, discussion of which occurs under those headings.

Connections. This issue focuses on connections between primary forms in structure. Connections between nonstructural members will be examined where it helps clarify the nature of the basic material in question. Form, strength, and durability properties of each material combine to produce an assembly with a configuration and refinement natural and unique to the material. Components can connect by butting, overlapping, merging, or a combination of these conditions (Fig. 1–15). In *butt connections* one member meets the face of the other. Members pass by and extend beyond each other in *overlapping connections.* In *merged connections* the members become one at the intersection.

The consideration of durability has its greatest impact on a connection configuration where joints are designed to shed water. This concern has a visible effect in the overlapping of some cladding materials, for example.

The configuration of a joint is an indicator of refinement. Butt joints require that two components have an exact position and size while overlapping joints have a variable in the length of the overlap. Butt joints require permanent precision as they readily reveal movement. An overlapping connection need not be precise nor maintain exactness during its life span, as its configuration makes irregularities difficult to detect. Butt joints, then, represent a more refined material than that represented by overlaps. For clarity in expression the level of refinement of the connection should match that of its material.

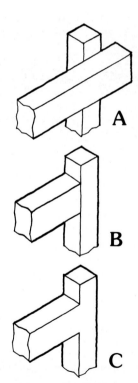

Figure 1–15 The configuration of A is an overlapping connection. B is a butt connection. C is a merged connection.

Surfaces. Included are both the surfaces of individual units and assemblies of units. Cladding is also considered. Form, durability, and workability of a material affect the configuration and exposure of a surface.

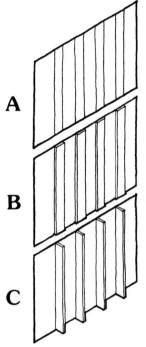

Emphasis on a material's primary form can occur in the configuration of a surface. Positioning the components out of the plane of the surface (back or forward) brings attention to the shape of the component because of its shadow and increased importance (Fig. 1–16). This three-dimensional emphasis of material form is a stronger expression than a two-dimensional emphasis (changes in color and texture only).

The degree of exposure of a surface can express a material's level of durabilty. If a surface is protected from the elements by a coating, the coating becomes an indication that the durability of the material is low. Bright coatings are more noticeable than neutral ones and are therefore deemed to be more expressive. Unprotected surfaces express a high level of durability.

Edges.   This group includes edges that are not corners (which are discussed with connections). The focus is on the top and bottom edges of walls and other components. The perimeters of openings are included. The ends of vertical linear members are included. Durability is the major influence in detailing edges, with form and workability taking smaller roles. The three combine to affect the characteristics of configuration and exposure. *Exposure* is the degree of contact with the atmosphere and earth.

Methods of protecting top edges from moisture can express a material's level of durability. Unprotected tops suggest high durability. Separating the bottom of a component from the earth expresses low durability. Contact with the earth suggests that the material is of high durability (Fig. 1–17).

Figure 1–16 The intensity of the surface expressions increases from A to C. A is a two-dimensional expression. C is a three-dimensional expression. B is three-dimensional but is weaker than C because its pattern projects less and will cast smaller shadows.

Figure 1–17 A hierarchy of durability is expressed with concrete submerged in the earth, masonry touching the earth, steel above the earth, and wood higher than the steel.

The primary form of a material affects expression at edges when it can be identified in the profile of the edge. The expression of workability in the profile of an edge is at the expense of primary form. Since it is only the edge of the primary form that is affected, it is possible that a balance between primary form and workability could be achieved.

ARCHITECTURE

Discussion of each material concludes with an analysis of the material's expression in architecture. Most of the buildings selected as examples were chosen because they are well known and often studied. Others were chosen because their forms and detailing are useful in clarifying certain principles of materials expression. The analyses are based on the exterior images of the buildings except where there is a close visual tie between inside and outside.

Each year scores of buildings are produced with varied levels of regard for traditional and contemporary design theories. While schools and schools of thought embrace one philosophy or another, numerous designers follow their own priorities. Buildings are good because of the creativity of the designer, not because rules were followed dutifully. The analysis of any building is likely to reveal violations of accepted rules and philosophies. They are not necessarily less successful because of the violations. In the complex art and science of building there is room for inconsistency. It is neither suggested that designing in harmony with materials leads to great architecture nor that violating them guarantees failure. Purposeful manipulation of form and detail regarding the nature of building materials gives the designer greater control of a building's visual impact than does accidental manipulation.

In the architectural analyses, judgment is made regarding the compatibility of a material's expression and its nature. Identifications of material violations are not negative comments about the architecture. The success of each building and the relationship of material use to its success are not evaluated in its analysis. Judging the architectural merit of the buildings is left to each person upon whom it is incumbent to use a broader range of criteria than those relating to materials.

Chapter 2

PROPERTIES
OF
WOOD

Wood is unique among structural materials in that it is both organic and occurs in nature. These conditions result in the properties of durability, workability, and precision of form being at the extremes of the ranges. Even though species vary in their properties, conclusions are drawn for wood in general. Although some aspects of form and strength are shared with other materials, wood's unique combination of properties gives it the potential for a clear identity in architecture.

FORM

Identifying the primary form of wood is both simplified and confused by the well-known image of trees. The primary forms are not logs and poles but lumber. Log structures and pole buildings have been used in past eras and have some use today. The overwhelming majority of wood in architecture, however, is lumber. The characteristics of boards, dimension lumber, and timbers, therefore, establish the nature of wood in architectural design.

Primary Form. Like trees, lumber is straight and linear (Fig. 2–1). The longest members available have lengths that are many times greater than their next-largest dimensions. For example, a 2 × 4 is commonly available in a length 75 times greater than its actual width. The essence of the side view of primary forms in wood is a straight line.

Lumber is rectangular, solid, and simple in all elevations and sections. It ranges from about an inch thick to a foot or so deep (Fig. 2–2). Sizes at the extremes overlap the images of other products and materials. Very thin sections approach the image of steel. Massive sections are similar to glued laminated timber and small concrete beams and columns. Consequently, the most clear expression of the primary form of wood is with the sizes between the extremes.

Figure 2–1 Lumber reflects the rectilinearity of trees and the rectangularity compatible with contemporary manufacturing and construction practices.

Figure 2–2 These timbers are near the upper limit of the range of standard sizes available in lumber. Glued laminated timber and concrete beams also come in these sizes.

Form characteristics are the most important to expressing the spirit of wood. They are the most readily understood by the general public as well as professionals. Wood's linearity readily distinguishes it from masonry and concrete (Fig. 2–3). The expression of other characteristics is necessary to isolate wood's image from that of steel, which is also linear. Wood's solid, simple rectangular profile and relatively low level of refinement distinguish it from steel.

The form of wood is the least refined of that of the four materials. Dimensions vary among species, manufacturers, and within a product itself. As delivered, ends may not be square and warpage is common (Fig. 2–4). Checks and splits may be present, especially in larger members (Fig. 2–5). The precision of wood form is likely to decrease after weathering (an issue of durability). Precision varies with the grade of wood. Higher-quality wood has fewer flaws, is more precise, and warps less than do lower grades.

Wood's relatively low level of refinement is recognized by professionals and laypersons alike. When wood buildings and other structures are called rustic, it is their lack of refinement that is being described. Low refinement is not a negative property as the term "rustic" suggests. To subdue a sense of rusticity in exterior applications is to subdue the nature of wood. To detail so as to accommodate this property is to express the nature of wood.

Figure 2-3 Upon approaching this structure, the linearity of the wood is apparent before other characteristics.

Figure 2-5 The checking in the surface of this timber is a result of the natural seasoning process. The fibers separated due to shrinkage as the wood dried. This irregularity of form is typical of the larger sizes of single-piece timbers.

Figure 2-4 The curve of the shadow on the board reveals an imprecision of form known as cupping. Boards with this and other imperfections of form are received periodically from the supplier.

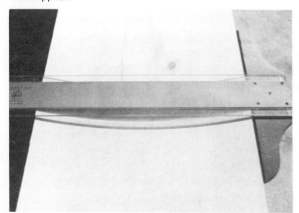

Figure 2-6 This assembly fails to exploit the roundness of the column because the beams form a right angle. If the beams formed an acute or obtuse angle, it would give the roundness of the column a more meaningful role in the expression of the system.

Secondary Forms. Round logs and poles are secondary forms of wood because of their limited use in architecture. They have primary-form characteristics except in section. In addition to the primary-form characteristics that may be expressed, the property of roundness is available for expression. Simply exposing the members is the least sophisticated expression of the characteristic. Bringing special attention to the roundness or using it to some advantage will produce more intense expressions. The round profile accommodates all angles of connecting members, while a rectangular section works best with components at right angles. Connecting beams to a round column so as to form right angles between the beams fails to exploit the roundness of the column and therefore fails to add to its expression (Fig. 2-6).

Laminated timber (glued laminated) is a secondary form because of the second manufacturing process required to produce it from lumber. Like the primary form, it is linear, solid, and rectangular in cross section. In contrast to lumber, it may be manufactured in curved or tapered shapes and is available in much larger sizes. These characteristics make laminated timber special among wood products. They distinguish the spirit of laminated timber as being slightly different from that of lumber and are worthy of expression (Fig. 2-7).

Figure 2-7 Glued laminated timber's potential for nonrectilinear shapes has been exploited for a clear visual effect. The option is not available in lumber and thus the aesthetic order of the structure is, to large degree, based on a unique characteristic of the product. (Courtesy of American Institute of Timber Construction, (AITC), Vancouver, Washington.)

Figure 2–8 The overall form of these trusses (stored upside down) differs from that of lumber in its greater size, triangular elevation, and openness.

Caution is warranted in expressing laminated timber in sizes at the extremes available. The smallest members overlap with sizes available in lumber. The larger sections are similar in size to concrete columns and beams. Avoiding the images of lumber and concrete is a discipline useful for achieving a clear identity for glued laminated timber. No attempt is made to justify the practice based on utility.

Since trusses are assembled from lumber, they are secondary forms of wood. Truss components as individual pieces exhibit the traits of the primary form. The truss itself varies from the primary form when it has sloped or curved chords (Fig. 2–8). Its large size and openness offers visual options not possible in lumber. Utilizing the open space between members as windows is one way that these secondary product characteristics may find expression in a building facade.

Plywood falls into the secondary category because it is laminated. It is rectangular and solid like the primary form but is not linear. It is significant that much plywood (and hardboard) siding imitates the linearity of lumber (Fig. 2–9).

Figure 2–9 Grooved plywood siding imitates the linearity of boards. The grooves weaken the panel and obscure its identity once installed.

Grooves in the panels imitate joints between boards and thus give an impression of "real" wood. Much of the plywood visible in facades is of this type. The grooves misrepresent the identity of the panel and therefore violate the nature of this secondary wood form. The popularity of the linear surface illustrates the significance of linearity to the image of wood. The major property of plywood that makes it different from lumber is its nonlinear rectangularity. To express plywood is to draw attention to this characteristic.

Shakes and shingles are considered secondary forms of wood here because they are not structural. Like plywood, an isolated shake or shingle is rectangular without being linear (Fig. 2–10). Widths vary, but the exposed halves of shakes and shingles are nearly square. To cover approximately half the shingle by overlapping cannot be considered a violation of the product's nature. It is the standard system and is what makes shingles shed water. An expression of rectangularity is achieved if the shapes of the exposed halves are clear in a facade. Tight joints and flush butts subdue individual identities. Spaced units and staggered butts clarify them. Curved and angled butts help clarify the identity of each shingle as the shadow line changes direction at each joint.

The small size of shakes and shingles gives them visual options not available in the larger components. Shingles may be positioned out of alignment with adjacent units to produce curved or undulating shapes. Such patterns express the uniqueness of shakes and shingles among wood products.

Beveled board siding is not structural and, therefore, is a secondary form of wood. It is like the primary form of wood except for its section, which is approximately triangular. Expression of the triangular profile is possible and legitimate but not likely to have a strong visual impact. The standard installation of beveled siding yields a linear image. The visual impact of the linearity is not great because it is so common. Expression may be enhanced by causing the linearity to be more remarkable than the standard pattern of horizontal parallel lines.

Figure 2–10 Installation of this shingle will hide the upper half from view. The expression of the lower half's rectangularity will reflect the spirit of the whole, if not its exact proportion.

Figure 2–11 The rough texture was cut into the lumber after the basic manufacturing process. It does not reflect the nature of wood texture, as it does not result from standard and routine processes.

Texture. The texture of wood relates to the process that produced it. Hand-hewn surfaces have maximum roughness, reflecting the axe or adz that chipped away a piece at a time. Surfaces produced early in the sawmill process are more regular but still reflect impressions of the cutting blade. The most common surface of modern lumber is produced by a planer. The surface is relatively smooth with no teeth marks. Because it is standard and the most common, a smooth surface is considered compatible with the nature of wood. Rough surfaces resulting from the standard cutting processes prior to planing or sanding are also compatible, especially for larger timbers, where they are common. Special ordering is typically required for rough-sawn surfaces in the smaller sections, but they have the advantage of being slightly stronger than their smooth counterparts since sanding reduces the size of the section. Rough surfaces produced after planing for decorative effect will not be considered compatible with the nature of wood (Fig. 2–11).

STRENGTH

The range of working stresses available in wood is above that of masonry and below those of concrete and steel. It has moderate strength in tension, compression, and bending. Using wood to resist all three stresses is standard practice. There is merit in expressing wood in all three modes simultaneously rather than focusing on one. Focusing on compression is the least clear expression of the uniqueness of wood.

All four materials have useful compressive strength. Expressing compression in wood does nothing to suggest that wood is different from the other materials. The expression of wood's moderate compressive strength will yield a neutral visual statement if the spirit of wood is to be maintained. Wood is the lightest of the four materials. An intuitive view of stability suggests that heavy materials belong at the bottom of an assembly, with lighter materials above. Since the material at the bottom is likely to be in compression, it follows that heavier materials seem more compressive in nature than the lighter material. The reasoning does not discourage the use of wood in compression. The expression of the uniqueness of wood, however, is not achieved by focusing on a compressive visual image.

Since it is the steel in reinforced concrete that resists tension, wood and steel are the only materials that can resist significant pure tension. Focusing on tension in the expression of wood, however, is not an efficient way to demonstrate the nature of wood. Wood's inability to compete with the tensile

Figure 2–12 Tensile elements are needed to prevent the two trunks from splitting apart. Wood has adequate tensile strength, but the bulk required would interfere with the tree's appearance. The choice of two barely perceptible steel rods illustrates wood's inability to compete with steel on a visual basis.

strength of steel on a utilitarian level is readily apparent in a comparison of allowable stresses. More important, wood cannot compete with steel in tension on a visual basis (Fig. 2–12).

Wood's moderate tensile strength requires a cross section thick enough to make recognition of tensile members difficult. A very thin member such as a wire can resist only tension and is therefore easily identified as a tensile member. Moderately thick wood tensile members can also resist compression, due to their ability to resist buckling. The ambiguity between tension and compression in wood is illustrated in trusses, where only trained personnel can identify which members resist which stress. Often, detailing is not adequate to distinguish between hangers and columns (Fig. 2–13).

Figure 2–13 The expression of the vertical members is ambiguous. Neither their form nor detailing indicate whether they are in tension or compression.

Figure 2–14 The cantilevered spans are extremely large for wood. They overlap the potential of steel. Since steel also shares wood's linear geometry, the expression is ambiguous. Less heroic cantilevers would more clearly express the nature of wood.

Even though significant tensile ability is not available in all four materials, its exhibition alone is not an efficient vehicle for expressing the nature of wood. The usefulness of wood in tension as a utilitarian matter is not challenged.

Wood is one of three materials that can resist significant bending stress. Only masonry cannot. The expression of wood's moderate bending strength cannot (by definition) have a remarkable impact. Since wood cannot span farther than steel, pushing wood to its limit lacks the visual impact of pushing steel to its limit. The longest spans in wood overlap the moderate range of steel, thus reducing the efficiency of strength as a distinguishing property. Each material's uniqueness can be enhanced by limiting wood to moderate spans and steel to long spans. The conclusion of the reasoning is that heroic spans do not express the spirit of wood (Fig. 2–14).

It is in the nature of wood and steel only to express bending resistance in a linear geometry. (Concrete is not a linear material.) Given the absence of reasoning to the contrary, the expression of bending in wood is a reasonably efficient method of demonstrating its nature. Wood's distinction from steel in the expression of bending depends on contrasts in profile characteristics and span limitations.

Wood's ability to perform as linear members in tension, compression, and bending is also shared only with steel. An expression of all three modes without a focus on a particular mode is in the spirit of wood.

DURABILITY

Wood is the least durable of the four materials. Exposure of raw wood to weather turns its light tan to dark gray. Unprotected wood decays in the presence of intermittent moisture. It may be eaten by termites. Weathering may cause the adhesives of laminated products to fail (Fig. 2–15). Cycles of wetting and drying may cause warpage (Fig. 2–16). Wood is far less resistant to weathering and insect destruction than is steel, masonry, or concrete.

Figure 2–15 Weathering of the wood and adhesive of the laminated beam has produced separations between layers and checking of the lumber.

Figure 2–16 Weathering caused the warpage of this wood cladding despite its fasteners.

Protecting wood from deterioration has long been standard detailing policy as a practical necessity. The expression of this limiting property is found in the methods of protection. Many practices that prevent water from penetrating a building also protect the wood of the construction. Because of their role in keeping interior space dry, sloped roofs, overhangs, sills, and similar detailing are not associated with any particular material. Venting louvers for attics and crawl spaces that reduce condensation fall into the same category. Even though these methods protect wood from decay, they are not strong vehicles for expressing the very low durability of wood.

The separation of wood from the deteriorating elements of the earth may be exploited for purposes of expression. A tendency in contemporary detailing is to bring structural and cladding members very close to grade to avoid exposing the foundation. Holding the wood above the ground an exaggerated distance expresses the vulnerability of wood while affording it greater protection. Eight inches is a common dimension between grade and the closest wood. Distances greater than 18 inches are large enough to draw attention. This device is not an exceptionally strong one for expressing wood's low durability. The detailing occurs below eye level and its purpose may be misunderstood. It is certainly a more positive statement than bringing wood into contact with the earth. It is worth exploring as one element in a system of many that collectively express wood's low resistance to deterioration.

Since coatings protect wood from moisture penetration, paint is compatible with the expression of wood in exterior applications. This concept is somewhat controversial. The highly favored appearance of raw wood over paint tends to prejudice reasoning. Unprotected wood cannot maintain an appearance acceptable for most contemporary purposes in most climates of the United States. Its nature is to deteriorate. Interior wood is, of course, an entirely different matter. Clear coatings of exterior wood have proven to be too temporary for most owners (Fig. 2–17). It is common to find clear coatings replaced by opaque coatings upon premature failure of the original.

Bright or contrasting coatings have greater visual impact than do neutral ones and are therefore stronger expressions. Chemically preserved wood is very durable. By the same reasoning, the noticeability of impregnated chemicals is a measure of their expression of the nature of wood. Creosote is highly noticeable by its black color and pungent odor. The brown color of oil-based preservatives is readily apparent. The least noticeable preservatives (water base) are the most common in building construction (Fig. 2–18).

The near invisibility of chromated copper arsenate (CCA) is used as a selling point by producers. CCA-treated wood has a faint green tint. The expression of the chemical is nil compared to the extreme protection afforded the wood. The near absence of expression gives the impression that wood naturally has high durability. Since the message is incorrect, the expression violates the

Figure 2–17 The clear coating on this exposed laminated beam has deteriorated, leaving most of the surface unprotected. After about a year's exposure, it remains only in the dark area.

Figure 2–18 Due to its treatment with a water-based preservative, the post is far more durable than are the other fence components. The nearly identical surface expressions of all the wood illustrate a failure to express the protective system of the post.

nature of wood. It is common to apply a coating to the treated wood. In this case the burden of expression rests with the coating. The chemical protection becomes a safety factor. The fact that the chemicals are hidden is too academic to consider. Chemically treated wood that is hidden from view is not an issue.

WORKABILITY

Wood is the most workable of the structural materials. The ability of wildlife to peck, bore, and fell trees illustrates the ease with which wood may be worked (Fig. 2–19). Anyone that whittles a stick may do so because of its high workability. Cutting similar thicknesses in steel requires more sophisticated equipment. Wood is often worked in three dimensions, whereas steel is rarely worked in more than two. Cutting masonry typically has little effect on its proportions.

Figure 2–19 A beaver cut down the tree with its teeth. The impossibility of felling a steel, masonry, or concrete column by the same process illustrates the significantly higher level of wood's workability.

Figure 2–20 Although entirely hidden in the finished building, the numerous angular cuts at the ends of the beams and joists are expressed in the octagonal building form for which they were necessary.

Working cured concrete is very difficult, as attested by a lack of examples. A sign of wood's very high workability is the ease with which adjustments to its shape may be made in the field, where conditions make working any material more difficult.

The effect of worked wood on building expression takes many forms. A subtle but effective method is the working of structural members that are not exposed but cause the building to have a special shape (Fig. 2–20). A wood building that is triangular, octagonal, free form, or otherwise nonrectangular in shape may have structural members that have been cut or bent and joined at angles other than 90 degrees. Since curves connecting at acute and obtuse angles require more working than do straight segments, curves are more expressive of wood's workability than are rectilinear shapes. In exposing reshaped structural members, workability is less subtly expressed (Fig. 2–21).

Figure 2–21 The curved top of the canopy subtly expresses the workability of wood when viewed from across the street. The exposure of the joists under the roof intensifies the expression by adding linearity to the image in this view. Each joist is a single unit cut from a wider piece of wood.

Figure 2-22 The simplicity of this contemporary worked beam compared to more complex historic examples reflects the prevailing need for economy.

If they are numerous, superficial changes to the form of structural members may affect the character of a building. The shaping of ends has more visual impact than the shaping of edges. Contemporary examples typically show less extensive working than do historical examples (Fig. 2–22). As the cost of labor continues to rise, labor-intensive activities are minimized. The result is fewer and simpler examples of worked structural components and the near-extinction of worked decorative elements.

Superficial but visually effective worked elements are decorative elements such as spindles, balusters, brackets, and trim. They have the advantage of existing, for the most part, only for visual purposes (Fig. 2–23). Few have functional assignments, as demonstrated by their absence on contemporary buildings. Their small size facilitates working in all three dimensions. Turning rounded shapes on a lathe is a simple exercise.

Working wood is less in the nature of the material than it once was, due to increased labor costs. Since the cost of working other materials has also increased, the relative economy of working wood still exists. It is more reasonable, both philosophically and economically, to base an aesthetic system on the working of wood than to base it on any of the other materials.

Figure 2-23 The extensive decorative image of these brackets is achieved by numerous pieces of wood cut and assembled to give the illusion of three-dimensional working.

Chapter 3

ASSEMBLIES IN WOOD

STRUCTURES

The geometry of a structure is derived from the form and strength of its material. Post and beam, platform, and other rectilinear frames and framing systems are compatible with wood's straightness and linearity. They are dependent on wood's bending, compressive, and tensile strengths. Equal spacing of members is a typical characteristic of framed systems, as it increases the efficiency of the system.

Philosophically, wood is less compatible with arches, vaults, and domes. Traditionally, these structures require nonlinear materials having only compressive strength. Numerous European cathedrals illustrate the point with wood gabled roofs built above vaulted masonry ceilings. The wood is straight, the masonry curved. The curved structures can, of course, be produced in wood. Arches express the unique ability of laminated timber to form curves. Lamella vaults and geodesic domes can be made from lumber with extensive shaping of the ends or through the use of steel connectors (Fig. 3–1). Laminated arches

Figure 3–1 Wood lamella and brick vaults are similar in concept. Both use straight pieces to approximate a curve that spans many times the component length. Both develop thrust.

are the most successful of the trio in terms of expression. The small radii of most wood geodesic domes are compatible with the image of material strength but cause problems with cladding. The raggedness that occurs when covering the multiple bends of a geodesic surface with wood or asphalt shingles expresses the mismatch of straight cladding materials with a system that is not. Economical long-span steel systems compete with wood lamella vaulting. Consequently, the wood vault has limited use in contemporary construction.

Expressing the nature of wood is made easier by avoiding structures that do not consist of straight elements. If arches, vaults, and domes are built in wood, much can be done to bring them closer to the spirit of wood than they philosophically are. If a system has no thrust, expressing this fact indicates that the material must have bending strength (Fig. 3–2). Expressing the linearity of the components is a significant distinction from the image of masonry or concrete. Maintaining short spans helps separate the wood image from steel.

Totally exposing a structure is neither the only nor necessarily the preferred way to reveal form characteristics of the wood components. The enclosure or cladding can reveal size, spacing, linearity, and general configuration (Fig. 3–3). Partial exposure can suggest the nature of the characteristics that

Figure 3–2   The structural expression of the curved component over the entry is ambiguous. It is not clear whether the walls at each end resist thrust. If they do, the form is an arch. If not, it is a beam.

Figure 3–3   Although the trusses are covered, detailing reveals their length, span, height, spacing, chord size, strut angle, and quantity.

cannot be seen. In exposed structures the form characteristics of wood may be expressed in a range of intensities. Components exposed flush with the surface form a two-dimensional pattern. The expression of a component on top of a wall surface is slightly more intense, as its depth is revealed and a shadow is added. Freestanding members express their forms most intensely. Nearly all sides of the components may be observed (Fig. 3–4). Exaggerating the number of members needed increases their visual impact. Detailing so that the members cast shadows increases the sense of linearity, as there are twice as many lines in view (Fig. 3–5).

The visual mass of a structure is also related to the form and strength of its material. More cross-sectional area is required in wood to carry a load than is required in stronger materials. The area required may be achieved with a few thick members or numerous thin ones (Fig. 3–6). Maximizing mass and reducing the number of units have the disadvantage of overlapping with images common in concrete. In large single-piece members, availability and surface checking may be a problem. The image of laminated timber may to some degree be separated from that of concrete by minimizing thickness.

Minimizing mass increases the expression of linearity due to the corresponding increase in the number of members. It also increases vulnerability to warpage and competes with the image of steel. Expressing a moderate number

Figure 3–4 The expression of linearity and other characteristics is maximized by the nearly free-standing status of the truss. Its image is transferred to the other trusses because their exposed ends match that of the completely exposed truss.

Figure 3–5 The sense of linearity is doubled by the second set of lines in the form of shadows.

(a)

(b)

Figure 3-6 The columns in A and B have about the same amount of wood in their sections. B is a stronger expression of wood because its linearity is stronger (four lines instead of one), the members are of moderate mass, and it could not be duplicated in concrete.

of members of moderate mass is a compromise that is compatible with wood's strength and other properties.

Linear structures have a common problem. The members act as long lever arms through which lateral loads apply rotational forces to the joints. The ability to resist rotation is dependent on the size of the cross section, which, in linear materials, is small relative to length. The tendency of the joints of a wood structure to change angle from the force of wind or other lateral loads must be accommodated (Fig. 3–7). The methods of stiffening wood structures are therefore expressions of the nature of wood.

Figure 3-7 The angular bracing in this barn has failed due to decay. Wind has forced rectangles in the framing into parallelograms, as the joints of the system do not have the strength to resist rotation.

Triangulation is one of three methods typically used to prevent wood structures from racking (leaning) (Fig. 3–8). Unlike a rectangle, a triangle is inherently rigid. Incorporating triangles with the rectangular shapes stiffens the structure. Triangulation has the advantages of size and recognition over the other stiffening methods.

Panels can also make a structure rigid. Their advantage is their match with the rectangularity of typical wood structures. Their disadvantage is lack of recognition. It is likely that an expressed structural panel will be mistaken for a cladding panel. Recognition can be increased by intermittent use of the structural panels superimposed on a cladding system. Reasoning must conclude that if the panels clearly serve no enclosure purpose, they must be something else. This method does not assure recognition but does expand the design and detailing vocabulary of the designer.

The third stiffening method is to enlarge the joints. This is the way laminated arches achieve rigidity between their vertical and sloped elements (Fig. 3–9). The tapered legs that broaden at the bend of the product give it a unique identity. The expressive disadvantage of this stiffening method in laminated products is that its strong association with the image of the product itself obscures its role in stiffening the structure as a whole. The fairly rare wood gussets connecting the members of trusses are based on this concept. Gussetlike stiffeners between columns and beams have not found significant application, due to the greater efficiency of triangulation. They do have potential for expression since their structural role would be readily understood by an observer.

Given the visual or practical disadvantages of thickened joints and panels as system stiffeners, triangulation yields the greatest visual impact. It shall be considered a major characteristic of structural expression in wood.

Philosophically, wood is an inappropriate support for heavier materials. Wood lintels are rarely used to carry masonry in contemporary construction but are sometimes expressed as doing so (Fig. 3–10). The lack of stability in the form of wood and its tendency to decay make it a poor choice to support

Figure 3–8 The triangular framing of this shelter prevents its leaning when subjected to wind load. They also contribute significantly to the visual character of the building.

Figure 3-9 The laminated component's ability to resist rotation at its bend is expressed in the thickening of the section at that point.

Figure 3-10 This contemporary wood lintel is decorative only; hidden steel carries the brick. The expression violates the nature of wood, as it projects an illusion that wood is a material of permanent rigidity.

a material that must remain permanently rigid. Historic precedents, which often are reasonable guides for pure expression, fail to justify this use (Fig. 3–11). The maintenance required for both the wood and masonry, once tolerated, is unacceptable in contemporary architecture. Hidden steel that actually carries the load in contemporary versions of this detail does not purify the expression. If the wood appears to carry the masonry, the expression violates the nature of wood. Although there are exceptions, a wood structure may be expected to contribute to the image of its architecture the characteristics of rectilinearity, triangulation, repetition of members and spacing, and moderate visual mass with balanced and moderate demonstrations of bending and compression.

Figure 3–11 The inability of the wood lintel to remain rigid permanently is revealed in the failure of the masonry, which must remain rigid to prevent cracking.

CONNECTIONS

The configuration of modern wood connections is derived from the form and strength of the material. The workability of wood once had a significant influence on connections but has diminished in importance with the evolution of steel fastening systems. Steel fasteners overcome the strength limitations of wood. Their expression is in the nature of wood because they reveal information about a wood property. Connections vary in their need for steel. The expression of the connectors therefore may vary in intensity in relation to their need. Hiding steel on which the existence of the connection is entirely dependent violates the nature of wood. Hiding steel that acts only as a safety factor can be a positive expression of the nature of wood.

Historic log construction defines the low extreme with regard to steel use. Overlaps and notches define the image of wood connections with no steel. The length of overlap may diminish with an increase in the sophistication of the notches, and vice versa. The absence of notches in a split-rail fence requires lengthy overlaps to assure stability (Fig. 3–12). No apparent lap is required in

Figure 3–12 In the absence of fasteners or notches, a long overlap of rails is necessary to prevent collapse from occasional lateral loads, such as from an animal.

mortise-and-tenon joints, where the notching system is highly sophisticated. A sentimental view of such connections tends to see them as being the ultimate expression of the nature of wood. They are not considered to be so here because they are not common in contemporary detailing.

Connections that are extensively cut and fit so that the members are flush and tight tend to obscure the identities of the components at their interface (Fig. 3–13). The apparent merging of the wood misrepresents reality. The fibers of each component do not become one at the joint even though they appear to do so. These joints readily reveal warpage, shrinkage, and other movement that is likely upon weathering. Component identity can be clarified if the members are not flush and if visible reveals occur between them. The expression of workability increases as the system of notching becomes more apparent. These characteristics also make warpage less apparent. Even with the incorporation of these variations, the merged-type connection does not best reflect the nature of wood.

At the other extreme, we find extensive use of steel brackets and plates. In these connections one member tends to butt the other, with the steel holding them together. Different types of butting conditions call for a range of steel expression. A column that rests on the top of a beam needs steel only for lateral and uplifting forces (Fig. 3–14). The connection resists the force of gravity

Figure 3–13 The original tightness and flushness of this joint contributed to an initial impression that the members merged (physically became one). Shrinkage opened the joints to help clarify that the members actually bypass each other as separate pieces.

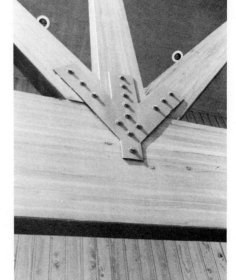

Figure 3–14 The connector plays a minor role in securing the center strut (in compression) to the chord of this truss. It is extraordinarily important in securing the angled struts (in tension). Its image does not express its significance to the angled struts.

without the help of steel. If a beam butts the side of a column, steel connectors resist gravity loads as well as the others (Fig. 3–15). It is reasonable to express the steel in the second example more intensely than the first because of its greater structural significance.

The expression of the connectors is enhanced by increased visibility and signs of importance. Large size, contrasting color, and decorative configuration are characteristics that intensify the expression of steel connectors. The butt configuration expresses the nature of wood in connections having a significant amount of steel visible.

Although butt joints with steel connectors are important, they are not the configuration closest to the nature of wood. They are relatively precise in that the members tend to be flush and the joints tend to remain tight. This level of precision expresses the nature of a wood and steel composite, not of wood alone. Butt connections without plates or brackets are not compatible with the nature of wood. Wood lacks the dimensional stability necessary to keep the joint tight (Fig. 3–16). It lacks the strength to resist significant forces except those which push the members together (Fig. 3–17).

A mitered joint is a particularly delicate type of butt joint. Typically, such joints express little or no steel. They require greater precision than do other butt joints and are less able to maintain it. The angled cuts leave very thin edges that are vulnerable to weathering and provide little material for securing the joint. The initial high precision of the joint is temporary. Examples of mitered joints, failed from weathering, are plentiful. Mitered joints in the exterior violate the nature of wood.

The nature of wood in connections without steel brackets and plates is expressed by overlapping members (Fig. 3–18). Overlapping accommodates the same properties that butting (without expressed steel) violates. When members

Figure 3–15 The importance of the steel plate connectors to the structural system is reflected in their large size. It is not reflected in their utilitarian shape or finish (galvanized).

Figure 3-16 Weathering has caused this butt joint to fail despite its threaded fasteners.

Figure 3-17 Minimizing the expression of steel in this system of butt joints contributed to its failure from impact. The weakness of the joint illustrates the incompatibility of butt configurations with minimal steel.

Figure 3-18 The exaggeration of the overlaps emphasizes conditions compatible with wood and gives the connection a strong visual impact. The image of the fasteners is enhanced by their detailing, which demonstrates some degree of planning and care.

overlap, the rectangular solid profiles fit snugly against each other, which is physically convenient and develops friction to help carry the loads. The visual impact of existing and future irregularities in the wood are subdued by the rusticity of the configuration. Unlike butt joints, the tight fit between members is likely to remain so because of the nature of the bolting. The expression of linearity is enhanced as is the strength of the joint.

The longer the overlap, the farther the fasteners are from the end of the member. This reduces the likelihood that they will pull out of the end, a possibility if they are too close. There is reduced need for steel plates to align the wood or add tensile strength. The overlap and through-bolt provide equal resistance to a push or pull (making this method particularly compatible with connections between the members of a truss). Members are not flush in an overlapping joint, giving it a rusticity compatible with the nature of wood. Bolting through lapped lumber is accommodated by members that are not extraordinarily thick. The easily bolted moderately thick members are more compatible with the expression of wood for reasons described previously. If a beam overlaps a column so that the beam is entirely dependent upon its bolts to resist gravity, the bolts warrant expression. Reduced expression of the fasteners is justified if the beam is "let-in" to the column. Notching the side of the column to receive all or part of the overlapped beam section can eliminate the gravity load on the bolts while expressing the workability of wood.

Overlapping also has advantages in cladding. The horizontal edges of shingles and clapboards are lapped. Movement as well as watertightness are accommodated. The details are so common that no expressive mileage can be expected from them. The vertical edges of these and other cladding units typically butt, which tends to obscure component identity. Distinct detailing, and therefore expression, can result from lapped vertical edges. To maintain the plane of the surface, these laps would take the form of gaps between the cladding units to express their lap with units behind them (Fig. 3–19).

Overlapping wood with minimum steel (no plates or brackets) is the configuration most compatible with the properties and philosophical implications of wood. The usefulness of butted members with steel connectors is recognized. It is noted that this system is most necessary for large sections which coincide with the sizes of small concrete beams and columns. Another consideration is the fact that the steel connectors produce a composite expression. The overlapping configuration is compatible with wood of moderate mass and has an expression that is entirely that of wood.

Figure 3–19 The lap of the shingles over the sheet metal accommodates movement and avoids the need for precise joints on the corner. The detail expresses the nature of wood but is slightly subdued by the color of the steel, which blends with the shingles.

SURFACES

In a building facade, the forms of the surface components contribute to the character of the surface. The geometry of building surfaces can be influenced by both structure and cladding. Since lumber and much cladding are linear, linearity is likely to be in the nature of wood surfaces. Some degree of linear expression may also be appropriate where nonlinear cladding such as panels or shingles are used.

Boards produce surface linearity to a degree equal to the clarity of their long edges. Tightly butted edges reduce but do not eliminate the visibility of the joints between boards. Without shadow lines defining the edges of each board, the sense of linearity is limited. Overlapping the long edges of boards, using battens and leaving gaps between boards make thin but visible shadows. The shadow lines increase the intensity of the linear expression over flush and tightly fit cladding. The linear expressions of clapboard siding or vertical boards and battens are noticeable but lack visual impact because they are so common.

A stronger expression may be achieved if the linearity draws attention to itself. A slight increase in intensity is achieved by installing the cladding at a 45-degree angle. The popularity of this pattern has made it fairly common; thus its visual impact is limited. A sloped pattern will be more special if alternated with sections of standard siding. Linear patterns that are less common will draw more attention. Multiangled configurations can increase the intensity of the expression if the boards are not cut so short that they lose their linearity (Fig. 3–20).

Linearity may be intensified by increasing the projection of the members from the surface (Fig. 3–21). Boards may be pulled out from the surface plane, turned on edge or otherwise detailed so their shadows and identities as individual units are stronger. As the expression of individual boards becomes stronger, so does the linear character of the surface.

Figure 3–20 Attention is drawn to the wood surface because of its unique pattern. The expression is in the nature of wood because the pattern is dependent for its existence on wood's linearity and, to a lesser degree, workability.

Figure 3-21 The linearity of this surface is emphasized by the significant depth of its lines (boards on edge). Contrast of the boards with their background further strengthens the image. The inability to cast strong shadows on the metal screen has a subduing effect.

The linear expression of a board is proportional to its length. A board whose length is no more than two or three times its width expresses rectangularity. This expression is exploited in the imitation of stone in certain historical applications. Short wood pieces that imitate stone quoins at building corners are not in the nature of wood (Fig. 3–22). They are in the nature of stone, which is the intent of the detail. Significantly changing the form of wood has the potential of expressing the property of high workability. The quoin detail fails to achieve this redeeming quality, as the cutting required is remarkable in neither configuration nor extent.

Grooved plywood siding mildly expresses linearity at the expense of product identity. Vertical joints between panels disappear but horizontal joints do not. The misrepresentation lacks credibility, as an interruption occurs in the line

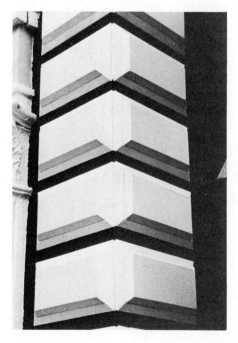

Figure 3-22 The key to wood's imitation of stone in these quoins is their blocky (nonlinear) image. The expression doubly violates the nature of wood, in that it lacks visual properties of wood while exhibiting visual properties of another material.

Figure 3–23 Grooved plywood lacks credibility in its imitation of boards as the joints between the 4-foot edges of panels are nearly impossible to conceal. Typically, trim or flashing occurs at the joint.

pattern every 8 feet (Fig. 3–23). The expression of rectangularity is in the nature of plywood siding surfaces. The form of the panels and thus rectangularity may be expressed by clearly revealing the outline of the panels (Fig. 3–24). This can be achieved by applying battens to all panel joints.

It is ironic that a fairly pure expression of panels is found in imitations of medieval half-timber framing. The cheap version covers the panel (often hardboard) joints with battens and includes a few pieces of diagonal trim (Fig. 3–25). It could be argued that the diagonal trim is an academic reference to the triangulation that sometimes occurs in the framing. In the final analysis, however, the purity of the expression is completely overshadowed by the historic reference of the image.

Figure 3–24 Expression of the panels is emphasized by their isolation on a contrasting background and the trim around each one. The linear patterns subdue the panel expressions slightly, as they suggest the possibility of a series of boards.

Figure 3–25   The elements necessary for an aesthetic order derived from panel form are present. The opportunity is lost, however, in this particular detailing due to the unmistakable attempt to imitate the Tudor style.

Expression of entire 4-foot by 8-foot panels is difficult in small facades such as in residences. Windows, doors, roof slopes, and other interruptions prevent enough repetition of whole panels to give the unmistakable impression that it is a purposeful element in the aesthetic system. The expression of the system is significantly stronger if the panels can dictate the placement of openings as well as facade proportions. This is more feasible in large facades than in small ones. Patterns created by subdividing panels so as to obscure actual joints but still express rectangularity are workable on small facades (Fig. 3–26). The panel expression is less intense than showing actual joints but has greater design flexibility.

The expression of a standard shingle or shake installation is more linear than rectangular. The tight vertical joints have less visual impact than do the long shadow lines created by the lapped courses. The system is so standard that

Figure 3–26   The pattern of battens is derived from the dimensionns of the panels covering the upper wall. Panel expression is subdued by the reasoning required to locate their positions but is enhanced by the importance of the pattern to the image of the facade.

Figure 3-27 The undulations of the fancy butts prevents the image of linearity typical of standard shingle installations. Contrast with the straight butt courses makes the special shingle forms more noticeable.

it cannot be said to violate the nature of shingles, but it does have an appearance similar to that of beveled siding. The standard installation lacks noticeability, which nearly eliminates its ability to make an impression on observers. Its expression of the nature of the product can be intensified in several ways.

The shingles may be spaced slightly to strengthen the image of the vertical joints and interrupt the horizontal shadow line. Butts can be staggered to attract attention and to further interrupt their shadow line. Fancy butt shingles achieve this in their standard installation (Fig. 3-27). Attention can be drawn to staggered or fancy butts if they are alternated with straight butt lines. The standard shingles are a reminder that the fancy butts are special.

The expression of shingles and shakes can be intensified by stepping the perimeter of shingled areas, which emphasizes unit form (Fig. 3-28). Patterns that depend on the small size of shingles and that would be impossible in linear cladding intensify the expression of shingle size (Fig. 3-29). Rounded and undulating surfaces are stronger demonstrations of the relative smallness of shingles because they are three-dimensional expressions.

Figure 3-28 The nature of shingle form is strongly expressed in this stepped edge.

Figure 3-29 The surface pattern expresses the nature of shingles with regard to their relatively small size. The pattern would not be practical in other wood products.

The methods of protecting exterior wood surfaces from deterioration are the vehicles of expressing wood's low level of durability. Coatings and chemicals, the major protective systems, have a range of visibility from very strong to nearly invisible. Paint that is unusually bright or of unusual color draws attention to itself and thus expresses wood's low durability more intensely than does a neutral color. Multiple colors have the same effect, with an additional benefit. The form of the wood components can be emphasized by painting them colors that contrast with those of surrounding surfaces (Fig. 3–30). Painting adjacent

Figure 3-30 This facade draws attention because it is painted with strongly contrasting colors (red and white) which identify forms of components and protect the wood from deterioration.

members with contrasting colors will intensify the linearity of a board surface. Painting shingles to produce an irregular pattern where graphic shapes follow the joints and butts of shingles expresses the rectangularity of the product.

Coatings that are not easily seen (clear ones, for example) are not expressive. They deny the presence of protection and therefore deny the low durability of wood. The denial is a violation of the nature of wood. Wood treated with nearly invisible water-based chemicals has the same expressive problem. The stains that are popular for lumber and cladding are an expressive compromise between the extremes of exposed wood grain and bright paint. Their intensity of expression varies with the intensity of their colors.

EDGES

The nature of wood can be expressed in the configuration and exposure of assembly and component edges. The low durability of wood is important in the treatment of edges. End grain is especially vulnerable to water penetration. Expression of this unique condition occurs in methods of protecting the end grain of wood. Although not as critical as end grain, side grain on the top surface of horizontal wood warrants protection also. The tops of exposed vertical members are often protected by caps that prevent the penetration of rain (Fig. 3–31). The caps provide an opportunity for expression, as they are a visible response to a wood property. If the visual impact of a cap is minimized, its importance is denied, as is the property of wood for which it compensates.

Painting the cap a color that blends with the wood, minimizing its size, and using a shape that is unremarkable are ways of subduing its presence. Drawing attention to the cap expresses wood to a degree proportional to the noticeability of the cap. The use of metal for caps is compatible with the nature of wood. Whenever materials are mixed, each warrants expression compatible with their properties and the importance of their role in the design. Sloping the tops of wood components facilitates the shedding of water and is therefore also an expression of wood's generally low durability.

Bottom edges of members have the advantage over tops that gravity assists drainage rather than penetration of the end grain. The earth, however, presents an additional hazard for wood near grade. In many climates, the earth contains moisture and insects. While some species of wood are more resistant than others, contact with the earth is a visual denial of wood's low level of durability (Fig. 3–32). The expression opposes the nature of wood. The violation diminishes as wood is moved farther from grade.

Figure 3–31 The minimal size and blending color of the two column caps deny their existence and wood's low level of durability. Their expression is stronger than would be a hidden protection such as flat sheet metal, occurring only on the top surface.

Figure 3–32 Contact of this wood to the ground denies its vulnerability to decay and termites. The expression of the detail is not in the nature of wood.

A lapped connection at a foundation allows gravity to pull water away from the end grain (Fig. 3–33). Wood that is butted to a broader pedestal compromises the expression and the protection afforded by the pedestal. If the top of the pedestal creates a shelf around the wood, water will be caught and absorbed by the end grain. Although lacking maximum compatibility with the nature of wood, the expression is stronger than setting the wood directly on earth or paving.

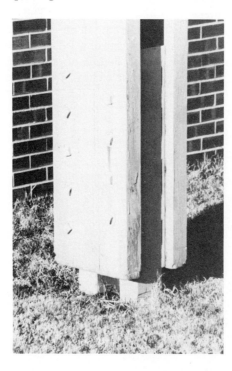

Figure 3–33 This foundation detail drains water away from the end grain and separates the wood from moisture in the earth. It expresses the nature of wood.

Protecting the top of wood framing from water penetration is accomplished automatically when a roof overlaps the wall. The detail is so common that it has little potential for expression. Greater protection is provided by longer overhangs, but the role of keeping the interior space dry overshadows the function of protecting the wall itself. Some potential for expression occurs in parapet walls. Reasoning regarding the expression of parapet copings is the same as for caps on posts. Expression of wood's low durability is directly proportional to the visibility of the coping.

The edges of wood systems tend to be straight in response to the rectilinear nature of wood framing. This characteristic neither violates wood nor has a significant visual impact. Curving wood edges expresses the workability of wood but is limited to applications where water penetration is unlikely. Openings and the tops of systems are particularly vulnerable. The cutting of the framing for a circular opening is simple. Trimming the opening to prevent water penetration is not. The shaping of the curved trim typically involves the lamination of thin pieces.

Turning the trim broadside to the opening requires bending the wood. Bending even thin strips typically requires radii larger than that of the average window. This orientation exposes the joints of the laminations to the weather and to view, which is often considered visually unacceptable. Turning the joints of the laminations toward the opening requires cutting many pieces of trim into curved sections. This results in numerous joints, which are especially vulnerable to water in the bottom half of a circle (Fig. 3–34). Because of these problems and due to the fact that circular openings are easily produced in other materials, they are not considered to emphasize the nature of wood.

Straight-sided openings eliminate most of the problems found in curved trim. Diamond-shaped (rotated square) openings have straight sides. Their drainage of water to the joint at the low vertex prevents them from being most compatible with wood. Although hexagons, octagons, and triangles can be oriented to avoid this problem, the rectangle is identified as the opening shape most compatible with wood. Rectangles match the geometry of the framing and are most easily trimmed to prevent water penetration.

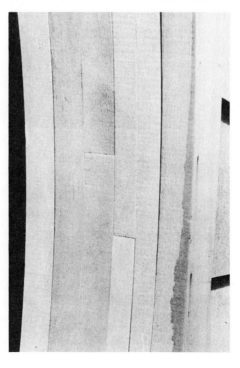

Figure 3–34 Numerous straight boards were cut into curves and assembled to trim this circular opening. The many joints in the lower half of the circle deny wood's vulnerability to decay from water penetration.

Chapter 4

WOOD
IN
ARCHITECTURE

CHECKLIST FOR ANALYSIS

The expression of wood in historic and contemporary architecture is analyzed in this chapter. The quality of the work is not judged. Its degree of compatibility with the principles of expression discussed previously is determined. Listed below are the major characteristics considered to express the nature of wood. Refer to Checklist C-1 in Appendix C for this list in a worksheet format with additional notations to assist analysis.

1. Linearity in the building image
2. Straightness in the building image
3. Contribution to the building image by form characteristics of secondary products (if any)
4. Low level of refinement (rustic spirit) in the building image
5. Demonstration of moderate strength as a significant part of the building image
6. A sense of frames or framing as a significant part of the building image
7. Demonstration of wood's very low resistance to deterioration as part of the building image
8. Demonstration of the relative ease with which the shapes of wood products may be changed as part of the building image

A building need not demonstrate all the compatible characteristics to be expressive of the nature of wood. The number required varies with the intensity of each expression and the magnitude of expressions that oppose the nature of wood.

ANALYSIS

Carson House
Eureka, California; Samuel and Joseph Newsom; 1885

The visual impact of the house is, to a large degree, based on the working of wood (Fig. 4–1). This is an example of exaggerated exploitation of a property. The images of Victorian buildings would be significantly subdued without their decorative brackets, dentils, balusters, spindles, finials, spandrels, and vergeboards. The ornaments are turned and cut from lumber which has little in common with the shapes of final products.

The extensive use of worked components has left limited room for repetitive long slender members (Fig. 4–2). The few that exist are overwhelmed by the shaped details. Consequently, linearity has scarcely any role in establishing the image of the building. There is just enough linearity to prevent the building from having a blocklike or planar sense in its form and detailing.

Figure 4–1 *Carson House.* Worked wood is so extensive that it has visual impact at a distance. The image of the working is made more apparent by the coating that protects the wood from decay.

Figure 4–2 *Carson House.* Although linear elements are present, they have a secondary visual role to the ornamental treatment of the wood.

The expression of refinement is mixed. It is generally higher than is in the nature of wood today. Numerous butt joints and repetitive small details demonstrate a high level of refinement. Overlapping members (balconies over brackets) and the busy facade allow imprecision without visual impact. It is recognized that the high quality of skills and materials required for high precision were available for the construction of the building at a more reasonable cost than would be true today. It is also noted that the high level of precision has been matched by a high level of maintenance.

Spans are moderate and therefore woodlike. The low durability of wood is expressed, as the visual impact of the paint is considerable. The paint colors are cream and dark violet. The contrast emphasizes the worked and linear forms and draws attention to itself.

The house expresses the nature of wood despite the absence of extensive linearity. It does so on the strength of its workability expression. The shaped components have a purposeful role in the aesthetic order of the building which makes their visual contribution stronger than mere exposure to view.

Gamble House
Pasadena, California; Charles and Henry Greene; 1908

The house emphasizes both the linearity and workability of wood (Fig. 4–3). The combination is remarkable since the two characteristics are usually in conflict. The basis for the linear expression lies in the exposed rafters, which may be seen in three dimensions at the porches and gable overhangs and in part at the eave overhangs (Fig. 4–4). The totally exposed rafters establish a

Figure 4–3 *Gamble House.* Upon approach to the building, a sense of linearity is apparent before the working of the wood is noticeable.

Figure 4–4 *Gamble House.* The base for the linear expression is established by the exposed rafters of the overhangs and porches.

(a)

(b)

Figure 4–5 *Gamble House.* Numerous beamlike elements expressed in three dimensions contribute to the sense of linearity.

strong rhythm of parallel lines. The rhythm is continued where only the rafter ends are visible, thus expanding the image of the linear system to encompass the entire building. Other details supplement the linearity of the roof system. Decorative beamlike elements parallel exposed beams, thus increasing the number of lines (Fig. 4–5).

The ends of rafters, beams, and other linear members are rounded. Profiles change slightly along their lengths. Some components are cut down from larger shapes so that their axes take a slight but sharp jog. The working is subtle but frequent. Nearly every linear member exhibits some reshaping. Beams and headers are visible in the shingled surface of the walls (Fig. 4–6). Headers and sills extend beyond building corners, thus moving from expressions of two dimensions to those of three dimensions (Fig. 4–7). Protrusion from the wall plane emphasizes both the linearity and worked ends of the members. While the reshaping of the members changed their forms only slightly, the large number of worked components increases the effect of the expression. The intensity of workability expression falls below that of the Carson House.

(a)

(b)

Figure 4–6 *Gamble House.* The expression of linear members is intensified by their projection beyond the minimum, which at times requires the cutting of shingles to receive them.

(a)   **(b)**

Figure 4–7 *Gamble House.* The extension of headers and sills beyond the corner and into three-dimensional expression emphasizes their presence and linearity. The detail violates the expressions of durability and refinement.

The relatively low level of refinement expressed is strongly in the nature of wood. The rounded ends reduce the normal level of "sharpness" afforded to lumber by right-angled corners. Overlapping connections are used extensively. The apparently merged corner sill plates and headers are exceptions. The fit of the crossing members is tight, their surfaces are flush and the notches are not apparent. The members lose their identities at the crossing. They seem to become one piece. This condition is in contrast to other detailing which maintains the identity of members as they pass through each other (Fig. 4–8). Pegs suggest fasteners at connections, which indicates that two separate pieces are present.

Figure 4–8 *Gamble House.* The identities of the members are enhanced by the emphasis given to the hole by its rounded edges. The apparent fasteners suggest that two pieces must be present.

In another connection, the holes are cut larger than the components (Fig. 4–9). Wood wedges driven into the holes alongside the lumber give the impression that a loose fit exists between the meeting members. The sense of looseness strengthens the separate identities of the members, as looseness does not occur if the members merge into one unit at their intersection.

A scarf joint maintains the identity of its two members in two ways (Fig. 4–10). First, the edges around the joint are rounded, which makes the joint more apparent. The rounded edges are compatible with the low level of precision natural to wood in that they would obscure movement or an imperfect fit. Second, two pegs invite scrutiny of the joint. As apparent fasteners, they suggest that two pieces have come together.

While the lumber has moderate mass, the very long cantilevers of the porch roofs express more than moderate strength. They are one of the very few ambiguous statements of wood in this building. Other spans are shorter and therefore more woodlike. Many connections bring attention to wood's moderate strength. Wood pegs suggest the position of numerous otherwise hidden threaded fasteners (Fig. 4–11). While the pegs are not themselves fasteners, they are more visible than flush screw heads would be. Their interruption to the smooth surface adds to the rustic image of the building. Some pegs do not cover fasteners, thus exaggerating the number of actual fasteners. A greater number of fasteners is associated with a material of moderate strength than with one of very high strength.

Figure 4–9 *Gamble House.* The identity of the members as individual components separate from each other is supported by the wedges. They exaggerate the presence of the hole, which, in turn, verifies that all pieces do not become one at their intersection.

Figure 4–10 *Gamble House.* The identity of the joint is maintained by the rounded edges of the meeting faces and the pegs. The rounded edges make the joint more visible, and the pegs draw attention to it.

Figure 4–11 *Gamble House.* Although the wood pegs are not themselves fasteners, they are visual reminders that fasteners are present. Some pegs do not cover screws; thus the number of fasteners is exaggerated.

Fancy metal connectors are strongly expressive of wood's moderate strength (Fig. 4–12). The clamps, straps, and braces are designed as compositions within their own right. They are clearly visible and attract attention because of their unique design. These conditions magnify their importance to the wood (whether they are actually important or not) and thus contribute to the sense that the wood needs assistance in its structural role.

The forms of the shingles are expressed, as they are spaced and have butts that are not perfectly aligned (Fig. 4–13). The gaps are visually as strong, thus producing an expression of rectangularity.

The protective stain on the wood is visible but not intense. Much of the detailing that so strongly expresses other properties exposes wood to the elements and catches water. The exposure of rafters beyond the roof line resulted in decay and required the replacement of a number of rafter ends. Renovation and continued maintenance has subdued the consequences of the vulnerable detailing.

Given the clear and numerous expression of many properties of wood, the Gamble House strongly expresses the nature of its material.

Figure 4–12 *Gamble House.* Metal straps are designed and expressed as entities in their own right. The apparent attention and care given their design implies importance.

Figure 4–13 *Gamble House.* Their spacing and slightly out-of-square butts make the rectangles of the shingles more apparent, thus nearly eliminating the linear image of typical installations.

Roos House
San Francisco, California; Bernard Maybeck; 1909

This house reverses the relationship between workability and linearity seen in the Carson House (Fig. 4–14). The wood trim gives the building a two-dimensional linear character. The impact of the linearity is subdued by the lack of repetitive proportions and freestanding linear elements (Fig. 4–15). Porch columns contribute to the linearity of the building but are too few to establish themselves as the base for the aesthetic order. The workability expressed in brackets and balcony detailing affects the visual impression of the building but to a degree much less than that of its linearity.

There are both butt and overlapping connections, which give mixed signals regarding precision. The sense of precision is slightly less than that of the Carson House because there are fewer pieces in the facade that must have an exact fit with each other. The expression of strength is moderate, as is the visual mass of most of the wood.

Figure 4–14 *Roos House.* At a distance, the worked wood has little visual impact. The dominating expression is linearity.

Figure 4–15 *Roos House.* The linearity afforded by the freestanding columns and the trim is subdued by the absence of long uninterrupted lines in extended series of equal spacing.

The durability of wood is neither violated nor expressed strongly. The wood is clearly protected from deterioration by a coating. The noticeability of the dark coating is enhanced by its contrast with the adjacent white surfaces. The expression of the coating is subdued by its brown color, which is less remarkable than most other choices. The contrasting colors also emphasize the linearity of the facade.

The building expresses the nature of wood. The conclusion is based mainly on its linear quality supplemented with lesser expressions of workability and durability. The linearity is not exaggerated to the degree that workability is in the Carson House.

Suntop Homes
Ardmore, Pennsylvania; Frank Lloyd Wright; 1938

The linear image of fascias and balconies is extended by a long fence which is clad with the same board siding (Fig. 4–16). The extensive visual roles of these elements give the brick facades a strong linear quality. The linearity of the composition is further enhanced by the long narrow proportions of the wood-clad sections. The contrasting masonry sections of the walls act as visual spacers between the wood masses, helping them maintain their separate slender identities. The linelike quality of the siding is exaggerated by the butted ends of each course. The detail subdues the visibility of the actual board length and thus eliminates interruptions in the long narrow strips and their shadow lines.

The unique overlap detail between courses give a rare emphasis to the thickness of the siding, which adds a subtle three-dimensional influence of the material. The faces of the fascia and balcony boards remain vertical while they lap (Fig. 4–17). Consequently, the face of each board is positioned forward of the one below for a distance equal to the board thickness. The top edges of these clad surfaces project beyond their bottom edges a distance of 4 or 5 inches. The fence lacks this characteristic.

Figure 4–16 *Suntop Homes.* The vertical joints in the cladding lack visibility. Consequently, the length of the boards and therefore their linear expression are exaggerated.

Figure 4–17 *Suntop Homes.* The projection of the upper boards beyond the lower boards is an expression of component form (specifically, thickness).

The expression of wood's limited durability is stronger than average. The protective coating on the wood is a subdued reddish hue. It is a stronger statement than would be had by clear, brown, or gray coatings. The wood is held above the ground, a detail most notable in the fence, where the brick base has the visual (as well as actual) role of a pedestal for the wood.

The cladding expresses the nature of wood by virtue of its essentially two-dimensional but strong linear statement and its relatively clear recognition of wood's low durability.

Herb Greene House
Norman, Oklahoma; Herb Greene; 1961

The building expresses the workability of wood in its free-form shape (Fig. 4–18). The expression is subtle since the significantly worked wood is not visible but is strengthened by the fact that it is structural. A supplementary working of wood is visible in the cladding. The ends of numerous cladding boards are cut at an angle. Although this working is decorative and two-dimensional, its expression is strengthened by the gaps between many boards, which provide a contrasting background. This detailing also gives the facade a limited sense of linearity, the noticeability of which is enhanced by the unique cladding pattern. At one end shingles clad a curved form, thus expressing a potential afforded by their small size.

The building expression violates the low durability of wood by the lack of apparent protection for the exposed wood, its close proximity to the earth, and the detailing of the cladding. Most of the board siding is not lapped and is therefore vulnerable to end-grain water penetration and seepage between cladding and sheathing.

The compact and generally inward-leaning form has a feeling of compression. A sense of frames is not present. These conditions do not support a sense of wood structure. The small vault over the window at the west end lacks a sense of thrust, as no masses are present at each side to resist it. The absence of a compressive image in the vault helps it seem woodlike. The expression of strength in general is not great and therefore is within the potential of wood.

(a)

(b)

Figure 4–18 *Herb Greene House.* The free form of the building is apparent at a distance, which increases the significance of the working of hidden framing.

The relatively low refinement of wood is accommodated by the random spacing of the cladding boards and the free form of the building. The absence of uniformity makes irregularities and movement in the wood impossible to detect.

The net expression of the building is somewhat in the nature of wood, although the substitution of concrete could achieve an approximation of the image.

Tennis Court Canopy
University of Oregon, Eugene, Oregon; Unthank Seder Poticha; 1971

Several properties of wood are expressed in the structure, including an uncommon contribution by its steel connectors (Fig. 4–19). The exposure of the numerous components in a variety of orientations confuses the structural pattern. An adequate number of parallel systems are apparent enough to establish a strong sense of linearity in the image. The overlapping of several major members is compatible with the rustic sense natural to wood. The numerous butt joints are accomplished with steel connectors that have unusually strong expressions afforded by their bright yellow color (Fig. 4–20). Their noticeability is enhanced further by their contrast with the darker wood. The higher sense of precision produced by the butt joints is justified by the clarity of the steel components on which they depend.

Figure 4–19 *Tennis Court Canopy.* The numerous parallel lines, some expressed in three dimensions, give the structure a sense of linearity. The actual and visual crossing of so many members tempers the expression.

Figure 4–20 *Tennis Court Canopy.* The yellow paint on the metal connectors gives them visual importance and therefore a role in the aesthetic order of the structure.

The durability of wood is neither violated nor expressed to a significant degree. The dark tone of the wood surface is clearly not that of raw wood but does not draw significant attention. Much of the wood is clearly protected by the roof system. Some of the larger spans overlap into the realm of steel. The largest members nearly overlap the image of concrete. Their thicknesses, however, are not quite large enough for concrete. Workability is not an issue.

Based on its linearity and connections, the structure has an overall expression compatible with the nature of wood.

Lath House at Heritage Square
Phoenix, Arizona; Robert Frankeberger; 1980

The open-air pavilion expresses the linearity of wood at two levels of intensity. From a distance the exterior expression of linearity lacks strength due to the blending of the numerous thin strips on the facade (Fig. 4–21). The columns are unable to establish a strong linear statement, as an uninterrupted view of a long colonnade is not available. At close range the linear expression is very strong. It is maximized from a vantage point within the structure. This is accomplished by exposing members in three dimensions, silhouetting a large number against the sky, and casting numerous long slender shadows on the large blank floor (Fig. 4–22). A large number of parallel lines are clearly visible in all directions, including downward.

Figure 4–21 *Lath House.* At a distance, the slender strips of wood in the curved fascia blend and thus lose their identity and linear expression.

(a)

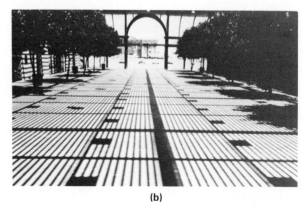

(b)

Figure 4–22 *Lath House.* The linearity of the structure is magnified by numerous long, equally spaced lines expressed in three dimensions and repeated in the two dimensions of their shadows.

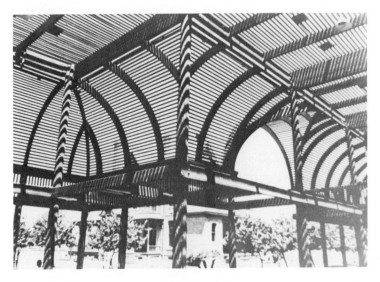

Figure 4-23 *Lath House.* The curves do not violate the straightness of wood or express workability. They express a characteristic of laminated timber that make it unique among wood products.

The form potential of laminated wood is partially exploited, as many units are curved (Fig. 4–23). The arched members overlap with the spans possible in masonry and generally have resistance to thrust available in the form of buttresslike framing or cross-ties (Fig. 4–24). The linearity and moderate mass of the curved timbers keep their images out of the realm of masonry. The span of the laminated beams in the central area is enormous. The expression of strength in this area overlaps that of steel.

The connections of the major members fail to express the nature of wood. The roof slats, which overlap their supports in a way compatible with wood, are farthest from view. Extensive use of butt joining occurs closer to eye level. Butt joints with minimum steel demand precision greater than that natural

Figure 4-24 *Lath House.* The linear quality and moderate mass of the arch help maintain its image within the realm of wood. Masonry would be more massive, while steel would be less so.

to wood (Fig. 4–25). The mitered and other joints that require neat flush fits are incompatible with wood's imprecision of form and movement. Both are apparent. The expression of steel connectors that secure many butt joints is ambiguous (Fig. 4–26). The steel is painted a slightly contrasting color but has ordinary or haphazard configurations. The forms of the connectors suggest that they are unimportant when, in fact, they are structurally very important. Since wood's expressions of strength and refinement are partially dependent on the nature of connections, ambiguity is the result of this mismatch.

Durability is not strongly expressed. The chemical treatment of the wood, which gives it significant protection, makes a weak visual statement. Workability is not an issue. Despite the incompatibility of many connections with the nature of wood, the structure does express the spirit of wood. The doubly emphasized linearity overcomes other shortcomings to carry the image.

Figure 4–25 *Lath House.* The natural imprecision of the wood contrasts with the high precision required for the mitered joint.

Figure 4–26 *Lath House.* The awkward shape of the large connector on the right suggests that it was designed after a number of other decisions had been finalized. The implication reduces the visual importance of an important contribution by steel.

Figure 4–27 *Thorncrown Chapel.* The entry facade has a strong linear expression due to the exposed frames, their reflection in the glass, the frame embedded in the curtain wall, and the partially visible interior frames.

Thorncrown Chapel
Eureka Springs, Arkansas; E. Fay Jones; 1980

The linear expression of the chapel is extraordinary, especially in light of the fact that the structure is not an open-air pavilion but an enclosed building (Fig. 4–27). Large frames of long slender members are exposed at the entry and in the curtain wall, and are visible through the glass in the interior. The exterior frames are reflected in the glass of the facade, which extends their visual statement. The frames continue through the interior of the space with a magnified presence due to their downward-projecting struts, which bring the structure relatively close to the viewer (Fig. 4–28). Unlike other structures, which tend to hug the walls and roof, this one fills the upper half of the space.

Figure 4–28 *Thorncrown Chapel.* The linear expression of the frames is intensified by their filling of the upper volume of the chapel with lines expressed in three dimensions.

Most of the members are expressed in three dimensions. The wall components are virtually expressed in three dimensions, as they are surrounded only by glass.

The frames are equally spaced and exhibit triangulation, which typifies the essence of wood structure. The connections, with a significant exception, are overlapping. The overlaps are exaggerated, with members extending long distances past the fasteners. This very woodlike joint is repeated many times. Workability is exhibited to a small degree in the angled cuts of the exposed ends of struts.

Durability is expressed in the stone base for the structure, which holds the wood away from grade. The wood's protective coating is not as strong an expression as it is a neutral gray. The lumber is relatively thin and stretches fairly long distances without lateral bracing. The image of the slender exterior members is one of vulnerability to warpage. The fact that the wood is of high quality, which makes warpage less likely, is not apparent to the untrained eye. While little of the wood is exposed to the elements, the impression is the reverse because of the strong relationship of the interior to the exterior. The curious result is that while a relatively small percentage of the total wood is exposed to the elements, the overall expression of durability is not strong.

An important visual element of the building is a series of connections that violate the refinement and strength images natural to wood (Fig. 4–29). The detail occurs twice in each frame, at the center "crossing" of the upper set of struts and at the crossing of the lower set of struts. At these connections, the members seem to remain secured to each other merely by touching corners. The steel connectors that make the joints possible are visible but very much subdued. Each is cut into the members so as to be flush with the surfaces of the wood. Their finish blends with the color of the wood. The connectors are fairly thin. These conditions diminish their visual impact to a level below their significant structural role. The result is an image so highly refined at this joint that it matches that of steel.

The sense of refinement in this small area has a significant effect on the image of the building. The connection occurs on the centerline of the building and is repeated many times in a clear pattern (two straight series). Being open, the joint seems to emit light in many views, thus drawing attention to itself. This violation of the sense of wood differs from those of many other buildings. This detail lacks an accidental image. It has an important and extensive role in the building image.

Figure 4–29 *Thorncrown Chapel.* The steel connector has almost no visual importance, while its contribution to the image of the connection is of exceptional importance.

The uncharacteristic sense of refinement afforded by the subdued steel connectors and the thinness of the members are somewhat reminiscent of the image of steel. The numerous solid profiles revealed in the struts coupled with the lapped joints and exceptionally strong linearity maintain a sense of wood. The combined effect of all expressed properties is a building expression in the nature of its material.

Hult Center for the Performing Arts
Eugene, Oregon; Hardy Holzman Pfeiffer; 1982

The mostly concrete building includes a wood structure at the location of greatest visibility, the entrance (Fig. 4–30). The structure is detailed with a sense of precision higher than that natural to wood. The steel hidden in flush butt joints performs a significant structural service with no expression of its own (Fig. 4–31).

Figure 4–30 *Hult Center.* The use of wood occurs under the gabled roofs that surround the entrance and lobby.

Figure 4–31 *Hult Center.* The wood is unable to maintain the initial precision facilitated by the hidden steel. The end of the beam refuses to be flush with the left side of the column. Surfaces refuse to maintain smooth uniform finishes.

Figure 4–32 *Hult Center.* The checking in the surface of the beam is typical of other wood components in the building. It is a symptom of low refinement that is not compatible with the flush plugs and other precise detailing.

Consequently, the connections misrepresent the nature of wood with regard to strength. The flush wood pegs that conceal bolts lend a sense of refinement that is unlike the significant checking in some of the wood (Fig. 4–32).

Adjacent bays of roof structure have contrasting expressions regarding refinement (Fig. 4–33). Purlins in one are cut flush with the side of the beam on which they bear. The flush detail adds a sense of precision to the connection, which would otherwise have a character more compatible with the rustic character of wood. The purlins of the adjacent bay overlap their beams to a significant degree, thus expressing more strongly the low precision of wood.

Expressions of linearity and strength with regard to span are compatible with the nature of wood. The wood is of moderate mass. Workability is not exploited visually, although working was necessary to bury steel in the connections. While the roof system protects most of the wood, that at the perimeter is exposed to the weather. The wood has no expressed protective coating. Since this is the most visible wood, a sense of durability higher than that natural to wood is projected.

While detailing harmonious with wood exists, the majority of the most visible details oppose its nature. This results in the overall image of the wood portion of the building being incompatible with the spirit of the material.

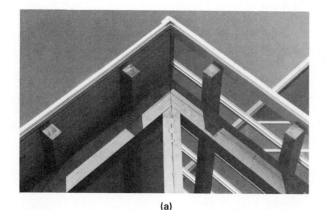

(a)

(b)

Figure 4–33 *Hult Center.* The overlapping of purlins on the beams of A express the low refinement compatible with the nature of wood. The flush ends of B represent a higher level of precision, which is more likely to reveal movement and warpage.

Shelly Ridge Girl Scout Center
Miquon, Pennsylvania; Bohlin Powell Larkin Cywinski;
1983

The pediment of the swimming pool bathhouse expresses the workability and linearity of wood in several tapered and spaced boards forming sun rays (Fig. 4–34). In doing so, the linear surface behind and between the rays is subdued. The two-dimensional expression of the vertical board cladding is diminished by its failure to relate to the roof, the arched opening, or the sun rays. An opportunity to express the nature of the roof trusses was missed by the failure of the sun rays to relate to the struts of the adjacent truss.

The absence of a column under one end of the arched opening gives the form a sense of lightness that helps it seem woodlike rather than like masonry. A sense of great strength is avoided by the thick columns and the large bracketlike forms above them. The brackets make the span seem smaller between the two columns. The steps in the stepped form of the brackets are too long to classify as a masonry corbel, which helps to maintain an image of wood. They also express the workability of wood in the overall shape and rounded corners. The nature of the component spanning between the columns is not clear. The mass of the wood at the center of the span seems thin for the image of structural wood.

The column pedestals lift the wood slightly above grade but provide a shelf that catches water. The incompatibility of the detail with the durability of wood was revealed in the premature decay of at least one column base on another building in the complex. The low durability of wood has mixed expressions. The more intense are the dark green of the pediment cladding, the red of the sun rays and columns, and the yellow of the sun form. Protection of the remainder of the wood is neutral in color. The foundation's holding of the wood above grade is emphasized slightly by trim at the bottom of the siding (Fig. 4–35).

The walls exhibit a rare expression of light framing. The studs are exposed between the top of the cladding and the eave. The studs do not contribute to

Figure 4-34 *Shelly Ridge.* The working of wood is evident in the tapered strips of wood forming sun rays and the brackets on the column capitals.

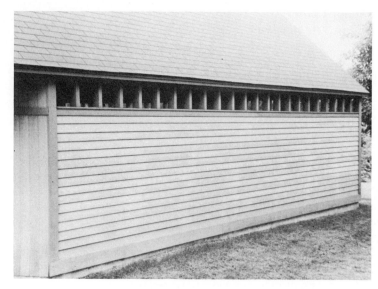

Figure 4–35 *Shelly Ridge.* The exposed stud ends at the top of the wall do not contribute to the linear image. Their shortness is unable to compete with the long uninterrupted line system of the cladding in establishing an image.

the linearity of the facade because the exposed length is too short. The expressive benefit of exposing the studs is subdued by the probability that they will not be recognized as the wall framing. They could as well be mullions. Greater exposed length or an additional exposure at the base of the wall could have bolstered their recognizability. The linearity of the clapboard siding is stronger than the usual application because there are no interruptions to the lines.

The overall expression is in the nature of wood, with the massiveness of the columns and the curve of the arched opening adding some ambiguity.

Germania Street Housing
San Francisco, California; Donald MacDonald; 1984

The cladding of the houses makes rare references to the low durability of wood and the form characteristics of plywood (Fig. 4–36). The square pattern of the wood trim reflects the rectangularity of the plywood siding on which it is superimposed. The noticeability of the reference is strengthened by its contrast with the more common practice of ignoring the panel image with a linear texture. The purity of the expression is dampened slightly in that, unlike the vertical joints, the horizontal panel joints do not coincide with the trim (Fig. 4–37). The

Figure 4–36 *Germania Street Housing.* Although the grids are derived from lines, their statement is one of squares, and thus the rectangularity of the plywood siding is reflected.

Figure 4–37 *Germania Street Housing.* The horizontal trim allows water to drain behind it. The relationship of trim to plywood panels lacks ultimate purity in that a match at the horizontal joints does not occur.

influence of the plywood is not felt in the placement of openings, as their perimeters rarely match the grid vertically or horizontally.

The nearly two-dimensional expression typical of most trim is augmented with the positioning of the horizontal strips on top of the verticals. This places the horizontal strips in a three-dimensional expression and strengthens their shadow lines. The lap joints are more compatible with the nature of wood than butt joints would have been. The laps also express wood's low durability, as they allow the drainage of water between the horizontal trim and the plywood.

The red color of the plywood contributes further to the expression of durability, as it is an intense hue. Its contrast with the light-colored trim emphasizes the presence of the strips and therefore everything they express. The surrounding fence, which extends the image of the houses, brings the wood into contact with grade and thus dilutes somewhat the otherwise strong compatibility of the design with the durability of wood. The expression of strength is limited, for the most part, to the lintel spans at the openings, which are moderate and compatible with the image of wood.

The overall image is in the nature of wood based on its reasonable compatibility with plywood form and wood's low durability.

Chapter 5

PROPERTIES OF MASONRY

Masonry includes clay brick, clay tile, concrete block, concrete brick, and stone. This group is unique among the structural materials in that individual units are small, compact, and have relatively low tensile strength. Although some characteristics are shared with other materials, the combination of masonry properties gives it potential for a clear identity in architecture.

FORM

While slight differences in strength and forming processes allow shapes and proportions to vary, the forms of clay, concrete, and stone units are similar to each other and different from those of the other structural materials. Limited tensile strength prevents units from being very much larger in one dimension than another. Long shapes would act as lever arms which multiply the effect of applied bending forces. The likelihood of breakage would be increased. Slender shapes would tend to break into more compact pieces.

Stone's tendency toward compact shapes can be seen in nature. When silica and other minerals replace the decaying cells of a buried log, a stonelike substance (petrified wood) can form in the shape of the log (Fig. 5–1). When movement produces significant bending (and therefore tensile) stresses in a petrified log, it breaks into blocky segments. If slender forms of burned clay and unreinforced concrete occurred in nature, they could be expected to act the same way. The production of common masonry products in compact shapes reduces the likelihood of breakage from handling. Given the tendency of masonry toward compactness and rectangularity, the primary form of masonry is identified as being blocklike.

Stone. Stone has the greatest variety of shapes among the masonries. Some stone occurs in nature in a block form. Shrinkage from the initial drying of sedimentary stone and the fast cooling of molten stone (typical at the earth's surface)

(a)

(b)

Figure 5-1 Petrified logs have the linear form of wood in A but the substance of stone. The incompatibility of form and substance is revealed by movement which broke the logs in B into compact masses.

produces tensile stresses. At times, the evenly distributed stresses crack these monolithic masses into remarkably regular blocks (Fig. 5–2). Breaking due to movement in the earth also contributes to the natural occurrence of block shapes.

Stone is typically quarried in large blocks. Stone that is processed into load-bearing units maintains the blocklike (primary) form (Fig. 5–3). The relationship of the two largest dimensions can be as high as 5 to 1 but is more commonly around 3 or 2 to 1. The two shortest dimensions are typically below 2 to 1. Stone veneer that carries its own weight does also. Large relatively thin stone slabs (cladding)

Figure 5-2 The natural cracking of this stone mass is similar to a formation called checkerboard limestone, the cracking of which is so uniformly blocklike that it was first thought by area residents to be a highway made by an ancient civilization.[1]

[1]Malcom C. Oakes and Ward S. Motts, *Geology and Water Resources of Okmulgee County, Oklahoma* (Norman, Okla.: Oklahoma Geological Survey, 1963) Bulletin 91, p. 60.

Figure 5–3 The blocklike nature of load-bearing stone is reflected in these limestone units, which are slightly thicker than the height of a course.

that hang from a building frame do not have the proportions typical of load-bearing units. They are secondary forms because they are not structural. The hanging veneers tend to be broad and thin. They are almost always rectangular. They are not considered planar, as the units are too thin to carry a structural load as a vertical or spanning plane (Fig. 5–4).

Carved stone falls into the secondary form category because it is not the standard unit and because of its second manufacturing process (carving) occurring after shaping the basic unit. Carved stone often maintains the compactness typical of the primary form. It is least like the primary form when it imitates organic forms such as leaves or human beings. Its long history suggests that carved forms should be considered to be securely in the nature of stone. The shortage of production skills, its relatively high cost, and its limited use in contemporary architecture suggest that carving is not as much in the nature of stone as it once was.

Figure 5–4 The stone slab has the form of a structural plane. Its display on a pedestal is an inidication of its uniqueness. If the form were in the nature of stone, it would not warrant such a display.

A range of textures are available in stone. Splitting produces slightly irregular faces, no two of which have exactly the same shape. The sawing process produces a smoother matte finish. A shiny surface can be produced by polishing. Stone surfaces in nature have irregular or matte finishes. A texture's remoteness from primary form is related to the extensiveness of production that is required to produce the texture. Roughness is therefore the surface quality closest to the primary form of stone, and highly polished finishes are the most remote.

Splitting is both a traditional and a contemporary process for shaping stone. The natural appearance of a split face is compatible with the naturalness of the material. Sawn faces fall between split and polished surfaces in their closeness to primary form. This reasoning does not require that polished surfaces be eliminated from stone in architecture. It suggests that different textures call for different roles in design. It is logical to treat primary forms and textures as the standard and special forms and finishes in a more special way.

Clay. Clay brick comes in a smaller variety of shapes than is available with stone. The two largest dimensions of standard modular brick are in a proportion of 2 to 1, with the two shortest being slightly less (Fig. 5–5). The same comparisons in Roman brick are 3 to 1 and 2 to 1. These units and others easily qualify as blocklike. Units are typically rectangular in both sections. Curved and angular shapes are identified as secondary forms because they are not the most common form of brick. They require some special handling in their production. Some shapes require second manufacturing processes, such as sawing or sawing and assembly (Fig. 5–6).

Figure 5–5 The brick has the compact and rectangular form identified as blocklike and representative of load-bearing masonry.

Figure 5–6 Assembling clay components from cut units sacrifices some compactness and blocklike qualities. Their forms are still closer to those typical of masonry than are those typical of wood or steel.

Structural clay tile is blocklike. Comparison of the two largest and two smallest dimensions of a unit are typically 3 to 1 and less. Ceramic tile is not considered masonry and is not part of this study. Terra-cotta is a secondary form because it is usually nonstructural and has limited use in contemporary building. Ratios of dimensions are often greater than primary clay forms, as they may take the shape of relatively thin panels. Terra-cotta is least like the primary forms of masonry when it imitates delicate shapes from nature.

The primary surface form of clay masonry is the texture of extrusion, the most common forming process. The relatively smooth surface may be roughened by processes following extrusion. The more textured surfaces are considered to be secondary forms (Fig. 5–7). Textures produced by molding differ only slightly from extruded textures. The glazing of masonry is an extra step in the manufacturing process and is therefore a secondary surface form. The carving of clay units prior to firing interrupts the production process significantly. Units are removed from the conveying system for hand carving, after which they are fired. The resulting texture, typically an artistic composition, is a secondary form.

Figure 5–7 Although a texture such as this one is easily achieved in brick, it does require extra equipment and processes beyond simple extrusion. The additional effort required prevents it from being the primary surface form.

Concrete. The name "concrete block" reflects the blocklike shape of these units. The most common form has ratios of 2 to 1 (length to depth) and 1 to 1 depth to height. Concrete bricks may have ratios up to 4 to 1. Slight variations to the typically rectangular profiles of block occur in secondary forms (Fig. 5–8). Tabs, recesses, sloped surfaces, and L shapes are available. Special-use units qualify as secondary forms because they are not as common as the standard block. Some require special handling during manufacture. Their forms are often compact and have some rectangular characteristics. Most of the special forms are utilitarian in nature. Often their special form characteristics are hidden in an installation and therefore have no effect on expression.

The majority of concrete masonry is molded with a flat matte surface. The enormous quantity of units thus produced establishes the texture as primary. Textured surfaces are created by producing two units face to face and splitting them apart. The split-face texture imitates split stone. The fact that it is similar to stone moves the texture away from the nature of concrete masonry. The popular texture is not the strongest expression of the spirit of concrete block.

Other textures are produced by molding (Fig. 5–9). Impressions and protrusions express the uniqueness of the forming process if they are not parallel to the sides of the block or not continuous across the face (avoids duplication in extruded clay). While grooves and ribs could be produced by molding or extrusion, deep undulations are not feasible in clay products due to the small size of brick and the thin walls of tile. Deep grooves and ribs can express the uniqueness of block's relatively large size.

Figure 5-8 This sill unit lacks rectangularity in one profile but is still rather blocklike and compact.

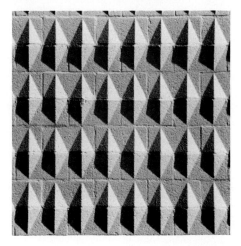

Figure 5-9 Three-dimensional surface patterns exploit the moldability of concrete, thus providing a vehicle to express block as unique among masonries. Only the linear patterns, however, have found broad acceptance among architects.

Masonry.   Clay and concrete masonry are available in hollow or solid units. Stone units are solid. Since a typical installation does not reveal the open cores, the visual impression is one of solidness. Masonry is commonly understood by the public to be heavy. The blocklike and solid appearance of masonry combined with its reputation of great weight give it an image of massiveness. Clay and concrete units are not always precise in their dimensions. Clay units have increased shrinkage with increases in burning temperature or time. As forms wear, concrete block loses precision of shape. Block shrinkage varies with curing procedures. Slight changes occur in concrete and clay units after installation but are imperceptible unless a failure results.

Masonry's massiveness and lack of perfect uniformity call for a rating in the area of refinement to be lower than that of steel. The ability of irregularities to be accommodated by mortar joints and the ability of units to maintain their shapes and positions under most conditions call for a refinement rating higher than that of wood. Wood's lower refinement, despite its lower visual mass, is due to its tendency to warp. (For interior wood and masonry, the ratings are reversed). Masonry is identified as having a medium level of refinement compared to wood's low rating.

In summary, the primary form of masonry is blocklike, rectangular, and of medium refinement. Texture varies among the three types and can be exploited to emphasize some individuality in each type. Detailing that allows these characteristics to affect the visual impact of a building is compatible with the nature of masonry and exploits its potential. Constructions that obscure these form properties violate the nature of masonry. Standard practices that neither exploit nor hide the form of masonry are not necessarily impure, but neither are they particularly expressive of the nature of masonry regarding form.

STRENGTH

Unreinforced masonry is the subject of this analysis. The use of steel reinforcing gives masonry the apparent structural properties of steel. Although this condition is common and useful, reinforced masonry must be considered as a material separate from pure masonry. Metal ties, wire joint reinforcing, and bond beam steel dilute the expression of masonry strength. They allow walls to be less massive and have fewer pilasters. Walls with these steel components are not considered to be reinforced masonry, however. Steel accessories and bond beams are an integral part of contemporary masonry construction, which is not pure but is as pure as is feasible. Steel in lintels is considered to be reinforced masonry for purposes of this study and is excluded from "pure" masonry.

It is common knowledge that masonry has low tensile strength both within units and in the bond between units and mortar (Fig. 5–10). Because of this strength limitation, stone, clay brick, and concrete block require significant mass to develop resistance to stresses from incidental impact. The mass at right-angled corners is adequate for installations where impact is limited to contact with people. Where carts, bicycles, and larger vehicles are present, right-angled corners are vulnerable (Fig. 5–11). Acute-angled corners provide even less mass and are therefore less appropriate for these areas. The brittleness of the

Figure 5–10 Due to its relatively low strength, the bond between mortar and masonry usually fails before the units themselves upon movement.

Figure 5–11 Thickness is needed to compensate for masonry's brittleness. This 90-degree corner was too delicate for its proximity to the adjacent sidewalk.

masonries affects their image of refinement. Since it forces the mass upward to compensate in many installations and prohibits delicate sections in most applications, the refinement level of masonry can be no higher than the medium rating assigned, from reasoning offered in the preceding section.

Masonry has a surprisingly low compressive strength compared to wood, steel, and reinforced concrete. Still masonry is thought of as a compressive material and has a history of use in that realm. Its image stems from the fact that without reinforcing steel, masonry has limited usefulness in any condition of stress except compression. Stone's ability to resist bending is too limited to dilute the compressive image.

The expression of compression seems more in the nature of masonry than wood, although the allowable compressive stress for some wood (parallel to the grain) is higher than that for assembled masonry. The unit weight of masonry is significantly higher than that of wood. The ability of masonry to resist deterioration from elements in the earth is greater than that of wood. Both conditions encourage the use of masonry at the base of a structure where compression is sure to occur. Wood's bending strength, the more unique property, draws attention from its compressive ability. It is common for wood joists to span between masonry walls. The reverse never occurs.

Similar reasoning applies to the image of steel compared to the image of masonry. Reinforced concrete is stronger than the masonries in compression. Its weight and ability to contact the earth suggest that it could have a compressive image. It does to some degree, but its ability to span draws attention away from its compressive potential.

Given the fact that the other materials can meet more difficult structural challenges, whereas masonry is virtually limited to one, masonry is identified as the material most appropriate for the expression of compression. Masonry in compression is so common that detailing to bring attention to this condition is necessary if significant expression is desired. Spreading the base of a masonry form suggests compression, as does great mass. Exaggerating these characteristics and others described in the structures section of Chapter 6 will increase the expression of compression in masonry.

DURABILITY

The masonries are, with some exceptions, compatible with the chemicals in the earth. Burned clay and concrete are relatively close to their raw states as mined from the earth and therefore do not have a strong tendency to return to them through chemical change. In certain parts of the country concrete is vulnerable to sulfate attack but can be resistive if cements designed for that purpose are used. Stone is in its original state and, logically, should be highly resistant to chemical breakdown. The stone of many historic buildings, having endured for hundreds of years, however, is now deteriorating from air pollutants. This vulnerability, although a real problem, is not quite the same issue as moisture's threat to wood. Everything considered, the substances of masonries are highly resistant to chemical deterioration.

The masonry substances have some vulnerability to physical deterioration. If water penetrates a unit and freezes, its expansion pushes particles apart. The resulting stresses can be too great for the low tensile strength of the material. If so, particles break away from the surface (Fig. 5–12). This type of deterioration, known as spalling, is usually a result of human error. Inadequate detailing or failures of adjacent systems can encourage water to penetrate masonry. Brick may be used that is inappropriate for the weathering conditions

Figure 5-12 Water penetrated the brick from above when the coping failed. Due to expansion of the freezing moisture, the faces of the brick failed in tension and fell off.

(more common with used brick, where properties are often unknown). Since physical deterioration is the exception rather than the rule, it does not significantly diminish masonry's rating in the area of durability.

The high resistance to deterioration of stone, burned clay, and concrete is compromised by the numerous joints in masonry systems. The anticipation of leakage through mortar joints requires the installation of flashing and weep holes to return water to the exterior as standard practice. This vulnerability does not destroy masonry's otherwise high durability, but it does prevent it from being the highest of the four materials. Masonry systems are, for the most part, able to maintain dry interior spaces.

Masonry is generally resistive to visual deterioration. Exceptions occur in porous materials. Limestone darkens with the absorption of pollutants. During construction, rain-splashed mud can produce a lasting stain on stone, concrete, and clay units at the base of a wall.

Masonry's ability to withstand deterioration of all types significantly outweighs its vulnerabilities. It can withstand attacks from agents that would damage wood or steel. The use of stone, concrete block, and clay brick in foundations and paving testifies to its significant ability to resist deterioration. Masonry is therefore rated as having high durability.

Expression of this quality is, at best, subtle. Exposing raw masonry surfaces to the weather is a sign that the material is durable. The practice is so common that recognition of the message is unlikely. Negative expressions are more noticeable. Painting brick violates its nature, as it suggests that protection is needed. The opportunity for expressing the vulnerability of joints is discussed in the section on edges in Chapter 6.

WORKABILITY

Traditional masonry practices include cutting units to form arches (Fig. 5-13). This is necessary for the units in the horizontal coursing that touch the curved course of the arch (the extrados). Small units (usually brick) may be broken with a hand tool or cut with a power saw at the job site. The new shapes of the cut units are not very much different from the originals. They remain compact and lose their rectangularity in only one profile. Cutting stone (after the cutting of the manufacturing process) and concrete block is not as common, but where it occurs, the reasoning is the same as for brick.

Figure 5-13 The cutting of brick to meet the curve of an arch is a standard process in masonry construction. This extent of cutting is accepted as being within the low workability of masonry.

With a saw, it is possible to produce shapes that are not blocklike (Fig. 5–14). The delicate slivers of brick and L shapes that it is physically possible to cut are not compatible with the sense of mass and compactness with which masonry is associated. On a practical level, they violate the strength properties of masonry. Some, depending on detailing, are likely to crack (Fig. 5–15). These forms, which reflect the greatest change possible to masonry units, do not influence masonry's image of workability because they violate the nature of the material.

Figure 5-14 The sliver of brick in the coping is not compatible with the blocklike and compact image of brick. Excessively sophisticated working was required, as revealed by the inaccuracy of the cut, which does not match the slope of the adjacent unit.

Figure 5–15 The inside cut that produced the L-shaped unit violates the nature of masonry. The delicate unit, half of which supports the lintel, is subject to differential loading and periodic impact. Its breakage into two more compact pieces is likely.

Working masonry is nearly limited to cutting. Bending is impossible and drilling is difficult. It is more difficult to work than wood. Working masonry produces forms of more limited contrast with the original than does working wood or steel. Consequently, masonry is identified as having low workability, below that of wood and steel.

Limiting the working of masonry to the extent necessary for arches is a policy compatible with the nature of the material. The policy does not produce an effect that will be recognized as a philosophical message. It is too common to draw attention. Stronger expression is possible if unique detailing results from a self-imposed discipline to work no masonry at all (Fig. 5–16). This approach is compatible with the low workability of the material and achieves expression through exaggeration. The compatibility of worked masonry with the nature of the material may be judged by comparing its extent to that required for traditional arches. Working of significantly greater sophistication or quantity is a violation.

Figure 5–16 The construction of this arch required almost no cutting of brick. The pattern resulting from this exaggeration of brick's low workability has visual impact. The achievement of the detailing (minimal cutting) is reasonably recognizable.

Chapter 6

ASSEMBLIES IN MASONRY

STRUCTURES

Masonry has low tensile strength both within units and between assembled units. It follows that structures which appear to depend on significant tensile strength in masonry violate its nature. Conversely, structures that exhibit the absence of tension and the presence of compression express the nature of masonry strength. Traditional compressive elements such as columns and walls can express the structural nature of masonry. If they are compact, bulky, close to the earth, and have blocklike characteristics, they also exhibit other properties of masonry.

Since the tensile strength between units is low, compactness in an assembly has structural advantages. It is less likely that a thick mass will develop tensile stresses by leaning than will a thin element. It is also less probable that a thick mass will develop tension due to buckling. Practical considerations restrict the mass of contemporary structural components for buildings. The less compact assemblies do not necessarily violate the nature of masonry. Other characteristics can demonstrate masonry's strength characteristics.

The potential for tensile stress from lateral loads or buckling becomes greater as walls or columns become more slender. The use of hidden steel tends to yield forms that violate the apparent strength properties of masonry. It allows walls and columns to be too slender for the tensile strength of masonry. Methods that allow thinness by visible means express the tensile weakness of masonry systems. Geometry can be used instead of mass to stabilize a thin masonry construction. Buttresses, for example, can transfer lateral loads to the ground through compression, thus allowing a wall to be relatively thin without developing tension from leaning (Fig. 6–1). The buttresses are the characteristic that expresses masonry's low tensile strength.

A zigzag or serpentine geometry has a buttressing effect (Fig. 6–2). Segments of the wall that are not perpendicular to the wind act as buttresses for adjacent sections that are. A wall that is a circle or part of a circle has the

Figure 6-1 The significant visual presence of the buttresses expresses the masonry's weakness in tension. They prevent tension from occurring when the wind blows on the opposite side of the walls (the prevailing direction).

Figure 6-2 The geometry of the serpentine wall expresses masonry's inability to resist significant tension. Its effectiveness in preventing the wall from leaning from lateral load is expressed in the thinness of the wall.

same structural advantage. Curved walls are compatible with the small size of masonry units. A unit is easily set at a slight angle to an adjacent one. Repetition of this misalignment will form an apparent curve. Small units can form curves of smaller radii than can large units. Masonry is therefore more compatible than wood or steel with curved structures. Without working, curved walls made from the linear materials would have radii too large to be useful. Curved walls can express both the strength and form properties of masonry.

A canopy cantilevered from a single central column will tend to tilt when the wind blows. This structural condition is not compatible with masonry as tensile stresses develop when the canopy bends the column. Three or more columns spaced equally at the perimeter of a canopy eliminate the cantilever and therefore the buckling effect of its lever arm (Fig. 6–3). The multiple columns providing a broad base for the structure give an image of stability that is compatible with the nature of masonry. A stable structure is less likely to develop tensile stresses than one that appears to be unstable. This is not to say that cantilevered concrete, wood, or steel cannot be used with masonry. The relationship of cantilever size to the dimensions of the base support determines the image of stability, which affects the degree of compatibility with masonry. The more stable the image, the more it expresses the strength properties of stone, brick, and block.

The lateral stability of masonry buildings is easily accommodated by internal shear walls, which also support gravity loads and act as partitions. The fact that its role as a stabilizing element is obscured prevents an internal shear wall from contributing to the masonry strength image of a building. Exterior shear walls could contribute to this image if they resembled buttresses. Undulating walls may not be necessary to stabilize a masonry building, due to the geometry of the building and internal shear walls. Nevertheless, they contribute to the image of stability and thus to the image of masonry in a building. The fact that their stabilizing contribution is likely to be superfluous makes the gesture an exaggeration—a legitimate tactic in materials expression.

Tensile strength in a unit of masonry is very low but not nonexistent. It is enough to resist small bending stresses that result from short spans. Stone is available in sizes large enough to span some window openings (Fig. 6–4). Stone

Figure 6–3 Positioning columns at the extremes of the canopy expresses a visual stability that is compatible with the strength properties of masonry. The stability is exaggerated slightly by one column standing beyond the perimeter of the main roof.

Figure 6–4 The stone lintels express the low bending strength of masonry in their short spans and relative large depth (upper lintels). The long vertical dimension of the windows emphasizes the shortness of the lintels and therefore their expression of limited strength.

lintels are less common than they once were but continue to be available. They can express the structural nature of masonry if their limited tensile strength (in bending) is exaggerated with very short spans. Attention can be drawn to this characteristic by remarkably narrow openings or numerous closely spaced columns. Neither are common in contemporary architecture and are therefore likely to have visual impact.

The nature of masonry strength is commonly violated by spans that are impossible without steel. Occasionally, stone, brick, and concrete block appear to span horizontally over open space. Cantilevers are particularly flagrant violations, as even the remote reference to a flat arch is missing (Fig. 6–5). The spans that are most far removed from the structural realm of masonry are those where the units cover the steel completely, including the bottom of the beam. The masonry seems to hang when positioned under the hidden steel. Beams where the masonry rests on an exposed steel flange are slightly less impure. Such detailing is economically inspired, as it is cheaper to leave the bottom flange exposed. It is usually painted a color that blends with the masonry, illustrating that even its nearly nonexistent contribution to the expression of the structure is not wanted.

This type of structural image violation is further magnified when masonry seems to span as a horizontal plane. Examples may be found in brick soffits at windows, overhangs, and entry foyers. It is possible to demonstrate control over masonry expression by violating the nature of the material so clearly and purposefully that the intent to do so for effect is obvious. A ceiling of brick (interior) is likely to be in this category, whereas a brick soffit (exterior) is not (Fig. 6–6).

The common horizontal spans of unit masonry over glass violate the image of masonry strength. The glass seems to support the masonry because the actual support, steel, is rarely visible beyond an exposed flange (Fig. 6–7). Common use of the detail encourages its acceptance as being in the nature of masonry systems, but its philosophical violation is too strong. Setting the masonry on top of a visible concrete or steel lintel is compatible with the strength properties of all the materials involved (Fig. 6–8). The masonry stacked on the beam would demonstrate its ability to accept compressive loads. The visual presence of the beam would express unit masonry's lack of bending strength.

Figure 6–5 The incompatibility of long horizontal spans in unit masonry is magnified in this concrete block cantilever. Something seems wrong, even to untrained observers.

Figure 6-6 The hanging sensation of this brick ceiling is emphasized by its separation from the walls by the lighting. The intensity and unusualness of this violation indicates that it was done for effect. Consequently, it demonstrates control over the material.

Figure 6-7 The hidden steel violates the nature of masonry, as it appears that the brick is setting on the glass. The slight reference to the hidden lintel made by the soldier units is diminished by their continuing in the wall where no lintel is needed.

Figure 6-8 The concrete lintels contribute to the expression of masonry's nature in two ways. A violation is avoided by its preventing the stone from appearing to make the span. The stone is expressed in compression as it is stacked on the concrete beams.

If the true lintel is not exposed, a special condition is created. Masonry seems to do what it cannot. The special condition may be acknowledged by detailing that is different from that of adjacent masonry. Turning units into soldier coursing over the opening is a minimal change from the expression of stretcher units. It is common enough to lack significant impact. Projecting units and turning them to soldier or rowlock coursing to create a decorative effect is stronger (Fig. 6–9).

Covering the lintel with units that contrast in color with the wall makes an academic reference to the presence of the hidden beam. The intent of this technique is more likely to be recognized than that of decorative detailing. The celebration of the hidden lintel is not as clear nor as strongly in the nature of masonry as is revealing the actual beam. It does provide alternatives that violate the nature of the material less than the pretense that no support is needed for the unit masonry.

Arches, vaults, and domes can be compatible with the compressive strength of masonry because, theoretically, they develop no tension in spanning (Fig. 6–10). Tensile stresses can occur if the nature of loading is not compatible with the shape of an arched form. Thick masonry accommodates a greater range of stress configurations than thin masonry because of its broader section. The weight of thick masonry is also a greater percentage of the total load than thin masonry, thus reducing the significance of live-load variations. Thick masonry is therefore less likely to develop tensile stresses as load patterns change (such as on a bridge). Great mass, then, can reflect the nature of masonry with regard to strength.

The integrity of an arched system is dependent on its rigidity. Movement tends to produce tensile stresses which are likely to crack, if not collapse, the structure. Movement in the earth is common enough to merit caution in spanning with masonry. Unlike in ancient building, where options were more limited, the availability of steel and reinforced concrete eliminates the motivation to achieve great heights and spans in unreinforced masonry. The greater catastrophe likely from the collapse of a large span encourages small spans in masonry today.

Masonry arches over doors and windows seem reasonable. Vaults over residential spaces and chapels are feasible. Vaulting a cathedral nave with unreinforced masonry in contemporary construction is a borderline application. An unreinforced dome of stone, brick, or block for a sports arena seems unnecessarily risky. Large spans in reinforced masonry raise the same issues as

Figure 6-9 The expressive violation caused by the hidden steel lintel is abated slightly by the decorative masonry detailing, drawing attention to this special condition. Although this was probably not the original intent of the detailing, it is the effect.

Figure 6-10 A strong example of masonry's compatibility with arched spans is demonstrated by the Pont du Gard. The fact that the two lower series of arches were constructed without mortar demonstrates that tensile strength is not required in these structural forms.

those raised by reinforced masonry lintels. Hidden steel is likely to make a masonry arched system span farther with thinner mass than is comfortable. If a particular span seems difficult for the masonry that appears to achieve it, the nature of the material is violated.

A true arch develops thrust, an outward push at the base. Steel, wood, and concrete can take the form of an arch without developing thrust. Masonry cannot. The expression of thrust resistance is a major distinction between true arches and curved shapes that are not. Thrust resistance is, therefore, an important vehicle for expressing the nature of masonry. The flying buttresses of Gothic cathedrals are well-known examples of thrust resistance that play an important role in the visual images of their buildings (Fig. 6–11).

Thrust may be resisted with a tie across the base of the arch. A steel tie rod, while a legitimate element of a masonry system, has little visual impact. Expressive intensity is proportional to the visibility of the thrust resistance. The rod contributes a minimum to the sense of masonry. Emphasizing the visual contribution of a tie system (increasing the number of rods, decorative detailing) would add to the structural expression of the masonry.

Masonry arches that appear to have no thrust due to the contribution of hidden steel violate the nature of the material (Fig. 6–12). Setting an arch on slender masonry columns or a few inches from the edge of a facade requires that no thrust exist. Thrust would push the unit out of alignment at the base of the arch in these cases. Steel in the arch can reduce or eliminate its thrust, while steel in its supports can prevent their movement. Arches that appear to have thrust and thrust resistance may have hidden steel that does not interfere with the image of masonry. If the visible conditions adequately accommodate thrust and in general masonry's lack of tensile strength, hidden steel is inconsequential, serving only to provide a safety factor. Such steel does not violate the nature of masonry.

Figure 6–11 The visual impacts of Gothic cathedrals were due in part to flying buttresses such as these. They are an example of a structural solution expressed as an integral part of the aesthetic order.

Figure 6–12 The steel embedded in the arch eliminates thrust. To rsist thrust, therefore, the mass of the columns is not forced to be significant. Their moderate size leaves the structure with an ambiguous image, neither wholly that of masonry nor that of steel.

The corbel depends on the limited ability of masonry to resist tension in bending (Fig. 6–13). This demonstration of tensile strength is compatible with the image of masonry if tensile strength is shown to be very low. This is achieved by minimizing the overhang of each brick so as to produce a corbeled edge with an angle of no less than about 63 degrees. A mass twice the total projection is required behind the corbel.[1] The embedding of steel can give corbels smaller angles and greater projections, which violate masonry's image regarding strength (Fig. 6–14). Corbels also have the potential for expressing masonry's form (thickness and rectangularity) and durability (protection of joints).

[1] *Recommended Practice for Engineered Masonry* (McLean, Va.: Structural Clay Products Institute, 1969) pp. 128–129.

Figure 6-13 These cantilevers are short enough to maintain tensile stresses within the limits of masonry. In its contribution to the character of the building, the steep slope of the corbel expresses the nature of masonry.

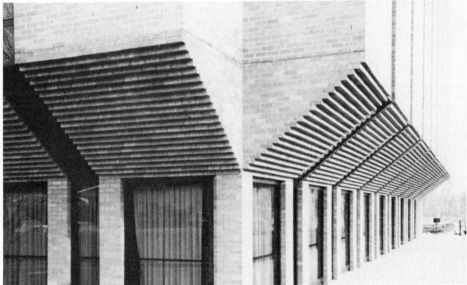

Figure 6-14 The cantilevers of these units are too great for the strength of masonry. Hidden steel supports the relatively low angle of the corbeled soffit. The expression violates the nature of masonry.

CONNECTIONS

Two masonry wythes may meet so as to emphasize or subdue form characteristics of the units. The intersection may require cutting units within or beyond philosophical limits. The connection may acknowledge or ignore the vulnerability of masonry joints to water penetration. These issues determine the compatibility of a connection with the nature of masonry.

Wythes of different masonry types (color, substance, size) meeting in the same plane will emphasize unit form if they overlap (Fig. 6–15). If each masonry section ends in a straight vertical line, the connection will demonstrate only

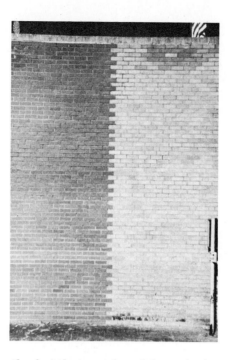

Figure 6–15 The overlapping of the two colors of brick expresses their rectangularity, height, and one-half their length.

the fact that an edge of the units is straight and vertical. In most bond patterns the straight vertical line will also require cutting units. The forms of whole units are not emphasized. An overlap in a running bond clearly expresses the heights of the units but only half their lengths. Recognition that the emphasized length is exactly one half a unit is likely. The standard meeting of wythes at a 90-degree corner with flush surfaces and a straight vertical edge is compatible with the form of masonry. Its common use, however, prevents the detail from being expressive of masonry properties. Projecting one wythe beyond the corner, projecting alternating units of both through each other, or stepping the wythes to create several corners more strongly express the form of masonry (Fig. 6–16). The details express the blocklike form of the units in three dimensions.

Figure 6–16 The blocklike image of brick is stressed in this corner detail, which expresses the thickness and rectangularity of the units.

Corners that are angles other than 90 degrees do not match the rectangular form of masonry. Acute-angled corners can violate the refinement level of masonry in proportion to the intensity of traffic that could damage them. A solution to a sharply acute corner is to detail it as two obtuse angles (cut off the point). Obtuse-angled corners can be detailed to be more blunt than 90-degree corners and meet masonry's need for compactness.

Special unit shapes with angled faces form a corner with flush faces and a straight vertical edge (Fig. 6–17). Acute-angled shapes produce corners of maximum sharpness and maximum violation of masonry's brittleness. A special shape with a rounded face would pull the acute wall corner closer to the bluntness that is more compatible with masonry. Special units with obtuse-angled faces may form blunt corners and, consequently, do not violate the nature of masonry. Such a corner is much like the standard 90-degree corner, however, in that it is likely to go unnoticed.

Acute- and obtuse-angled corners can also be solved by cutting units. The compatibility of these corners with the nature of masonry can be judged on workability and expression of form (with regard to refinement and mass). Since the cuts typically produce miters, their angles are half that of the building corners (Fig. 6–18). This produces acute angles in units, even for obtuse building corners. Cuts producing very sharp corners violate the workability of masonry because of the difficulty of the cut, the delicacy of the unit produced, and the large number of cuts required.

Figure 6–17 The specially formed units contribute to the sharpness of this corner, which violates the level of refinement natural to masonry. The violation is magnified by the close proximity of the detail to the sidewalks.

Figure 6–18 The vertical mortar joint on the corner violates the nature of masonry in that the brick seems to have no thickness. In reality, it makes the units especially fragile, as the mitered corners have angles half that of the wall.

Mitered corners that are acute violate the sense of blockiness in masonry because the vertical joint on the vertex of the corner gives the illusion that the units have no significant thickness. It is like the joint that would occur between hardboard panels that have brick shapes pressed into their surfaces. This illusion is not as strong in the larger obtuse angles. A joint on the edge of an acute or obtuse corner violates the rectangularity of masonry. The visual message is that if the units have thickness, they cannot be rectangular in plan.

Constructions that have non-90-degree angles in both plan and section violate the workability of masonry if they achieve smooth straight corners by cutting the units (Fig. 6–19). The sophistication of cutting required for the special fitting simultaneously in two directions is philosophically excessive for masonry.

Non-90-degree corners can be formed with uncut standard masonry. Alternating units may project beyond or stop short of the other wythe's surface (Fig. 6–20). The resulting visual image is very strong due to the texture and shadows produced. The expression of form and size is particularly clear in the projected unit version. The projected units are somewhat vulnerable to impact. If they occur in an area of high vehicular traffic volume, they violate the strength image of masonry.

Figure 6–19 The form of the masonry violates the nature of the material with regard to workability. The slope of the surfaces and the obtuse corner angles complicate the cutting required. Numerous slivers of brick are required at the corners.

Figure 6–20 Overlapping and extending standard bricks at the obtuse-angled corner strongly express the form of the units. The bricks also provide shelves that will catch water and challenge the durability of the adjacent joints.

Figure 6-21 The gap produced by the meeting of the back corners of the two wythes expresses unit thickness and rectangularity. The detailing traps no water, thus is compatible with the durability of masonry systems.

Projected or recessed units provide shelves on which water may stand. Since the shelves are adjacent to joints, this detailing violates the durability of masonry where leakage and joint deterioration is a problem. Problems are more likely to occur in areas of significant rainfall, numerous freeze–thaw cycles, and poor workmanship. Regardless of actual leakage, philosophical acceptance of holding water against a mortar joint is difficult. The violation of durability is not as strong as the positive expression of form. The violation is not clear to laypersons, failure is not certain, and if ramifications occur, they will do so at some time in the future. The form expression is immediate and recognizable by all.

The use of projected and recessed units where habitable space is not enclosed (freestanding columns and walls as fences) diminishes the concern over leakage. A significant roof overhang reduces the threat of leakage. Water catching shelves may be eliminated by touching the inside corners of two wythes that stop in a straight vertical line (Fig. 6–21). The intensity of form expression is reduced but remains in the exhibition of brick thickness.

Masonry planes may join with a curve instead of a corner. Curves are compatible with the strength properties of masonry. They are compatible with the small size of masonry. The degree of compatibility depends on the relationship of curve radius with unit length, as discussed in the next section.

SURFACES

A straight flush surface is the standard configuration for a masonry wall. It is compatible with the straight faces of standard units. While significant skill is required to align the small units to make large straight surfaces, it is commonly available among masons. The standard surface is too common to draw significant attention to the properties of masonry. Detailing can alter the standard system to be less or more expressive of the nature of the material.

Stone that appears to be stacked (load-bearing or veneer) gains visual stability as the ratio of unit thickness to height increases. Stones that appear to be stacked on edge (a characteristic of some veneers) produce a surface that lacks visual stability (Fig. 6–22). Physical stability is provided to stacked veneers

Figure 6-22 This veneer lacks the sense of stability that is important to masonry. The stones seem to be stacked on their thin edges.

by securing the stone to the building structure. The image, however, violates the nature of stone with regard to strength. Stone stacked on its broadest face produces the surface with the strongest stonelike quality. Stratified stone gives a more stable appearance if installed with the stratification horizontal (its natural orientation in the earth). It is also strongest and resists water most efficiently in this position.

The relatively thin stone panels hung from the frame of a tall building lack the appearance of either stacking or hanging. The apparent contact of the panels with each other and grade suggests stacking. Great height and the suspension of the stone over glass indicates hanging (Fig. 6–23). The structural expression is at best ambiguous. The movement of tall buildings from wind is

Figure 6-23 The expression of this stone cladding is ambiguous. It has neither a stacked nor a hanging sense. The double bend in the stone above each window prevents a sense of span, thus expressing stone as setting on the glass. The same form could be achieved in metal panels or concrete.

a problem for any cladding material but seems particularly incompatible with stone.

Although stone cladding may never achieve the spirit of load-bearing stone, detailing can draw stone into closer harmony with the properties of its products. As in plywood panels, the rectangularity of stone panels can be emphasized by wide joints of color contrasting with the panel. The wide joints also encourage the more accurate image of hanging instead of stacking. Thickness can be expressed by reveals at the joints. Lapping the panels like shingles would have a sense of hanging and would express thickness. Expressing the reality of hanging is a dubious achievement, however, since tension does not reflect the spirit of stone.

The highly polished surfaces typical of much cladding are the most remote from stone's natural texture. Surfaces that include both rough and highly polished stone exhibit the natural material and the nature of contemporary stone technology. Texture variations produced on different units or within units emphasize each other by their contrast (Fig. 6–24). The reference provided by the rough surfaces gives a sense of purpose to the polished elements that demonstrates control over the material.

The face form of unit masonry is expressed in flat surfaces by the joints. The expression is weak as the joints are small and the units are too numerous to appear as individuals. The expression is intensified if attention is drawn to the form of individual units. This may occur in two dimensions, with changes in unit color or texture (Fig. 6–25). Patterns in the masonry express the nature

Figure 6–24 The three textures on the stone express naturalness and the potential of stone in combination with manufacturing technology.

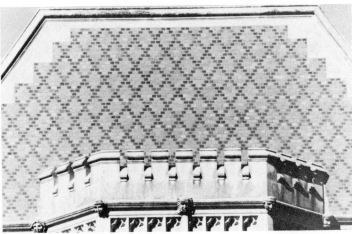

Figure 6–25 The pattern expresses the rectangularity of brick and the dimensions of the end faces (headers). The expression is subdued by the contact of dark units with each other and the strength of the grid pattern's own identity.

Figure 6–26 The expression of the brick faces is near the maximum. An increase in the number of projected units would obscure individual form. The projections express the fact that the units have thickness.

of unit form to the degree that their height and length are made more obvious. Patterns that isolate periodic individual members in a field of contrasting color clearly exhibit the size and shape of these units' faces. Patterns that amass groups of units emphasize only partial forms at the edges of each group. Regardless of the clarity of expression, two-dimensional patterns do not address unit thickness and thus ignore the blocklike nature of masonry.

Projecting and receding units add a third dimension to the surface expression. Although full unit thickness is not expressed, slight projections verify that the units have thickness, contribute to their blocklike image, and add to the overall sense of mass in the assembly (Fig. 6–26). Shadows strengthen the form expression of projected and recessed units. Clarity varies with the nature of the pattern. Color and texture may be combined with projections and recesses to maximize the clarity of unit form (Fig. 6–27).

Three-dimensional expression of masonry form can be achieved by turning selected units at an angle to the surface (Fig. 6–28). This technique can express the length, height, and full thickness of the units if the angle of the turn is just right. If the units are not square in plan, a 45-degree turn will expose only part of the length, a weaker expression of unit form. The fact that the turned units resemble triangular prisms interferes only slightly with their blocklike image.

Figure 6–27 The blocklike nature of brick is emphasized by the recessing of units with contrasting color. Individual unit forms are subdued slightly in that they are not isolated but appear in groups.

Figure 6-28 The turned stacks of units express the blocklike nature of brick in the exhibition of both unit length and thickness. Height is less apparent, as it is not expressed in three dimensions.

Projections and recesses violate the durability of masonry in that they catch water. A sloped mortar wash may drain water from small shelves. The expressive violation remains, however, if the method of protection (the wash) does not have visual impact. Tall stacks of units may be projected or recessed as a group, thus minimizing shelves. The expression of unit height remains two-dimensional in this detail, as the individual stacks are flush vertically. The reasoning and conclusions regarding the significance of the water shelf issue are as discussed for connections in the preceding section.

Battered surfaces, in which each course sets back from the one below, emphasize the height, depth, and rectangularity of the units (Fig. 6–29). The detail does not produce shadows on the faces of the units, which limits the intensity of the expression. The potential for water penetration increases with the distance of the setback. As the expression of depth increases, so does the violation of the durability of masonry (except in arid climates).

A similar expression of form is achieved by corbeled masonry without the violation of durability (no water is caught). Corbeling also has the advantage of casting shadows on the unit faces and always having the soffits in shade. The dark undersides of the projected units contrast with the light faces to produce a strong three-dimensional expression. This is apparent when seeing corbels from below, which is the usual view (Fig. 6–30).

Figure 6-29 The stepped surface strongly expresses unit height and rectangularity. Durability is challenged in the shelves that hold water against every horizontal joint.

Figure 6-30 The strong association of corbeling with the nature of masonry is illustrated by the decision to paint corbeling (and other projections) on the existing brick during the renovation of this building. Architects: Loftis Bell Downing and Partners.

The projections and recesses of sculpted (prior to firing) clay brick minimize the violation of brick's durability (Fig. 6–31). The slopes of many recesses and projections drain water and their relationship to mortar joints is random. The numerous shelves that occur within the borders of units do not hold water against a joint. The sculpted surfaces violate the form of the brick, as it is typically lost in the artwork. Patterns that do not relate to joints obscure the units,

Figure 6-31 The rectangularity of brick is obscured by the strong identity of the art. The cutting contributes to a sense of thickness in the masonry. Shelves occur at horizontal joints only intermittently. Artist: Mara Smith.

and the image of the art draws attention away from them. If the brick form has no meaning in the pattern, it is more logical to use a neutral shape such as a square instead of the standard rectangles. Nonrepeating patterns are compatible with the fact that the units are hand carved.

Surfaces of concrete block with patterned faces express the uniqueness of the substance among masonries (Fig. 6–32). They differ from carved clay units in that the patterns are cast. The casting process tends to be one of mass production, making repetitive use of molds. Commercially produced units typically form repetitive patterns which express the nature of the production process. Positioning blocks in various orientations offers a small variety of patterns that may be generated with one block design. Certain patterns require more than one unit to complete. Two- and four-block patterns are common. Surfaces that have a complete pattern in every block express the nature of unit form. The expression of form diminishes as the number of blocks required to complete a pattern increases.

Expression of unit form decreases as the intensity of the pattern identity increases. The image of block is diluted by patterns that are similar to forms of other materials. Grooves and ribs tend to have strong identities and are similar to surfaces in the linear materials (Fig. 6–33). Typically, the mortar joints of these installations follow the contour of the block face so that their role in defining block boundaries is limited. The linear form of many ribbed or grooved block surfaces are similar to that of wood battens or corrugated sheet metal. Without participation of unit form, the surfaces are essentially those of cast-in-place concrete.

Loss of unit identity significantly violates the nature of the material. Some identity could be regained by alternating ribbed units with standard units. The borders of each ribbed unit would be clear. The linear image would be eliminated. Some overlap with the image of extruded clay units would occur in units having shallow grooves. The distinction between the larger cast units and the smaller extruded ones would increase as the size of the ribs increased.

Figure 6–32   The three-dimensional faces of the blocks express the formability of concrete. Unit form is emphasized by isolating the special blocks between standard units. The shelves will catch little water, as the locale has a dry climate.

Figure 6-33 Individual unit form nearly disappears in this ribbed block installation. The blocklike nature of the concrete units is further obscured by the strength of the linear expression.

The nature of curved surfaces is one measure of the designer's control over the material. A common goal in designing a masonry curve is to produce a smooth surface. The use of curved units to accomplish this violates no principle, nor does it produce an expression of particular note. If the curve of the unit is not apparent, this important secondary characteristic has not been expressed. This is common in large radius curves. Very small radii (typical of round columns) require units with such sharp curves that they are easily recognized as curved units in the installation. Consequently, the image of the building component and possibly the building is served significantly by the secondary form. This condition adds philosophical legitimacy to the nonstandard product.

The production of a curved wall with standard units offers greater opportunity for expression or violation of masonry's nature. Smooth surfaces are physically compatible only with curves of radii that are large compared to unit length. If the radius is too small, the curved surface will not appear smooth (Fig. 6-34). A tight radius forces the corners of each unit in a running bond to overhang the center of the units below it. A texture results which is emphasized when triangular shadows are cast from each pair of overhanging corners.

A nominal 8-inch stretcher in a curve of radius 10 feet 8 inches will project a nominal $\frac{1}{16}$ inch beyond the face of the unit below. The radius is measured to the center of the exposed face. The same unit in a curve of radius 5 feet 4 inches will project a nominal $\frac{1}{8}$ inch. The projection is proportional to radius for a given unit length. (See Appendix D for other projections.) A $\frac{1}{16}$-inch projection seems small but will cast a long shadow in certain orientations to the sun. The movement of the sun makes the duration of certain shadows brief. Their temporary presence does not eliminate their effect on building image. Once a wall has demonstrated that it has an accidental texture, the periodic absence of shadows has only a partial effect in abating the image.

Judging the intensity of the accidental texture will vary among lay persons and practitioners. The minimum ratio of radii to length cannot be fixed for all

Figure 6-34 The radius of this curved wall is too short for the length of the units. The resulting texture seems accidental and reads as an error in the design. Consequently, this surface is not in the nature of brick.

tastes. Probably most observers would judge the texture from $\frac{1}{8}$-inch projections to be disruptive to the image of smoothness. Probably $\frac{1}{32}$-inch projections would not be judged to produce such a texture. The accidental textures produced by straight units are considered objectional here because they demonstrate a loss of control over the masonry and violate the unity of the masonry design. Control and unity can be secured by eliminating the textures or their image as accidents.

A number of techniques are available to avoid the textures of projections. The obvious tactic is to produce only curved walls of adequately large radii. For borderline radii, textured units may obscure the projections and their shadows (Fig. 6-35). The bumps and depressions in split-face concrete brick, for exam-

Figure 6-35 The fact that the radius of the curved wall is too short for the unit length is noticeable only upon very close inspection. Shadows cast by protruding corners of the split face concrete brick are lost in the shadows of surface irregularities.

ple, are at least $\frac{1}{16}$ inch. Corner projections about this size would blend with the face textures, as would their shadows. Extruded mortar joints would have a similar subduing effect on small textures and shadows.

If the corners of units align vertically instead of occurring at the center of the units below, no projections occur. This is the case in the stack bond pattern (Fig. 6–36). A smaller radius may be achieved with a stack bond without a texture than with any other bond pattern. Very small radii require cutting the thickness of stack bond stretchers. Although no shadows are produced, stack bond masonry with very small radii produces curves that appear to be more like polygons. These conditions may be avoided by using units in the soldier position to form stack bond patterns.

Reducing unit length produces less of a texture for a given radius. This may be accomplished by turning the units into header, sailor, rowlock, or soldier positions. The actual unit size does not change, but the length (measured tangent to the circumference of the curve) is shorter in these positions than in the stretcher position. The soldier has the advantage over the other positions, as it produces the shortest circumference length with minimal thickness (measured on the radius) (Fig. 6–37). Minimizing thickness is important in avoiding the cutting of units which small radii may require. The expression of a running bond of stretchers in a straight wall changing to a stack bond of soldiers at a curve is in the nature of masonry. It shows an understanding and a planned manipulation of material properties.

Figure 6–36 The stack bond eliminates bumpy textures from small-radius curves. The penalty for using a radius too small for unit length is the requirement to cut the units behind the surface. The violation does not affect the surface expression.

Figure 6–37 Soldier units in the stack bond produced an apparently smooth curved surface with a small radius. The visible change in units and bond at the curve expresses the nature of masonry and control over the material. Architect: Kaighn Associates Architects, Inc.

The philosophical compatibility of straight units with smooth curves is tenuous. If an apparently smooth curve is produced, a primary form characteristic is subdued. A smooth curved wall obscures the fact that the units are straight. The straightness of masonry may be expressed and the appearance of error in textured curves may be eliminated by the purposeful production of texture (Fig. 6–38). Units may be adjusted forward or back of the curve plane to intensify the texture. Such manipulation has the appearance of a planned and meaningful detail. Straight sections of the same wall may have a similar texture, thus tying the texture of the curve to the aesthetic order of the whole. This approach offers the most pure and flexible solution. Size of radius ceases to be an issue. The contribution of unit form to building image is emphasized.

The expression of veneers (that carry their own weight) can be clarified as being that of a surface rather than that of a structure. Exposing the structural frame around the masonry infill does this clearly. This expression is essentially a two-dimensional one, however, as unit thickness rarely plays a recognizable role. The third dimension may contribute to the visual statement if the edges of the veneer are revealed (Fig. 6–39). Overlapping the veneer slightly on the surface of the building frame and separating the veneer into sections with gaps between are techniques that can expose the thickness of the masonry as part of the facade image.

Figure 6–38 The brick texture in this small-radius curve has a planned and purposeful image. It is a strong expression of brick with regard to form and size. The detail demonstrates an understanding and control of the nature of the material. Architect: Noftsger Lawrence Lawrence and Flesher Architects and Engineers.

Figure 6–39 The detailing of the brick veneer clarifies its nonstructural role. The brick thickness is expressed in numerous exposed veneer edges. The steel carrying the veneer has nearly no expression, which leaves the brick with a hanging image that violates the strength nature of the material.

EDGES

The detailing of top, bottom, and vertical edges may recognize or ignore the nature of masonry with regard to form, workability, and durability.

Straight-sloped wall tops (along the long axis) do not express the unit nature of masonry. Such an edge could as easily be produced in linear or planar materials. The triangular or trapezoidal shape of the wall suggests that the units are not rectangular. When nonrectangular units are used to produce the sloped top, they are typically cut on the site. The challenge to the workability of masonry increases as the angle of the slope diminishes.

Slopes that are flatter than the diagonal of a stretcher (16 degrees for standard modular brick) require cutting through the long dimension of the units (Fig. 6–40). The cut is more difficult than most required for an arch. There are likely to be a large number of them, as the walls tend to be long. The slivers required for the low slope walls are too delicate for the image of masonry. Steep slopes are more compatible with the nature of masonry stretchers than are gentle ones. The cuts are easier and the resulting shapes are more compact. Soldier units are more compatible with low slopes than are stretchers. The cuts required for the soldiers would be simpler and would produce shapes that are more compact than the special stretcher shapes.

A stone course can eliminate the working of bricks. Stone can be shaped in the factory as part of the standard shaping process to produce the sloped top and fit with the bricks below. Using stone for the shaped units within a brick or concrete block wall draws attention to the special condition. Celebration of a special condition helps justify it.

Concrete could be used to provide the interface between the standard units and the sloped coping (Fig. 6–41). In this detail no masonry need be cut. The concrete strip, stepped on one side and sloped on the other, has visual impact. The visual statement of the concrete could be strengthened by increasing its size, recessing it, projecting it, or decorating it. The detail is a reasonably strong exaggeration of the low workability of masonry. Even with the concrete statement, the overall form of the wall does not reflect the blocklike nature of masonry.

The descending top can express the low workability of masonry (no cutting) and its blocklike form if it steps in increments equal to unit size (Fig. 6–42). Steps that are multiples of unit size are nearly as expressive. In this case, individual unit form and size must be visually sorted from each group that makes a step. The stepped parapet wall is a common historical form. The detail is not

Figure 6-40 The low slope required cutting brick through its long dimension. The cut is sophisticated and periodically produces slivers of brick. The detailing violates the refinement and workability natural to masonry.

Figure 6-41 No bricks were cut to produce this gentle slope. Mortar provides the stepped and sloped interface between the stretchers and the coping. The low workability of masonry is expressed.

Figure 6-42 The stepped edge matches the length and three thicknesses of the bricks used. A blocklike sense is projected, giving the wall a strong spirit of masonry.

restricted to parapet walls. Glass or other materials could provide an interface between the top of a stepped wall and the sloped roof that covers it.

Numerous joints, the pull of gravity, and a tendency to crack make the tops of masonry assemblies vulnerable to water penetration (Fig. 6-43). To expose the top edge of masonry is therefore a violation of the nature of masonry expression with regard to durability. Protective systems may express this property if they are visually prominent. Flashing hidden below the top course protects the masonry below but without visual effect. Such a wall looks unprotected and, therefore, violates the material in its expression. Tilting the top across its width helps shed water. If the slope is noticeable, it is expressive of the nature of masonry.

A cement mortar wash over the top of a wall is typically meant to have low visibility. Its violation is almost as strong as the hidden flashing. Unlike

Figure 6-43 The freeze–thaw cycle has damaged the unprotected column top, while the rest of the brick remains in good repair. The example illustrates the vulnerability to masonry joints to water penetration when subjected to the pull of gravity.

the flashing, the mortar is subject to the same cracking that is likely to occur in the wall. If the wall cracks, so will the wash. The detail fails in both expression and function.

Precast concrete, stone, and tile copings are expressive of the need to protect the top edge of masonry (Fig. 6–44). Although these units also have joints, they are fewer in number than the joints between smaller units of the wall. The intensity of the coping expression is related to its degree of visibility. Large coping units with color contrasting with that of the wall contribute to the visual order of the assembly. Projecting, decorating, or otherwise drawing attention to the units increases their expression.

Figure 6-44 The clearly visible coping protects the top of the wall and contributes to the aesthetic order of the facade.

Figure 6-45 The metal coping is a visible solution to the water penetration likely at the top of the walls. Its expression is emphasized by its contrasting color. Increasing the vertical dimension of the coping would further strengthen its expression.

The expressiveness of metal copings may be judged by the same criteria as those used for the other coping materials (Fig. 6-45). Because steel and aluminum are not ceramics does not diminish their potential to express the limitations of masonry durability. The metals have the advantage of contrasting more with masonry than the masonries do with each other. In addition, the joints between metal coping sections are fewer and less subject to failure due to movement. Minimizing the visual prominence of a metal coping is to deny its presence and therefore its need. The suggestion that masonry walls do not need their tops protected is a violation of the nature of masonry. A metal cap can be made visually important in ways that express its own material.

Poured-in-place concrete fascias used to protect the top of masonry walls have advantages over the shorter materials. Fewer joints are present in the poured concrete. Also, the plastic nature of the material allows it to interface with the form of masonry on its lower edge while taking any form on its upper edge (Fig. 6-46). The role of a concrete fascia in the visual order of the facade can be subdued or emphasized by size and detailing. To emphasize the component is to emphasize the nature of masonry with regard to its durability limitation.

Figure 6-46 The concrete portion of the sloped wall allows the brick portion to step down without cut units. The concrete also protects the edge of the masonry from water penetration.

The compatibility of masonry with the earth encourages contact with the grade. Grade contact expresses the ability of masonry to resist insect attack and corrosion. It is an ability that places masonry above steel in its level of durability. Masonry may suffer visual deterioration, however, when in contact with earth. Limestone may stain from absorption of ground moisture. Many masonries are subject to permanent discoloration from the splashing of muddy rainwater. The matter is usually not an issue with steel or wood. Steel and painted wood are not absorbent. Wood is typically held well above grade. A number of techniques may protect masonry from visual deterioration and express this vulnerability.

Grass prevents the splashing of mud but is usually absent during construction. Its role as wall protection does not have high recognizability. A strip of paving at the base of a wall would be an effective splash guard but is not very noticeable. Expression is achieved by providing a strip of material around the base of the building that is meant to receive the splashed mud. The strip may be any of a number of materials, including the exposed concrete foundation, inexpensive masonry, or glazed masonry. Staining utilitarian materials such as concrete or concrete block foundations seems planned and acceptable. Mud easily washes off glazed units. At the extreme of protection and expression is a horizontal shelf, projecting from the foundation, which provides a barrier between the mud and the masonry (Fig. 6–47).

Masonry walls with straight bottom edges flush with the foundation are standard but bring little attention to the characteristics of masonry form. Projecting the masonry wall slightly beyond the foundation emphasizes the third dimension of the material and sheds water. Its visual effect is subdued by its low position. Perception of the overhang is difficult and the detail is sometimes hidden by planting. The net effect is only a slight increase in the expression of masonry beyond the flush detail.

A more noticeable expression is possible when the grade slopes along the foundation. The issues are similar to those regarding a sloped top edge. If a foundation steps down a slope in dimensions that relate to unit size, the nature of masonry is expressed (Fig. 6–48). If the step size is the same as that of a single unit, the expression is clearer than if its dimensions are multiples of unit size. A stepped foundation that projects high above grade yields a stronger expression than one that is low. The high foundation has greater visual mass and is closer to eye level.

Rectangular openings are reasonably compatible with masonry. They are essentially expressionless, however, because of their common use in all materials. Reasoning involving all the basic properties leads to other options

Figure 6–47 The ledge at the top of the foundation prevents mud from splashing onto the building. It also contributes to the visual order of the facade.

Figure 6-48 The step, three bricks high and eight bricks long, is one of a series in the foundation. Its expression of brick form is further enhanced by the projection of the units beyond the surface of the concrete.

that have a stronger expression of masonry's nature. Strength considerations encourage arched tops or very short straight lintels of stone. Stone lintels may call for corbels at the jambs to shorten the span. Except for curves associated with arches, practical considerations encourage straight vertical jambs.

The durability issue calls for single-piece sills (such as stone) to minimize joints. Multiple-unit sills (brick) call for a curve to exploit the advantage that small units have over large ones in forming curves. The cutting required is of the same sophistication and quantity as that for an arch of similar size. Limiting the curve to a single radius is encouraged to minimize the sophistication required in cutting. Combining the individual conclusions yields two options for opening shapes that have stronger expressions of masonry than does the standard rectangle.

Very narrow rectangular openings with single-piece heads and sills project the spirit of masonry. A minor variation would be corbeled jambs supporting the lintel. The other option is a circular opening (Fig. 6–49). It lacks a sense of framing (unlike a rectangle) and has an image of mass and simplicity that relates to masonry's medium level of refinement. It is not suggested that all masonry openings take these shapes. They may be useful on occasion in punctuating the image of masonry. Using and expressing concrete or steel for lintels and sills is not discouraged. These materials lend their own properties to the openings and can alter their shapes accordingly.

Figure 6-49 The structure and shape of the circular opening expresses the uniqueness of unit masonry with regard to size and workability. The fact that gravity pulls water directly into only a few joints at the bottom is a mild reference to the durability of masonry.

Chapter 7

MASONRY IN ARCHITECTURE

CHECKLIST FOR ANALYSIS

The expression of masonry in historic and contemporary architecture is analyzed in this chapter. The quality of the work is not judged. Its degree of compatibility with the principles of expression discussed previously is determined. Listed below are the major characteristics considered to express the nature of masonry. Refer to Checklist C-2 in Appendix C for this list in a worksheet format with additional notations to assist analysis.

1. Blocklike characteristics in the building image
2. Characteristics of the building image derived from the opportunities in form afforded by relatively small building units
3. Contribution to the building image by form characteristics of secondary products (if any)
4. Medium level of refinement in the building image
5. Clarity of masonry's nearly complete limitation to compression resistance in the span systems contributing to the building image
6. Extensive demonstration of compressive strength in walls and columns
7. Demonstration of masonry's medium resistance to water penetration and deterioration as part of the building image
8. Absence of the sense that cut or broken masonry contributes to the building image

A building need not demonstrate all the compatible characteristics to be expressive of the nature of masonry. The number required varies with the intensity of each expression and the magnitude of expressions that oppose the nature of masonry.

ANALYSIS

Hockley House
Philadelphia, Pennsylvania; Frank Furness; 1875

In several buildings by Frank Furness the compressive nature of masonry is particularly clear. The Hockley House is not his strongest compressive statement but does exhibit characteristics that contribute to a feeling of compression (Fig. 7–1). Three round columns at the front entrance are short, with oversized capitals. Their stubbiness suggests large axial loads without a tendency to buckle. The short columns rest on blocks of stone that increase in size toward grade. The battered characteristic gives the bases a feeling of stability. The absence of a tendency to develop tensile stresses due to tipping prevents the sense of compression from being diluted. The battering is accomplished, for the most part, by sloped surfaces on the stone blocks, thus preventing the formation of shelves at each joint that could catch water. Large joints give the blocks individual identities. This emphasizes the expression of stacked blocks. The battered stone detail continues across the base of the street facade, lending the same sense of compression that is projected by the base of the columns.

The large bay window on the street facade does not have as strong a sense of masonry as do the other parts of the building. The massiveness of the cantilevered form does not match the less massive stone brackets below it. The brackets lack a blocklike or compact feeling, either of which would have contributed to their credibility as masonry structure. Corbeled rectangular units would have been more in keeping with the spirit of masonry than are the curved brackets. A shorter cantilever would also help. The short stone lintels at certain windows are more successful in expressing the limited bending strength of masonry. The resulting narrow windows emphasize this structural limitation, especially when they occur in a series with thick mullions (expressing compression) between.

Figure 7–1 *Hockley House.* The general sense of compression is diluted somewhat by the lack of thrust resistance at the corner of the two arches over the entry stairs.

Other windows are arched, a form compatible with the masonry's strength properties. The masses of brick to either side of the windows seem adequate to handle thrust. The arches have credibility, therefore, and express the compressive nature of masonry. The two large arches supported by the short columns at the entry steps do not have the same credibility. Their meeting at the corner does not have a buttress or other mass to resist thrust. No tie is clearly expressed that would eliminate the need for a buttress. The decorative components that fill the area below the curve of the arches are vague in their structural expression. They appear neither to tie nor to span. They seem to hang from the arches, thus failing to purify the ambiguous expression of the arches.

A number of details emphasize the form of the brick and stone. Some window jambs step back to form three corners instead of one (Fig. 7–2). The detail is a reminder that the brick has thickness. The detail is emphasized by its contrast to the standard corner detail in the upper one-third of the jamb. Extensive corbeling at the cornice and the chimney emphasizes brick height, width, and thickness (Fig. 7–3). A band of turned brick calls attention to the three dimensions of the units. The height of the brick is expressed in courses of darker brick. Dark brick patterns emphasize the height and length of units at the cornice.

Water-catching shelves occur at the turned brick and in a few other details. This lapse in attention to the durability issue is limited, however. The majority of the details shed water. The steep single-piece window sills have noticeable positive drainage.

Figure 7–2 *Hockley House.* The stepped jamb, short lintel, steep jointless sill, and stout mullions make the windows expressive of the nature of masonry.

Figure 7–3 *Hockley House.* A hanging sensation is avoided in the chimney by the structurally convincing and intensely form expressive corbeling at its base.

Working the brick is limited to the traditional degree required at the arches. Both smooth and textured stone are present. The rougher textured stone has a pattern of gouges, suggesting the use of a tool. The contrasting textures and tool marks express the nature of stone and stone-processing technology more strongly than the smooth stone would by itself.

The absence of purity in two major structural expressions on the main facade is balanced by numerous small expressions of the nature of masonry form. The stronger-than-average compressive expression in the column system and street facade further emphasizes the strength characteristics of masonry. The net effect of the design is an expression of the nature of the material.

Trinity Church
Boston, Massachusetts; H. H. Richardson; 1877
West porch by Shepley, Rutan, and Coolidge; 1897

The church is especially pure in its expression of masonry (Fig. 7–4). The building has compact proportions that give a sense of stability. The round forms express the relatively small size of unit masonry and contribute to the stable appearance of the building. The image makes the occurrence of tensile stress from tipping or leaning seem unlikely. The resulting overall feeling of compression is enhanced by numerous details. Spans are arched or served by very short stone lintels. The expression of the short lintels is magnified by their need for numerous columns. Many clusters of columns contribute to the spirit of compression, as the visual mass of a group is more compact than that of one column. A group, appearing as an individual visual unit, seems less likely to buckle than does an isolated column.

Attention is drawn to the short stone spans at the chapel steps (Fig. 7–5). Each lintel supporting the stone in the canopy wall is carried by a freestanding column at each end. Since there are numerous short lintels, there are numerous columns. They act as punctuation, defining the lengths of the lintels. The shortness of the lintels is also clarified by their change in height. Since they step

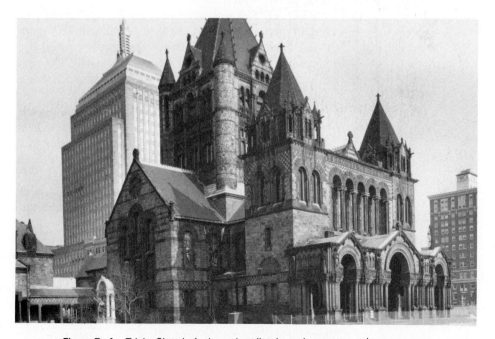

Figure 7–4 _Trinity Church._ Arches, short lintels, and numerous columns express compression. Most patterns created by light and dark stone emphasize the form of masonry.

Figure 7-5 *Trinity Church.* The unique stepped column system brings strong emphasis to the short lintels and the block form of the stone.

up with the stairs, they do not align with each other. Alignment would obscure the actual length of each unit. Here the length of each lintel is emphasized by its isolated position with respect to adjacent lintels. The color of the lintels contrasts with that of the adjacent stones that do not span. The change in color further clarifies the identity of the structural components. The stepped wall below the columns reflects the blocklike nature of the stone, as does the stepped canopy above. The unique assembly of stepped walls, columns, and lintels strongly expresses the nature of masonry and is a major element in the aesthetic order of the chapel facade.

The authenticity of the arches is supported by the consistent presence of adequate mass at either side to resist thrust. The arched forms are emphasized by the contrast in color between the voussoirs and the surrounding stone. The deep shadow under the arches does the same. The result is emphasis of a form that expresses compression and therefore the nature of masonry.

The size and shape of the stone is emphasized in many details by contrast of color. Bands of dark stone around the building clearly indicate the height of the units. Dark stone trim at openings projects periodically into the lighter adjacent stone, thus revealing the rectangularity and height of both. A checkerboard pattern of light and dark stone forms a band on several elevations. The height, width, and squareness of these units is expressed clearly.

A zigzag pattern requires closer inspection to identify the rectangular form of its units. Casual observation yields a sense of triangularity. In fact, triangular units are present at the edges of the pattern. The stepped nature of the pattern and therefore its compatibility with masonry form is obscured by the 45-degree tilt of the stones. A pattern of level rectangular stones such as the checkerboard would require no angular units. It is the detail least expressive of the nature of masonry with regard to form.

The issue of durability is adequately addressed. Generally, the detailing sheds water. The stones that cap walls are longer than the stones below them. They therefore provide protection, since they offer fewer joints for water penetration. One-piece stone sills have the minimum number of joints possible (one at each end). The detailing does not make an issue of shedding water. The result is that the aesthetic order does not depend on attention to the durability issue. Its visual effect is therefore nearly neutral.

The building strongly expresses the nature of masonry. Its aesthetic system is based on the expression of strength and form properties. It is remarkably pure compared to contemporary masonry buildings. Its purity does not contrast as much with that of other historic stone architecture.

Robie House
Chicago, Illinois; Frank Lloyd Wright; 1909

Attention to the durability level of masonry plays a significant role in the aesthetic order of the Robie House (Fig. 7–6). The visual impact of the stone cap protecting the top of the brick walls is emphasized by its contrasting color and large size. The cap overhangs the wall, thus providing greater protection than would a flush coping. Its visibility is also greater due to the shadow under its edge.

Although the stone base has no shadow line, it is larger than the cap. It holds the brick above grade, thus reducing the potential for staining from splashed mud. Since the base projects beyond the surface of the wall, it holds the exposed ground surface even farther from the brick. The base's vulnerability to being splashed with muddy water is not an issue, as that is its apparent role. The protective role of the base is, to a large degree, symbolic. It would not merit extensive discussion except for its association with the wall cap. The pair form a protective system that is visually prominent.

The stone trim plays a different role where it occurs over openings (Fig. 7–7). The stone is not structural, as is readily apparent for any opening over a few feet wide. It serves as recognition that the brick cannot span the opening in a horizontal line. Although the stone could not span the distance in most cases, it gives the brick a place to set visually. The fact that the brick has no structural role beyond compression is thus clarified.

The violation of structural potential is limited to the stone, which at least recognizes the need for a lintel. The detail is not of the highest purity but reflects the structural limitations of the brick. Both stone and brick are excluded

Figure 7–6 *Robie House.* The stone coping and base are an unusually strong expression relating to the durability of masonry systems.

Figure 7-7 *Robie House.* The stone trim above the windows and other openings acknowledge the need for lintels to carry the brick.

from a number of major spans where the top of the openings meet the soffit of the roof overhang. Since masonry does not exist at these spans, strength limitations of the material are not challenged there.

Little is done to emphasize the form or compressive nature of masonry. At some corners the brick forms a shape similar to that of a pilaster, which gives the wall surface a sense of thickness. The slight increase in a sense of mass at these details lends itself to both the expression of compression and the block-like nature of masonry. Battering and corbeling are not present. The working of masonry is well below its natural limit, as no cutting is featured.

The net effect of materials expression in the building is in support of the nature of masonry. The most significant materials expression is in regard to the issue of durability. It is visually strong enough to overcome the lack of purity of the nonstructural stone lintels. It is a unique condition, as structural expressions usually outweigh those relating to durability.

Ennis House
Hollywood, California; Frank Lloyd Wright; 1923

Wright exploited the potential of the forming process in the Ennis House as he did in other concrete block houses (Fig. 7-8). In doing so he expressed a significant difference between concrete units and the other masonries. The repetitive patterns are a logical result of reproducing numerous units from the same form. The use of smooth-faced units emphasizes the uniqueness of the patterned block by their contrast (Fig. 7-9). A sense of block mass is projected by stepping back walls, corners, and other details (Fig. 7-10).

Stepped surfaces have the potential of violating the durability of masonry. It is surprising to note that even in the mild climate of Los Angeles, deterioration has occurred at some of the water-catching shelves. The problem is magnified in the horizontal planes by the pattern recesses, which hold water. The tops of the walls have no apparent protective system, thus continuing the violation of the durability expression.

Figure 7–8 *Ennis House.* The nature of concrete block's forming process was exploited as a significant element in the aesthetic order.

Figure 7–9 *Ennis House.* The patterned block is emphasized by adjacent plain units. Pattern repetition distinguishes the unit material from poured-in-place concrete. The decay of the shelf created by these units is visible in the irregular upper edge.

Figure 7–10 *Ennis House.* Stepping the wall and the corners emphasizes block form, as it suggests that the material has thickness. The set back of upper sections suggests stability, thus expressing the compressive nature of masonry.

Stability, and therefore compression, is expressed by both those walls that take large steps back in a few tall sections and those that step back slightly at each course. The compressive nature of block is ignored, however, in several significant spans and details.

Calling certain strength expressions violations is not entirely appropriate, as the block was never promoted as unreinforced masonry. Wright designed the block as a composite system of steel and concrete units. This is significant-

Figure 7-11 *Ennis House.* Openings are spanned by block in a horizontal line. This expression of strength, which is exaggerated in the long span over the entry gate, violates the nature of masonry.

ly different from simply adding steel to a standard block assembly. The terms *knit block* and *textile block*, by which the system is known, reflect its composite nature. The profile of the units was shaped to receive steel rods that "knit" the units together vertically and horizontally. The structural expression of the system is criticized as if it were unreinforced masonry, because that is what it appears to be.

All openings have lintels of units that appear to stick together side by side and, as a group, resist bending (Fig. 7–11). The image violates the strength properties of unit masonry. A number of windows have blocks apparently hanging in the corners where jambs and lintels meet. The block steps are too large for a corbel. Although they strongly promote the blocky image of the unit, their tensile sense violates the spirit of masonry strength.

The workability of masonry is not challenged in the building, as the cutting of blocks is not apparent. The durability level of masonry is violated by numerous water-catching shelves and unprotected top edges. The form of the block is strongly expressed. An uninformed view of the building would conclude that the strength violations just about balance the positive expression of form. The general impression of the building, however, is unmistakably masonrylike.

Sowden House
Hollywood, California; Lloyd Wright; 1926

Attention is drawn to the concrete block masses by their central location and contrast with adjacent stuccoed surfaces (Fig. 7–12). The blocklike nature of the unit is strongly emphasized, as stepped surfaces occur in the face, top, and bottom of the masses. The formability of the concrete is exploited in the repetitive surface pattern of the units, thus demonstrating one of its differences from clay and stone masonry.

The potential of the surface manipulation is only partially realized, however, for two reasons. The face pattern lacks the angular geometry that would clearly distinguish it from broken stone (Fig. 7–13). Its texture is reminiscent of the imitation stone units once common in concrete block. The shadow line

Figure 7–12 *Sowden House.* Blank surfaces frame the visually active concrete block masses, thus encouraging attention to focus on the concrete units. They lack a sense of compression because no base is expressed on which they may set.

Figure 7–13 *Sowden House.* The relatively simple rounded forms of the block, while facilitating form removal, are reminiscent of broken and weathered stone.

across the center of the units reads as a joint, thus obscuring the actual size and position of installed units. The installation of blocks back to back causes the positive mass of the pattern to occur at the crossing of the joints rather than between joints. This contributes further to the vagueness of block identity.

The tops of the block assemblies violate the durability level of masonry systems. They have no apparent system of protection against water penetration of the joints on top edges. On the positive side, the faces of the surfaces drain water since the blocks align vertically. Because the small recesses do not occur at joints, any water that hesitates in draining has no adjacent joint to penetrate.

The major violation of the nature of masonry is in the area of strength properties. The masses appear to cantilever several feet. Masonry does not have the tensile strength in bending to achieve the cantilevers. The units are actually attached to a hidden concrete structure.

The workability of masonry is not challenged, as cutting is not expressed in the assembly. The durability issue is balanced with both a violation and harmonious detailing. Structural and unit form establish the greatest part of the facade's aesthetic order. The clear strength violation, however, is not balanced by an equally strong expression of unit form. The net effect is an expression that is not compatible with the nature of its materials.

Lloyd Wright House
Hollywood, California; Lloyd Wright; 1928

The visual prominence of the small amount of concrete block in Lloyd Wright's own house is enhanced by their location at the entry and between blank walls (Fig. 7–14). They contrast with those of the Sowden House in one respect. Their surface forms are based on rectangular geometry, which clearly distinguishes them from broken stone (Fig. 7–15). Their blocklike nature is expressed as depth is revealed in the recesses of the face pattern and the stepped configuration of the assembly. Some study is required to identify the form of each block, as they are partially obscured by the busy pattern. The projections in the texture of the block challenge the level of refinement expected to survive the incidental impacts typical at an entryway. The high position of the assembly helps protect and therefore justify the relatively fragile forms.

Figure 7–14 *Lloyd Wright House.* The visual prominence of the block detailing is enhanced by its placement at the entry and between blank wall surfaces.

Figure 7–15 *Lloyd Wright House.* The intricate pattern of cubes and squares distinguish the concrete block units from broken or cut stone. The horizontal strip has a sense of hanging rather than setting. The structural expression of the vertical mass is ambiguous.

The blocks seem to hang from the building. The sense of tension is in opposition to the structural condition natural to masonry. The exposed horizontal surfaces, both within the open faces of the units and on top of the assemblies, fail to respect the need for protection from water penetration. Block's natural level of workability is not violated, as none is attempted.

The net expression, like that of the Sowden House, is in violation of the nature of concrete masonry. The structural and durability violations are not overcome by the fairly strong expression of the formability of concrete.

Jacobs II House
Middleton, Wisconsin; Frank Lloyd Wright; 1943

The house expresses the compressive nature of stone in its simple stacking and curved plan (Fig. 7–16). The curved shape of the building is especially appropriate for the high earth berm pressing against it. The stability provided by the curved geometry lends to a sense of compression. Without a tendency to lean, the stone expresses no potential to develop tensile stresses. The curved form is compatible with the unit nature of the masonry. The large radius curve is easily achieved by turning each stone slightly with respect to adjacent units. The compressive expression is violated in a few openings over which the stone passes in a horizontal line, butted end to end and seeming to span. This condition is avoided in the major opening (the large window wall), where masonry does not occur over the glass.

The rough texture of the stone seems natural. The expression of the stone form is enhanced by the projection of numerous units from the wall plane. The projection, however, ignores the vulnerability of masonry to water penetration at the joints. The contact of the stone wall with the berm is compatible with the substance of stone but violates the durability level of the system because of the numerous joints. The waterproofing system applied to the stone wall is not visible and therefore does not purify the expression. An incorrect impression of the watertightness of masonry assemblies is the result. A detail that is compatible with the durability level of masonry is the roof's protection of the top edges of the building walls. The limited workability natural to stone is recognized in the use of simple blocky forms throughout.

The major durability violation does not have an overpowering visual impression, as the joints that are in jeopardy are out of sight. The visual effect

Figure 7–16 *Jacobs II House.* The curve of the wall stabilizes the mass against the berm. The passing of the joints into the earth suggests that they are able to resist the inevitable tendency of water to penetrate.

of the forms and detailing in support of the nature of masonry therefore outweighs that of the violations.

Morris Gift Shop
San Francisco, California; Frank Lloyd Wright; 1948

The entry facade, the only element visible to the public, expresses the form characteristics of brick (Fig. 7–17). An example of brick expressed in all three dimensions (rare in space-enclosing walls) occurs in a vertical strip near the entry (Fig. 7–18). The detail covers a lighting alcove and has unglazed voids to emit light. Every other brick is omitted, which exposes the full depth of the remaining units. The expression is strengthened by the units setting forward of an adjacent wall surface. Consequently, a significant portion of one end of each unit is exposed to view.

Four arched courses are corbeled at the entry, which expresses a sense of thickness in the units (Fig. 7–19). The top arched course projects from the surrounding wall to contribute further to the sense of a third dimension. The arched courses at the face of the entry express the compressive nature of masonry. Their credibility is supported by adequate mass on either side to resist thrust. The vault behind the arches, however, violates the structural nature of masonry.

Figure 7–17 *Morris Gift Shop.* The importance of the brick detailing near the entry is magnified by the simplicity of the facade.

Figure 7–18 *Morris Gift Shop.* The form of the brick has the maximum exposure possible at the lighting alcove because of its three-dimensional expression and the light that increases visibility. Visibility is further increased by its location near the entry.

Figure 7-19 *Morris Gift Shop.* The third dimension of the brick is partially revealed in the corbeling of the arch at the entry.

The entry vault is half brick and half glazing (Fig. 7-20). The glazing and its mullions are too delicate to resist the compressive forces transmitted by the masonry half. The expression is therefore one of tension rather than one of compression. The masonry half seems to hang from above, thereby transmitting no force to the curved glazing. The expression does not appear to violate for shock value. It reads as a serious detail and is therefore a significant violation.

The durability level of masonry systems is both violated and supported. The top of the brick facade has a protective cap, as does the top of a wythe a few feet lower. The bricks at the lighting alcove catch water. The projected arched course drains water but in the wrong direction. The cutting of brick is not excessive, so the workability of masonry is not violated.

The effect of the structural violation on the street elevation is nil, as it is not apparent when the entire facade is viewed. For this reason the building is judged to express the nature of its material. If the structural violation was more visible, the opposite conclusion would be drawn.

Figure 7-20 *Morris Gift Shop.* The hanging expression of the half-vaulted brick at the entry violates the strength potential of masonry.

Bavinger House
Norman, Oklahoma; Bruce Goff; 1955

The logarithmic spiral lends a sense of stability to the stone wall of the house (Fig. 7–21). The resulting expression is one of compression, as the likelihood of tensile stresses is reduced by the geometry of the curve. The sense of compression is not challenged by openings. Large openings in the exterior are spanned by the roof system (Fig. 7–22). The stone over other small openings is arched. Generous mass occurs on either side of the small arches to resist thrust. The natural form of the stone rubble is expressed in the irregular edges of the wall at its top and opening jambs. Attention is drawn to the edges by the presence of bluish chunks of glass mixed with the stone.

Figure 7–21 *Bavinger House.* The curve of the spiraled wall stabilizes the stone and contributes to the sense of compression.

Figure 7–22 *Bavinger House.* The potential for tensile stresses is avoided by spanning the opening with the roof system rather than the stone. The natural form of the stone is emphasized in the irregularity of the window jambs.

Figure 7-23 *Bavinger House.* The top edge of the wall expresses the irregularity of the stone rubble but seems especially vulnerable to water penetration at the joints.

The durability of masonry is violated significantly in the top edge of the wall (Fig. 7–23). Its irregularity catches and directs water to the many unprotected joints. The condition is aggravated by the drainage of the continuous skylight into the upper edge of the wall. The contact of the stone to the ground expresses the compatibility of the substance with the earth but fails to address the questionable water protection of the numerous joints adjacent to the living space below grade. No method of protecting these joints is expressed. The potential for visual deterioration of the stone near the ground is not an issue. The stone, which came from the site, has the same reddish-brown color as any mud that would splash on it.

Workability is not challenged, as the stone is not cut. The strong expression of stone form and the compressive image of the building are balanced by the significant violation of durability. Although freeze–thaw damage would have little visual impact among the irregular shapes, the dryness of the interior is in peril. The net expression of the building with regard to its material is, consequently, ambiguous.

Oreon E. Scott Chapel
Drake University, Des Moines, Iowa; Eero Saarinen; 1955

The curved wall of the chapel expresses compression, as its stabilizing geometry reduces the potential for tension from leaning (Fig. 7–24). The compact form of the building contributes further to this sense. Because of the extreme simplicity of the building, the compressive image plays a major role in the visual statement.

A three-dimensional surface pattern is created by recessed pairs of stacked headers (Fig. 7–25). The detail expresses a degree of thickness in the brick. It also emphasizes header width and unit height. The height expression is diluted slightly because the unit pairs are flush within the recesses. The expression of unit form is confused slightly because the bond pattern does not recognize the pattern of recesses. Since there is only a limited relationship between the

Figure 7–24 *Scott Chapel.* The geometry and compactness of the chapel gives a sense of stability and mass that is compatible with masonry. Square recesses give a sense of thickness and contribute to the blocklike image of masonry.

Figure 7–25 *Scott Chapel.* The extensive cutting done to force the recesses into the brick pattern is magnified by the fact that another bond pattern could have eliminated the cutting. The cement washes on the shelves are barely visible at close range.

two patterns, simple but extensive cutting of brick was required. Every recess required cutting brick. Workability is violated with regard to quantity but not sophistication. The violation is magnified because cutting could have been avoided by a change in the bond pattern.

The durability issue is addressed by the coping and base, which are both of adequate visual mass to contribute to the building image. The mortar washes at the bottom of each recess helps protect the joint from water penetration but have little visual impact. Their lack of visibility denies their existence and therefore denies the potential for a problem. The positive expression of the coping and base is diluted by the failure to express the protection at the recesses. The net result neither contributes to nor detracts from the expression of the building with regard to its material.

The expression of form and strength supports the image of the material. Workability does not. Durability is split. The composite expression of materials favors the nature of masonry.

East Building, National Gallery of Art
Washington, D.C.; I. M. Pei and Partners; 1977

The analysis is essentially one of the stone cladding, as the structure includes both steel and concrete. A sense of hanging is not apparent in the cladding (Fig. 7–26). A sense of stacking is. The low profile, blank walls, and extension of the cladding to grade gives an overall compressive sense to the building. An academic reference to the need for lintels is made by exposed strips of concrete over openings. In the larger spans (such as at the main entry) hidden steel trusses span the openings, as the concrete strips do not have adequate depth to do so. Although the concrete is not the lintel, nor is it large enough to be the lintel, it lets the cladding continue its stacked image by giving it a visual base.

The form of the stone has a limited role in the aesthetic order. The units have identity in the wall surfaces, due to their slight difference in color. The joints are too small to read when viewing the facade as a whole.

The extraordinarily sharp form of a building mass adjacent to the main entry violates the refinement level natural to masonry (Fig. 7–27). The violation is magnified by its prominent location and its position by a sidewalk. The potential for damage from accidental impact is high. The walk invites contact with the sharp edge, as is evident by its discoloration and deterioration from

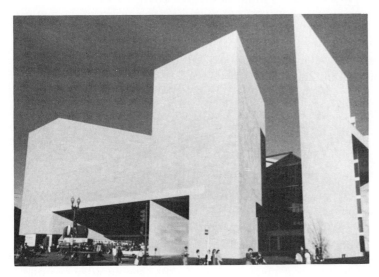

Figure 7–26 *National Gallery.* A subtle contrast in tone identifies a lintel-like band over openings such as in this main entry facade. The distinction between stone panels is minimal.

Figure 7–27 *National Gallery.* The sharp-edged marble form violates the compact and blocklike image of masonry.

Figure 7-28 *National Gallery.* The strangeness of the sharp stone edge is illustrated by soiling and wear from constant touching by curious visitors.

touching (Fig. 7–28). The stone is touched frequently out of curiosity, an illustration of its oddness. It is strange enough to qualify as a purposeful violation of the material for shock value. This approach recognizes the nature of the material in its violation.

The surface of the stone is very smooth but not glossy, which keeps it from being at the extreme of remoteness from a natural sense. Expression of a coping is nearly nonexistent. No base suggests protection from splashed mud at grade. The working of masonry is not an issue. The net effect of material expression with regard to the nature of masonry is nearly neutral in the building. Except for the subtle luster and natural variations in color and pattern in the marble, metal panels or concrete could produce similar expressions in the facades. This does not deny the aesthetic value of the subtle differences between the stone surface and those of the other materials.

Mandell Residences
Houston, Texas; Arquitectonica International; 1984

The apparent horizontal spans of brick over the openings of the townhouses violate the structural nature of masonry (Fig. 7–29). One circular opening is compatible with brick's compressive potential. The angles of the one triangular opening are just within the structural limit of a corbel (Fig. 7–30).

The cutting of the brick at the circle is twice the quantity required for a traditional arch but not more sophisticated. The cutting at the triangular opening produced sizes and shapes that seem more arbitrary than those of the circle. While the odd-shaped units at the arch participate in the transfer of compression, they do not at the triangular opening. The triangular units that occur about every third course seem to hang from the brick above. This appearance occurs partly because the triangular opening has no trim course as does the circular opening. The trim course at the circle provides a visual and physical support for the triangular units and lends itself to the impression of a compressive mass. The thin steel flange that provides support for the triangular opening is visible only upon close inspection. The expression of the opening is judged without it.

Figure 7–29 *Mandell Residences.* The numerous horizontal spans of brick over openings are not harmonious with the strength properties of masonry. Thickness is expressed in several openings that are not glazed.

Figure 7–30 *Mandell Residences.* The corbeled triangular opening is structurally feasible; thus the hidden steel is reduced to the role of providing a safety factor. The pieces of brick that seem to hang from the jambs violate the strength image of masonry.

The clear expression of the circular opening and the ambiguous statement of the triangular one are not enough to establish a structural pattern compatible with masonry. The violations of strength principles by the apparent horizontal spans of the brick are too numerous. The slight undulation of the back wall is too slight to be a significant stabilizing geometry (Fig. 7–31). Any sense of compression suggested by the undulation is obscured by the long horizontal spans of brick over openings in the wall.

The stepping of parapets at the corner townhouse emphasizes the rectangularity of the material. The height of a unit is not especially clarified by

Figure 7-31 *Mandell Residences.* The undulation of the back wall is too flat to provide significant stability in expression or reality. The numerous horizontal brick spans prevent a sense of compression from developing in this facade.

the stepping, as it occurs in multiples fairly high above eye level. The visual effect of the detailing is further limited by the difficulty of seeing any other stepped parapet. The stepped expression is countered by the more visually prominent sloped parapet in the front facade. Numerous openings without glazing occur in the masonry, which reveals the full thickness of the wall. This contributes to a sense of thickness in the individual units.

Durability is addressed with copings on the tops of parapets and sills at openings both with and without glass. The protective strips are not visually strong, as they are the same color as the brick. Since they play nearly no role in the visual order of the building, the expression of the durability of masonry systems is almost neutral. Workability is not pushed beyond its traditional limit. The cuts for the brick are simple and few compared to the total number of units.

The building does not express the nature of its material. Brick seems to have had little effect on the design. A number of other materials could have been used instead and, if painted the color of brick, would have caused little change in the image of the building.

Herring Hall
Rice University, Houston, Texas; Cesar Pelli; 1984

The expression of masonry form is strong in this veneered steel building (Fig. 7–32). The visual impact of the building is, to a large degree, the result of surface patterns created by a mixture of two colors of face brick, another color of glazed brick, and various sizes of limestone. Contrasting colors identify groups of units, single courses, and single units (Fig. 7–33). When viewed close enough to see the stepped edges of the diapering pattern, the shapes of the units both

Figure 7-32 *Herring Hall.* The surface patterns express unit shape to varying degrees of clarity. In this view, the building is nearly too far away to see that the diagonal lines consist of rectangular forms.

Figure 7-33 *Herring Hall.* The rectangularity of brick is expressed in the rectangular patterns. Unit height is expressed in the single courses, which contrast in color with the surrounding wall.

in and adjacent to the pattern are emphasized. Otherwise, the diagonal lines seem to deny the grid of the mortar joints. Stepped surfaces on the street facade and deep recesses near the corners of the end walls give a sense of thickness in the masonry (Fig. 7–34). Depth is further expressed at the exposed edges of the column veneers (Fig. 7–35). The revealed masonry edges at the columns express the role of the brick as a veneer rather than as a bearing wall.

The expression of the brick at spans over open space and glazing violates the strength potential of masonry (Fig. 7–36). Long horizontal runs of brick and stone are visually significant. The steel actually performing the spans is hidden except for the occasional flange barely visible below the units. The numerous

Figure 7-34 *Herring Hall.* The stepped detailing gives a sense of thickness to the masonry and does not catch water.

Figure 7-35 *Herring Hall.* The masonry is revealed to be a veneer in the exposure of its edges at the columns. The radius of the column is small enough for the curved nature of the units to be apparent; thus the secondary characteristic is expressed.

Figure 7-36 *Herring Hall.* Patterns over certain openings are reminiscent of lintels. The detail is unable to establish credibility as an academic reference, however, because it is used only intermittently.

spans prevent the solid masses and two curved walls from establishing a sense of compression.

Protection of top edges ranges from minimal to strongly expressed. The absence of a base for the masonry has resulted in the discoloration of the limestone in one area. Three-dimensional surface detailing sheds water, as the stepped forms are flush vertically.

The complex relationships between units in the facades have a highly planned feeling. The symmetry and sense of care projected in the placement of colors and textures obscures the fact that nonstandard sizes were needed. The net impression is that the working of units was not a significant part of the construction effort and thus the issue is not violated.

With the durability and workability issues failing to produce significantly strong expressions, form and strength are left to determine the overall sense of the building regarding the nature of masonry. The violations of strength are based on common contemporary detailing and in some cases there is nearly an academic acknowledgment of the violations. The numerous two-dimensional and occasional three-dimensional expressions of form, in contrast, are extraordinary compared to contemporary practices. The expression of form therefore overshadows slightly the violations of strength. The net expression favors the nature of masonry without being exceptional.

Chapter 8

PROPERTIES OF STEEL

The category of steel includes numerous alloys with varied properties. With the exception of stainless and weathering steels, which have significantly greater durability, common characteristics may be identified that represent the image of steel. While some aspects of shape are shared with wood and some aspects of strength are shared with concrete, its unique combination of strength and form give steel a clear identity in architecture.

FORM

Primary Form.   Products that are structural, are produced directly from raw steel, and are standards of the industry define the primary-form characteristics of steel. Hot-rolled structural shapes (wide-flange sections, channels, and angles) meet the criteria for the primary group (Fig. 8–1). So do bars, plate, and certain types of pipe. Although the products differ in profile, they tend to have several common characteristics. A length of 90 feet, the maximum for wide flanges (W shapes) at some mills, and a depth of 3 feet, another standard maximum, produce a length-to-depth ratio of 30 to 1 for wide-flange sections. While greater and smaller ratios are standard among the primary products, most may be considered to have a linear geometry. They are more like lines than planes or blocks.

Only the longest of the many plate sizes available could be classified as linear. The sizes commonly stocked by fabricators are more accurately described as rectangular. Since a single plate does not act as a structural plane, plate is not identified as being planar. Unlike wide flanges, plates tend to lose their identities in structural applications, as they are often cut and joined with other plates or components. Because their expression in buildings tends to be minimal or supplementary to that of structural steel, it is not important to define a new classification of geometry for them. They are simply called rectangular. They are much like plywood in this respect.

Figure 8–1 Hot-rolled structural shapes define the primary form characteristics of steel. They are rectilinear, visually light, and have a sense of precision.

All primary products are produced as straight members. Most profiles are rectangles or are rectangular, as in the case of perpendicular flanges and webs. Round bar and seamless pipe do not conform to this characteristic. These exceptions are considered to be minor since their influence on building form and detailing is small compared to that of the rectangular primary forms. Their effect is limited by their relatively small cross section.

The thickness of steel components is generally small compared to component size. Component cross sections tend to be small compared to the size of the structure which they form. The result is a material of small visual bulk. This characteristic is expressed by components whose thicknesses are exposed to view. Nearly all primary forms express the thinness typical of steel and have the potential for expressing precision in detailing.

While the closed perimeters of pipes and tubes limit the expression of thinness, some potential for it does exist (Fig. 8–2). A major difference in the expressions of wood and steel is with regard to visual mass. Unlike wood, steel has a potential for expressing a very high level of refinement. High strength and dimensional stability with regard to moisture make the longevity of visually delicate forms in steel more likely than it is in other materials.

Figure 8–2 The low visual mass natural to steel products is more strongly expressed in pipes and tubes if wall thicknesses are revealed at the ends and in cuts between the ends. (The example is a secondary form, as reflected in the seam on the far side.)

While recognizing that exceptions do exist, the primary form characteristics of steel may generally be described as those of linearity, straightness, rectangularity, and thinness. Rectangularity refers, here, to the 90-degree corners in sections and elevations of the linear members. This reference should not be confused with the reference to plate, plywood, or the faces of masonry, where the rectangles have closed perimeters with dimensions that are more nearly equal. Raw hot-rolled surfaces are fairly smooth but not slick or shiny. They are able to remain true (without undulations) throughout their life span, due to the substantial thickness of the products (compared to some cold-rolled products). Component surfaces are compatible with the precision and refinement natural to steel. Expressing these characteristics will contribute to a sense of steel in a building image.

Secondary Form. Secondary steel forms are those fabricated from primary forms, are not structural, or are not common. Plate girders, rigid frames, welded pipe, trussed components, cable, decking, and cladding are included. The secondary products exhibit most of the primary-form characteristics. They are nearly all linear and relatively thin.

The characteristics of plate girders are much the same as those of wide-flange members (Fig. 8–3). The larger size of the girder yields greater span potential but requires stiffeners to keep the relatively tall thin webs from buckling. While the stiffeners are themselves linear, they interrupt the linearity of the girder. The linear expression of plate girders is therefore diluted. The expression of thinness and precision is strengthened by the many exposed edges of the web stiffeners.

The rigid frames typical of prefabricated metal buildings are usually not rectangular in side elevation (Fig. 8–4). The need for more steel and larger dimensions at the moment-resisting connections yields legs that are rectangular in section but tapered in elevation. While linearity and thinness are much like that of wide flanges and channels, the variation from rectangularity offers the potential for expressing a contrast with primary forms. The relative economy (compared to hot rolling) of fabricating nonrectangular forms out of plate suggests a potential for the expression of tapered forms in plate girders also. It is an option that has not been thoroughly explored in architecture.

Because welded seam pipe is available in large diameters, it has potential for high visibility and therefore strong expression (Fig. 8–5). Pipe differs from the primary-form characteristics in its round profile. Besides the simple expres-

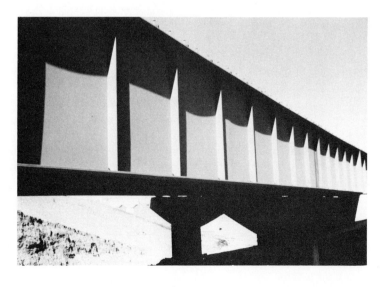

Figure 8–3 Plate girders typically fail to exploit the relative ease of cutting the web plates into shapes other than rectangles. The thin edges of the numerous web stiffeners give these components a sense of precision and refinement but reduce linearity.

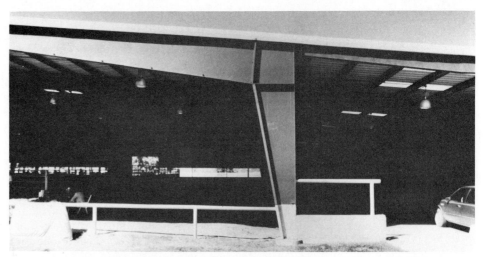

Figure 8–4 The tapered shapes of the vertical and horizontal legs of a rigid frame offer an opportunity for expression in building form.

Figure 8–5 The sculpture strongly expresses the unique characteristics of pipe as well and the thinness and precision of steel in general. Artist: Alexander Liberman.

sion of pipe roundness, the shape may affect building form indirectly. Round sections facilitate connections between members that are not on the *X, Y,* or *Z* axis (Fig. 8–6). Pipe is therefore not as closely tied to rectangularity as are the primary forms. Exploiting this flexibility is to recognize a major secondary form characteristic of pipe.

Trusses, truss girders, and open-web joists express linearity in both their parts and their overall shapes. They exhibit rectangles and triangles in their internal configurations (Fig. 8–7). Triangularity and internal openness are secondary characteristics that may be exploited to influence building image and demonstrate the uniqueness of trussed members within the family of steel components.

Cable differs from the other forms of steel in its flexibility (Fig. 8–8). This combined with its rounded profile gives cable even more freedom of configura-

Figure 8–6 The round characteristic of the pipe facilitates the attachment of struts from many angles. This is reflected in the polygonal building form. The product form has therefore contributed to the building image.

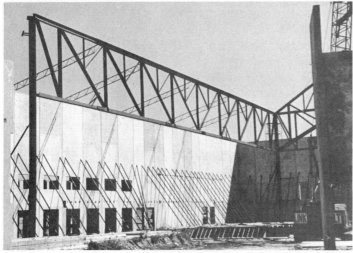

Figure 8–7 The triangles typical of trussed components offer a vehicle for expression beyond their simple exposure to view. They are large enough to receive glazing, ducts, acoustical materials, or decorative elements.

Figure 8–8 The storage of cable on spools reflects its high degree of flexibility. The property may be exploited in architectural expression while also expressing the linearity and precision typical of steel in general.

tion than pipe. Its relatively small diameter allows numerous pieces to come together from all directions via paths of many configurations. In exploring options such as these, the special nature of cable may be expressed as well as linearity, thinness, and precision.

The outline of much metal cladding is less linelike than that of a wide-flange member. Corrugated sheets have a three-dimensional linearity in their surfaces. This linearity is integral with the nature of the sheet, as it is necessary for rigidity. The condition is opposite that of plywood, where the grooves that achieve linearity weaken the panel. The shape of individual panels of industrial standing-seam cladding is linear (Fig. 8–9). Other standing-seam panels are long rectangles but are not linear. Smooth-faced panels tend to be rectangular.

Standard installations of sheet metal cladding vary in their recognition of panel form. Corrugated installations do not express panel form. The joints between smooth-faced panels define panel shape but without emphasis. Standing-seam units lose their identities, but the resulting linear expression is much in the spirit of the component form of the long industrial units. Panel rectangularity is a secondary-form characteristic that may be exploited in building expression. Because it is not the standard (and therefore not the economical) detail, the concept has received little attention in architecture.

The hot-rolled secondary products have the same surface characteristics as the primary forms. The surfaces of cold-rolled products are slightly smoother and therefore have even greater potential to express the high refinement of steel. The extreme thinness and broad surfaces of cladding make maintaining flatness difficult. Random undulations interfere with the expression of high precision and refinement.

High precision, relative sharpness, linearity, and visual lightness are common to both secondary and primary products. Exhibiting these properties is appropriate in secondary forms, as they express the nature of steel in general. A number of characteristics exist among the secondary forms that are not typical of all steel. Their expressions clarify the uniqueness of each secondary product.

Figure 8–9 These industrial standing-seam roofing components constitute one of the few metal cladding types that has linear components.

STRENGTH

Steel's great strength is the basis of its uniqueness among the four basic materials. The form characteristics of linearity and thinness exist because steel is exceptionally strong in tension and bending. This combined with its outstanding ability to resist compression make it the choice for the tallest structures and the longest spans. Consequently, strength affects expression in both detailing and building form.

Steel's great tensile, bending, and compressive strengths are not equally remarkable. It is nearly infinitely stronger than clay brick in tension and bending but only 100 times stronger in compression. A factor of 100 seems large except when compared to infinity. The ratio is further reduced when buckling is considered. The comparison suggests that the tensile and bending strengths of steel are more unique than is its compressive strength. It follows that expressing steel in tension and bending makes it more special than expressing it in compression.

The ability to resist bending stresses is not unique to steel. Concrete and wood routinely resist bending. It was once common and still possible in stone. The resistance of pure tension, while possible in other materials, seems most appropriate in steel. Wood has tensile strength but has problems in pure tension. It is difficult to recognize that wood is in tension. Failure at the fasteners is also a concern. Concrete may appear to resist tension, but only the steel in the concrete can actually do it. Steel's potential in tension is more unique than its potential in bending (Fig. 8–10). While the use of steel in all three modes is appropriate and practical, a hierarchy of potential exists for expressive uniqueness. Tension offers the greatest opportunity, followed closely by bending, with compression being a distant third choice.

Figure 8–10 The corrugated sheet steel was blown across a field and against the tree in a storm. It failed in bending but not in tension.

DURABILITY

The most common construction alloys are analyzed to determine the relative durability of steel. Other steels will be considered separately as exceptions. Steel falls between wood and masonry in its ability to resist deterioration (Fig. 8–11). While rusting may be likened to decay in wood, steel is not susceptible to termite attack. Steel is therefore considered to be more resistant to deterioration than wood.

The physical deterioration of masonry is usually a result of human error in detailing or specifying. Unprotected carbon steel rusts even if there is no error in its production. Deterioration occurs occasionally in masonry and always in unprotected carbon steel. Steel is therefore considered to be less resistant than masonry to deterioration.

Steel's vulnerability to fire also falls between that of wood and masonry despite the relatively good performance of heavy timber (Fig. 8–12). Wood is combustible. Steel is not. Both masonry and steel can melt. Construction masonry's highest melting temperatures are higher than those of construction steel. The durability level of steel (defined to include destruction by fire and corrosion) is identified as low compared to wood's very low and masonry's high ratings.

Figure 8–11 A construction delay left the structural steel exposed to the weather longer than is typical. Steel's vulnerability to deterioration is illustrated by the rust on the members where the paint has failed, and on the unpainted bolts.

Figure 8–12 The susceptibility of steel to fire is illustrated by the twisted trusses, which softened and collapsed from the heat of a fire.

Weathering and stainless steels are exceptions to the conclusions regarding durability. While the thermal properties of these steels are not remarkably different from those of carbon steel, they are far more resistant to deterioration. They compete with masonry and concrete in this regard. As exceptions, their guidelines for the expression of durability are not the same as those for carbon steel. Systems of corrosion protection (paint, for example) would not reflect the durability of these steels as accurately as they would for the more standard steels.

Raw carbon steel rusts in the presence of moisture and fails in fire because of the high temperatures. The methods of protecting steel from moisture and elevated temperatures are the vehicles of expressing the low durability of steel. The degree of expressiveness may be judged by the visibility of the protection and the magnitude of change in the essence of the steel. High visibility and low change of essence produce a strong expression of the nature of steel. A protective system of low visibility with a high change of essence is not expressive of steel's nature. Corrosion prevention tends to obscure the essence of steel less than does fire protection. Greater potential therefore exists to express the durability of steel with rust protection than with fire protection. Expressing both systems at the same time is difficult because of the probability that they would not be recognized for what they are.

WORKABILITY

The ease with which steel components may be worked compared to the potential for change in the products is less than that of wood. Like wood, steel may be cut, pierced, and bent. Steel is considered to be less workable, however, because of the higher sophistication of tools and skill required to reshape it. The contrast is clearer in the working of the materials on the site. Since site equipment is less sophisticated than shop equipment, steel components are cut to length with slopes, bevels, bends, and holes in place prior to their arrival at the job. This is in contrast to lumber, which typically is delivered in bulk and cut during installation. Another consideration, the potential for structural damage, contributes to minimizing the site working of steel (Fig. 8–13).

The cutting of steel tends to have a two-dimensional quality, as products are relatively thin (Fig. 8–14). Three-dimensional cutting (such as on a lathe) is not practical for the large steel components of building construction. Relatively major shape changes can occur in steel, due to its great strength. Cut-

Figure 8–13 The bolt holes were incorrectly placed at the shop. Welding the connection avoided the site working of the steel that would have been necessary to create new holes.

Figure 8–14 Steel's moderate workability is illustrated by the sculpture. Extensive cutting was done, but it occurred in only two dimensions. Artist: Alexander Calder.

ting and welding allow a member to have an angular bend but maintain its identity as a single component (Fig. 8–15). This is not practical in wood. With numerous angular bends, a steel member can approach the form of a curve. It is also possible to bend steel into a smooth curve. The size and orientation of the member are limited by the radius of the curve. A curved component is usually small. Stronger sections require greater radii.

The ratio of result to effort in working steel is greater than that of masonry. The relatively simple act of breaking or cutting a masonry unit yields a new form that is much like the original. Steel is therefore considered more workable than masonry. While worked steel can be more remote than worked wood from its initial shape, the comparison of equipment and skill necessary for each material prevents steel from being considered more workable than wood. Steel is therefore assigned a rating of medium workability compared to wood's very high and masonry's low ratings (Fig. 8–16).

Figure 8–15 A turn in the axis of the structural component illustrates a worked form unique to steel. It is not practical in the other materials.

Figure 8–16 The working of steel beyond its natural level (medium) contributes to the interest of the sculpture. As a focus of the work, the violation seems to have been done for effect and therefore demonstrates control over the material.

Steel's medium level of workability is an option for supplementing other characteristics of steel. It does not warrant a role as the basis for an entire aesthetic order as is an option in wood. While working steel alters some primary-form characteristics, it is possible to do so without obscuring the identity of the material. If the working of steel contributes to the imitation of another material, negative expression of the steel's natural image can result.

Chapter 9

ASSEMBLIES IN STEEL

STRUCTURES

Being linear materials, wood and steel structures have certain characteristics that are similar. Because steel is linear it is adaptable to forming frames. Functional requirements and economy usually dictate that the frames be rectangular in nature. Since a rectangle is not an inherently rigid shape, many frames consisting of only linear members forming rectangles are not stable.

By definition, a linear member brings a small cross section and significant length to its connections. The length of each member provides a lever arm through which lateral loads apply rotational forces to its connections. The relatively small amount of steel at the connections usually has neither the mass nor geometry to resist rotation. Consequently, purely rectangular frames tend to lean with the application of lateral loads. The methods by which leaning is prevented are vehicles for expressing this particular characteristic of steel structures.

A common stiffening method employs geometry. Unlike a rectangle, a triangle is inherently rigid. Incorporating triangles within a rectangular frame increases the rigidity of the structure (Fig. 9–1). The aesthetic order of a building is greatly affected by such triangulation if it is exposed to view. A subtle expression occurs when the triangular framing is not exposed but affects some aspect of the building, such as window shape. A range of expressive intensities exists between these possibilities.

Rigidity may be achieved by manipulating the geometry within the components themselves. Spreading the flanges of components increases their ability to resist rotation at a connection. One-story industrial rigid frames achieve rigidity in this way. The tapered web that results is easily perceived if exposed to view. The frame is sometimes exposed in a facade or detailed to affect the character of a building (Fig. 9–2). Exposure of all frames in their entirety outside the cladding is rare. The principle may be applied to taller buildings, but

146

Figure 9-1 The triangles of each × stabilize the rectangular framing. The necessary triangles may be generated by other configurations, such as V's, K's, or diagonals.

Figure 9-2 The contribution of the rigid frames to the aesthetic order is stronger than if they were exposed. The cladding allows their shapes to establish the character of the facade. The coordination of their cladding color with decoratively painted cladding increases their importance.

the challenge to rigidity increases with height. If the enlarged joints are hidden with cladding that completely obscures their shapes, no expression results from this method.

Large steel plates may be used to stiffen a frame as plywood does in wood framing. Plates have been used to achieve rigidity on both interior and exterior walls. Even in exterior applications, expression of this technique is limited. Designing the plate so that its structural role is clear is nearly impossible. Maximizing the visibility of the plate may be all than can be achieved. Recognition of its role is unlikely.

Steel frames may be stiffened by concrete or masonry in the form of core masses or shear walls. These materials may contribute to the expression of steel structure if they have high visibility and their role is clear. The difficulties in expressing masonry and concrete as rigidity-producing elements are the same as those for steel plate.

Steel frames tend to occur in series with similar sizes, shapes, and spacing. These characteristics contribute to the economy of structure in any material but are especially appropriate in steel. Steel components are prefabricated and mass produced by industrialized methods to a higher degree than is wood, masonry, or concrete. Uniformity is an important characteristic for the efficiency of these processes. Processes that employ a greater amount of hand work (carpentry, brick laying, constructing formwork) are more tolerant of unique conditions.

Because uniformity is slightly more important to steel structure than to structures in other materials, its expression contributes to an image of steel.

Rectangular framing is compatible with the rectangularity of steel. Other geometries have varying degrees of compatibility. Triangular framing requires cutting that is within a level of workability acceptable for steel. The acute angles of triangular forms express a higher degree of sharpness and precision than do the right angles of rectangular framing. Hexagons, octagons, and other shapes with obtuse angles do not have this ability (Fig. 9–3). Like the triangle, they are compatible with the workability of steel. The cutting required increases with the number of sides of polygonal framing. As cutting increases, workability is pushed closer to its natural limit and sharpness of form diminishes.

The workability of steel is limited by economy, if not philosophy. Whereas each designer may determine if the cutting required for a particular polygon is excessive, the infinite number required to produce a perfect circle is too many for any budget. Circles are in conflict with the straightness that characterizes primary steel form. The softness of circular form opposes the sharpness that is compatible with the high precision of steel.

Achieving curves in steel by bending avoids the cutting issue. Bending small structural components can be within the acceptable level of workability. Bending very large members taxes the limit. The smaller the radius of the curve, the harder it is to bend a given member and the less load it can carry as a beam (curved in the horizontal plane). Bending and assembling several small members into a large component creates an illusion (Fig. 9–4). The appearance is one of

Figure 9–3 The obtuse angles of the octagonal framing lack the visual sharpness that would emphasize the high potential for refinement and precision in steel.

Figure 9–4 The curved steel at the perimeter is a composite of members, the face of which is plate. Note the straight diagonal framing behind the curves. The rectangular decking at the upper levels shows its incompatibility with the round form as it awaits cutting.

a structural member strong enough to carry the loading but not too strong to be bent. The message is misleading. Hidden framing provided to assist the weakened curved form structurally contributes to the illusion.

Steel is least different from other materials in its ability to resist compression. Compression is therefore not the most efficient vehicle with which to express the uniqueness of steel. Ironically, steel's great strength makes the expression of compression more difficult than in weaker materials such as masonry. Intuitively, compression suggests a squashing effect such as occurs when sitting on a cushion. Although the compressive strains in structural materials are not visible to the eye, some historical applications of masonry have been wider at the base than the top. The detail increases stability and puts more brick where the compressive stresses are greatest and gives the impression of squashing.

Thickening the steel of lower columns in tall buildings has little or no visual impact. Significant increases in strength can be achieved in columns by slight increases in section size. The result is that while carrying the largest compressive loads, steel looks the least like it is in compression (Fig. 9–5). Exaggerating the size of components at the base of a structure to achieve a look of compression seems more appropriate for a weaker material, such as masonry. Steel's high strength makes the exaggeration redundant.

This does not mean that steel should not be used in compression. Steel is useful as columns and other compressive members. Columns may contribute to the expression of steel in ways other than compression. They may exhibit the form, durability, and workability characteristics that make steel unique. They may contribute to structural expression as part of the repetitive frame that is characteristic of steel. They may form sides of the triangles that are common in most steel frames.

Steel's great strength may be exploited in structures to achieve uniqueness by virtue of large size. Great building height can express the strength of steel in compression (gravity and lateral loads) and tension (lateral loads). High

Figure 9–5 The bridge tower defies an image of compression in its tall, slender, graceful shape. The broadening of the vertical elements toward the base only makes the structure seem taller.

strength may be expressed in large spans (Fig. 9–6). Large cantilevers are especially effective in expressing steel because of their attention-getting ability. A significant cantilever is more rare than a significant span between two supports as masonry is excluded from the former but not the latter. The challenge in pushing the upper limits of steel's span capability to achieve striking results is in assuring that the engineering feat is apparent in the finished building.

The structural reality of a large span that touches a nonbearing wall is difficult to perceive. If it can be shown that the curtain wall does not support the structure, the achievement of the span will be clearer. One way to isolate the girder or truss is to separate it from opaque cladding with glass. All-glass curtain walls touching the bottom of spanning members will seem less like supports if their mullions are thin. A recessed gap between a beam and the wall below would also reduce the wall's confusion with a bearing wall.

Short and medium-length spans may express the nature of steel but with more subtlety than that of long spans. Since a given span requires a smaller section in steel than in another material, emphasizing steel's visual lightness is a reflection of its strength. Expressing other characteristics in addition to strength is important to the image of steel regardless of span. The longer spans are dependent on steel's linearity and refinement to distinguish steel's image from that of the next strongest material, concrete. To distinguish steel from wood, shorter spans must depend on visual lightness and refinement, as they are both linear and similar in the areas of durability and workability.

Arches are not compatible with the straightness of steel's primary form and have limited compatibility with steel's workability. Since arches reduce the need for tensile strength (steel's great asset), certain strategies are required if the nature of steel is to be expressed. If no thrust is developed (more likely in shorter spans) demonstrating this condition would distinguish steel arches from masonry arches. If thrust is developed, the reduction of the tensile stresses with which it is associated could be reflected in the enormity of the span. If the span is not extremely large, extreme thinness in the members would help separate the image of the steel from other materials, which may also produce arches with thrust and moderate span (Fig. 9–7).

Figure 9–6 The steel trusses span diagonally across the sanctuary of this church without intermediate supports (270 feet), thus expressing steel's great strength. Architect: Planners Architects Collaborative.

Figure 9-7   The expression of the steel arches is ambiguous. The span is moderate, as is the visual mass of each member. The framing to each side is adequate to resist significant thrust, but it is not clear if thrust is developed.

Steel is most different from the other three structural materials in its ability to resist pure tension. This structural realm offers the greatest potential for combining strength and form characteristics into an expression that can only be steel. Flanged members commonly resist pure tension in trusses and lateral bracing. These components often fail to achieve steel's expressive potential for the same reason that wood has difficulty expressing tension. They are often stiff enough to resist compression, which obscures their tensile role. Rods, straps, and cable are too limber to resist compression (Fig. 9–8). They are able to resist great tensile loads, especially when used in groups. Cable has the added advantage of having enormous length. Great length with a small profile emphasizes linearity, thinness, and tensile strength.

Figure 9-8   The vertical cables are clearly in tension. Even to the untrained eye, they appear to be too thin to accept compressive loads.

Two potential obstacles must be addressed in the expression of tensile structures. Their thinness limits their visibility. Cables are more visible against a plain contrasting background than against a visually busy one. The sky provides such a background. Building surfaces are typically less plain and therefore obscure the cables more. More cables are easier to see than fewer cables (Fig. 9–9). Exaggerating the number of cables required would give the system greater visual impact. Some economy may be achieved with this approach. More cables can shorten the spans of the beams they support, thus allowing the beams to be smaller. The image of cable thinness is emphasized if multiple cables are spaced rather than bundled. Another tactic to bring attention to cables is to combine them with decorative elements such as fins and flags.

The natural geometries of hanging lines include both straight and curved shapes. A curve or approximated curve results when loads are uniformly distributed along a line that hangs from two points. Approximated curves result when the spacing between loads is long, the line is relatively flexible, and the loads are large. In these cases, the line will be straight between loads. It is ironic that greater flexibility yields straight segments which obscure the fact that the line is flexible. When a cable is suspended from only one point, it becomes a straight line to the load. If this line had a curve, it would indicate that the load was not significant.

Since large loads express great strength in their supports, a slack line does not express the great strength of steel. Since straightness is a characteristic of cables supporting large loads, it is the geometry that best expresses the nature of steel in tension structures.

The expression of steel's great strength in tension is obscured if tensile systems do not have structural clarity. Curtain walls obscure structural clarity if they seem like bearing walls. The techniques described previously to help

Figure 9–9   The thin cables of the bridge are more visible because of their great number. As fine lines they express the refinement of steel more intensely than would thicker cables.

clarify the nonstructural role of curtain walls may be used with the enclosure walls for tensile systems. Omitting the bottom floor of a multistory building to clarify the tensile nature of the structural system has limited potential. Doing so exposes the compressive element (possibly the utility core) from which the floor structures are suspended. If the same building configuration could be achieved with cantilevers from the central core, structural clarity is not achieved by this method.

Exposing cables above the roof of a building helps clarify the nature of the structural system for one-story buildings. In multistory buildings, the technique is a strong indication that the roof is supported by tension; it is not necessarily apparent that the floors below are, too. Exposing the cables outside the curtain walls as they pass from floor to floor would help clarify the nature of the system. The cables may not have a strong visual image against the building. They may not be recognized as the only supports for the ends of the floor beams at the perimeter of the building. Detailing that addresses these issues contributes to the expression of steel, especially with regard to its great tensile strength.

CONNECTIONS

A butt connection is most compatible with the characteristics of steel (Fig. 9–10). Securing a beam to a column as it passes beside the column is made extremely awkward by the profiles of flanged components. Rectangular tubes could come closest to achieving this overlap connection but would have complications if bolted. Bolting is likely to deform hollow tubes and the ends of the tubes are not sealed by the configuration. Eccentricity may be avoided in overlapping wood connections by positioning a column between two parallel beams or a single beam between two columns. While doubling the number of beams or columns is compatible with the medium strength of wood, it seems especially redundant with the very high strength of steel.

Overlapping a joist (cold-rolled channel or open web) on the top flange of a beam is common. These joists are secondary forms of steel and therefore do not dictate the connections compatible with the primary forms. Plate is

Figure 9–10 The requirement for exact dimensions in this butt connection is compatible with the high precision of steel.

sometimes lapped but not typically as the primary structural component of a building. Wide-flange beams typically connect to each other by butting the end of one web to the side of the other web so that the top flanges are at the same level. This requires cutting the flange from the end of one member to accomplish the fit. The configuration has construction advantages as well as having a high sense of precision that reflects the nature of steel. Butt connections in general have a sense of precision and refinement because of the requirement of exact fits, which involve a minimum area of contact.

Connections with components that seem to merge are compatible with the strength and precision of steel (Fig. 9–11). They create the illusion, however, that the members become one at the intersection. Structurally, the connection may act as if such is the case. Physically, this could happen only in connections cast as one piece. Typically, one steel member is continuous while the other is cut and butt joined by welding. The merged connection is closer than the overlapping type to the nature of steel, but not as close as the butt configuration (Fig. 9–12).

Welding contributes significantly to the refinement of steel connections. Grinding can make the welding nearly disappear between flush surfaces. While bolted connections are not as refined, the fasteners are usually installed in straight rows or grid patterns. Their repetitive size also contributes to the appearance of neatness. The image of precision increases as the size of components increases relative to bolt size. Rivets have a slightly more precise image, as their flatter heads produce a texture that is less rough than that produced by bolts. Although practical considerations often make bolting the choice for fastening, welded connections express more characteristics that are unique to structural steel.

Figure 9–11 Although steel's precise nature is needed to create an apparent merged joint, the expression of precision is subdued. The members appear to pass through each other, which is not an issue of precision. The image misrepresents the physical reality of the connection.

Figure 9–12 The interest of the sculpture is due, in part, to the oddness of the detail, showing two steel beams apparently merging at their intersection.

Cladding joints do not affect the reasoning regarding the type of connection natural to steel because of cladding's secondary classification. Cladding joints often do have butt connections and other characteristics that support the nature of steel. When thin sheets of cladding overlap, the appearance of the connection has a degree of refinement because a significant bump is not created. This is not the case in the overlapping of steel components that imitate beveled siding, shakes, or shingles. Butting panels with inward turned edges have a sense of precision, as a single straight line is produced at the joint.

Crimped connections such as in standing-seam cladding are a combination butt and overlap. They have the potential to project a sense of refinement because of the thin straight fin that good craftsmanship can produce (Fig. 9–13). Straight trim is sometimes used to cover the connection of two standing-seam roof planes at a hip or ridge. The mismatch of shapes does not reflect the refined potential of the steel (Fig. 9–14). The same issue must be addressed occasionally in corrugated cladding. Straight trim that does not match the undulations of the surfaces violates the nature of steel with regard to refinement. Tight-fitting trim that undulates with the corrugations makes a neat connection which is compatible with the spirit of steel (Fig. 9–15).

The similarity of metallic cladding materials makes comments regarding steel also appropriate for several other metals. Although the focus is on steel, the discussion applies to aluminum, copper, and other sheet metal alloys.

Figure 9–13 The butting of the panels with the lapping and crimping of the edges produces a fin-like joint that is thin and straight. The connection is in the nature of steel.

Figure 9–14 Covering a series of standing seams with a straight cap gives a sense of crudeness to the connection. The high precision of steel is further violated in this example by the irregularity of the cap.

Figure 9-15   The trim over the connection at the corner matches the corrugations of the cladding. The result is a highly precise and refined-appearing connection which expresses the nature of steel. Architect: W. Haskell Olivo.

SURFACES

Structural components and cladding can affect the character of a building surface. On low buildings mullions are useful in supplementing the column system in establishing a series of vertical lines. Without them, the columns may be too short and far apart to dominate the facade. In tall buildings, columns have a better chance to control the aesthetic order of the surface because of their greater length. Exposed flanges add a sense of refinement to the surface because of their straight thin edges.

Standing seam and corrugated cladding give surfaces a three-dimensional linear quality (Fig. 9-16). While the lines are not as deep as can be achieved

Figure 9-16   A strong linear image is expressed in this cladding by the long uninterrupted standing seams and their shadows. Thin lines and good craftmanship project an image of precision. Architect: W. H. Raymond Yeh and Associates.

by structural members, they are present in greater numbers and are deep enough to cast shadows. The vertical laps of the sheet metal are typically subdued by the visually stronger system of parallel ridges. The result is a system of very long lines. Linearity is therefore expressed. The thinness of the standing seams adds a strong sense of refinement to the surface.

Flat panels often do not express linearity in one direction. The lines of their joints express a grid pattern if the surface has multiple panels in both directions. When the panels are the full height of a building, some vertical linearity is expressed. The expression is weak if the joints have no trim and is stronger if they do.

Cladding usually has the smooth texture typical of metals. It often lacks the thickness to hold a flat surface plane when subject to thermal stresses, however (Fig. 9–17). Lumpy surfaces fail to achieve the precision and sense of refinement possible in steel (and other metals). A more highly refined image may be achieved by increasing the thickness of the metal or laminating it to a stiff backing. Irregularities are emphasized by reflections from the surface. A matte finish makes irregularities harder to see, thus refining the expression, if not the surface itself.

Visually interrupting the surface helps obscure irregularities. Standing seams achieve this while having relatively short distances between fins, which help stiffen the sheet. Corrugations visually interrupt the surface and stiffen the cladding significantly (Fig. 9–18). Corrugations are a subtle expression of thinness because the thinness makes them necessary for stiffness. They lack

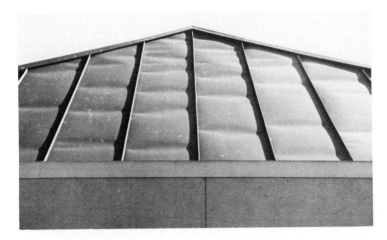

Figure 9–17 The lumpy appearance of the cladding fails to express the high level of precision that is compatible with metals.

Figure 9–18 Corrugations stiffen sheet metal and give it a linear quality. They visually interrupt the surface, thus obscuring imperfections. These have a higher sense of precision than most because their bends are 90 degrees.

the refined image of standing seams, however, because they are wide and undulate in obtuse angles, if not curves. The most refined appearances occur in panels where the undulations are very thin and the angles of the bends are 90 degrees. The acute-angled bends that occur periodically in some products are too few to overcome the blunter corrugations with which they are mixed. Shallow pyramids, rectangular impressions, and other three-dimensional patterns will stiffen sheet metal and therefore express its thinness.

The cladding of curved surfaces is often achieved with smooth panels that are manufactured in curved forms. The violation of the straightness of steel is less significant in cladding than in structure. Sheet metal is easily curved. The expression of curved panels is much like that of curved brick. The curve is a characteristic of a secondary form and warrants expression.

Curving the ribs of corrugated sheet is more difficult than curving flat sheet. The function of the ribs is, after all, to prevent curves. The increased difficulty in curving corrugated sheet (in the strong direction) increases the intensity of the violation of steel's straightness. The ripples introduced into the surface of some corrugated sheet in response to this difficulty purify the curved expression (Fig. 9–19). In spirit, they are similar to the ripples that tend to occur naturally, except that these are uniform in shape and spacing. Their planned appearance acknowledges the uniqueness of the curved material.

Metal cladding products, including corrugated sheets, are not able to resist significant impact. Ironically, steel's high strength is responsible for this vulnerability. Unlike wood, masonry, and concrete, steel can form a useful product when very thin. Unprotected applications of the cladding where impact is probable violates the nature of the product. The nature of the cladding can be expressed by the system that protects it. Brightly painted steel posts between automobile parking and a corrugated clad wall would express the thinness of the metal.

Many conclusions regarding the configuration of steel cladding apply to the cladding of other metals. Aluminum is of special interest, as it is frequently used to cover structural steel. Like steel, aluminum is a relatively thin, precise, and highly refined material. This allows aluminum to express itself while providing an academic reference to the nature of the steel it hides.

A major vehicle for expressing the low durability of steel is the surface treatment, which reduces corrosion. Finishes that are the most noticeable but change the physical aspects of the steel the least are the most expressive of steel and its durability level. Metallic coatings have an appearance not much dif-

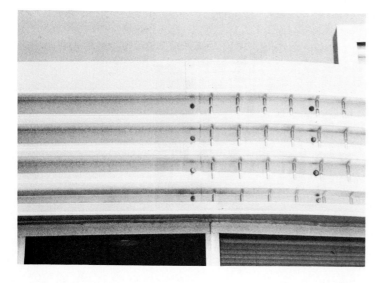

Figure 9–19 The straight section on the left joins a curved section on the right. The texture of ripples between the large horizontal corrugations acknowledges the special geometry of the curved panel. Architect: W. Haskell Olivo.

ferent from that of raw steel. Galvanizing, for example, is not very expressive of the need to protect steel from corrosion. It is highly protective but not highly visible. Galvanized steel looks almost like steel without protection. Since steel needs protection, the expression of the nature of steel is low.

At the other extreme of visibility are the vitreous coatings. Although the bright colors possible in porcelain enamel can be strongly apparent, the glass layer changes the physical nature of the steel. Its surface becomes as fragile as the glass itself. Striking the surface of raw steel with a stone has no effect. The same blow to porcelain-enameled steel is likely to chip the surface. The damage has a lasting effect, as it is difficult to repair. A tough material is turned into a delicate material by the coating. Porcelain-clad sheet steel is usually not perfectly flat (Fig. 9–20). The slight undulations are emphasized by reflections from the shiny surface. Consequently, the potential precision of steel is not served by the coating. While expressing its presence and therefore its protection of the steel, vitreous coating fails to express the nature of steel in other respects.

Paint changes the physical nature of steel very little and has the potential of being highly noticeable. After painting, the surface continues to have the texture of steel, sounds like steel when struck, and feels like steel. The toughness of baked-on enamel is illustrated by the fact that it is applied to sheet before the corrugations are rolled. The physical abuse during corrugating does not damage the paint. The loss of toughness of the surface is minimal from the application of paint. Bright colors are more expressive of the protective coating than are neutral colors. They draw more attention to the coating itself. Bright colors are therefore most expressive of the low durability of carbon steel.

The surfaces of stainless and weathering steels are unique. Weathering steel appears to be rusting away, which it usually is not. If functioning properly, it will stop rusting after several years. The apparent misrepresentation of the durability of steel is minimized because carbon steel systems that are rusting in their entirety are rare in architecture. The coatings that protect carbon steel isolate weathering steel as being the one that is not coated and is rusted. Because it is unique in this respect, it is more easily recognized. Leaving the rusty surface unprotected contributes to its recognizability.

Stainless steel, which is highly resistant to corrosion, can be coated with chrome oxide to achieve color or terne for improved durability. The terne (tin and lead) coating looks much the same as the silver color of stainless. Its lack of expression is compatible with its role as a safety factor. This is quite a dif-

Figure 9–20 The shininess of the porcelain-enameled sheets (dark strips above columns) emphasizes their undulating surfaces. The expression is imprecise and unlike the spirit of steel.

ferent role than that which zinc plays when it galvanizes carbon steel. The galvanized coating is more than a safety factor. Although a layer of chrome oxide on stainless improves its durability, that is not its main function. Its usefulness is in the metallic colors it can produce. Colors on stainless steel do not express the nature of the material, as they hide its natural silvery hue without being necessary to its survival. This is different from the relationship of paint to carbon steel.

It is difficult to express a system of fire protection for steel that is recognizable but does not obscure the nature of the steel. If water is contained in a hollow section, it provides protection without expression. If steel is protected by virtue of its location beyond the reach of fire (some distance beyond the building enclosure), the method of fire protection is recognizable only upon explanation. Sprinkler systems are not associated solely with the protection of steel since they protect everything. They also have limited visual impact. Gypsum board may protect steel without obscuring its linear form. It completely obscures its expression of thinness and refinement.

Sprayed fire protection leaves the general form of steel apparent but changes the surface significantly (Fig. 9–21). Sprayed steel is occasionally exposed in utilitarian applications such as basements, industrial buildings, and the occasional low-budget mall. The rough and usually soft texture of the sprayed material is the opposite of steel's nature. The surface material expresses itself but cannot be said to express steel. The coatings are usually covered because of their relatively delicate nature and unfinished appearance. When covered, the cladding material becomes the expressive issue instead of the fire protection. Intumescent paint does not obscure the form or texture of steel, but is not recognizable as fire protection.

Cladding steel for fire protection is much like cladding steel buildings. The cladding can reveal certain characteristics of the steel structure. It can make an academic reference to the steel.

Figure 9–21 The sprayed fire protection on the column gives the steel a soft lumpy appearance. The fragile quality of the coating is illustrated by the damage at the lower right. This application is designed to be covered.

The manufactured edges of flanged steel and cladding are relatively thin and accurate. Their ability to impart a sense of precision to a building edge depends on their detailing. If the edges of flanges are exposed at the edges of a building, a sense of refinement will be projected (Fig. 9–22). The high strength of steel assures that the thin flange will survive handling and impacts from feet, bicycles, carts, and even vehicles to some degree.

Steel cladding is thinner than hot-rolled sections, making component edges visually and physically sharper (Fig. 9–23). Cladding edges are too thin to resist significant impact. For exposed edges to express the refinement potential of steel (which they do not do if damaged), they must be positioned away from potential impact.

Figure 9–22 The straight relatively thin steel flanges give the building edge a sense of refinement and precision.

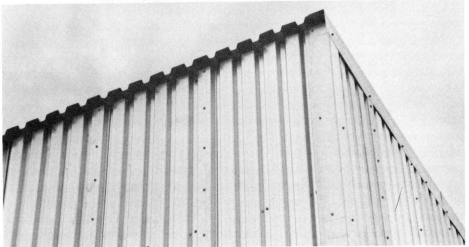

Figure 9–23 The thinness and regularity of the projected edge of the corrugated roof have a sense of precision. The height of the detail protects it from damage, thus extending the duration of the expression indefinitely.

Figure 9–24 The trim wrapped around the lower edge of the corrugated cladding visually blunts the expression of the edge and subdues the sense of precision. The mismatch between the straight trim and undulating surface also detracts from an image of refinement.

Since the edge of sheet metal looks unfinished and too sharp for some tastes, it is often covered (Fig. 9–24). Edge trim seldom matches the shape of corrugated cladding. Straight trim wrapping around an undulating edge lacks the precision and refinement of steel. Occasionally, one leg of a trim angle is slipped behind the cladding, with the edge of the cladding butting the other leg. The detail exposes another thin edge (the projecting angle leg) and is precise. This configuration expresses the nature of steel, whereas the wrapped trim does not.

Standing-seam panel edges tend to be folded under and flattened. Doubling the thickness strengthens the edge but leaves it relatively thin and precise (compared to other materials).

The relationship between the bottom edge of steel components and the earth affects the expression of durability. Steel's low durability discourages ground contact. Separating structural steel and cladding from the ground can lighten the overall expression if the base is set back from the steel (Fig. 9–25).

Figure 9–25 The recessed concrete base helps the steel sculpture drain water, holds it above moisture at grade, and lightens its visual image. Architect: Jones Hester Bates Riek Architects.

Visual lightness is a characteristic compatible with the nature of steel. In the case of large-diameter steel pipe columns, a base that separates the pipe from grade helps distinguish it from a round concrete column (Fig. 9–26).

Rectangular openings are compatible with the geometry of steel. Because they are the standard of the industry for all materials, they cannot be said to express the uniqueness of steel. While nearly all windows will be rectangular in steel buildings, other shapes are used occasionally to create special images or accents. Reasoning regarding the nature of the material can identify another shape that is more expressive of steel's unique properties.

Although working steel framing and cladding can produce circular openings, they do not express the unique properties of steel (Fig. 9–27). Sealing the edges with trim is not the problem it is with wood, but does have difficulties. The complication is in the need (for ease of installation) to have a uniform joint between the opening edge trim and cladding around the entire perimeter. If the trim laps over the cladding, it sheds water at the sill but catches it at the head. If the cladding laps the trim, the reverse occurs. A flush joint is a compromise that avoids the pulling of water into the joint by gravity but is susceptible to wind-driven moisture. A bigger issue is the image of softness projected by circles and other curved shapes. They do not reflect the spirit of straightness and sharpness associated with steel.

Triangles have the sharpness of steel, the form of much steel framing, and straight sides which are compatible with the straightness of trim. They are the shape of windows produced when triangular bracing is exposed in a curtain wall. They are easily framed and waterproofed. Triangles reflect the unique spirit of steel more than other opening shapes.

Pentagons, hexagons, octagons, and other polygons lack the sharpness of triangles and their compatibility with the typical lateral bracing systems. They are not as expressive of steel as triangles.

Figure 9–26 It is difficult to distinguish these steel columns from concrete. Setting them on a recessed concrete base would reduce corrosion and help secure their identity as steel.

Figure 9–27 The circular opening softens the image of the steel building. A sense of precision is projected in its trim, which is butted to the edges of the steel cladding rather than lapped.

Chapter 10

STEEL
IN
ARCHITECTURE

CHECKLIST FOR ANALYSIS

The expression of steel in historic and contemporary architecture is analyzed in this chapter. The quality of the work is not judged. Its degree of compatibility with the principles of expression discussed previously is determined. Listed below are the major characteristics considered to express the nature of steel. Refer to Checklist C-3 in Appendix C for this list in a worksheet format with additional notations to assist analysis.

1. Linearity in the building image
2. Straightness in the building image
3. Contribution to the building image by form characteristics of secondary products (if any)
4. Very high level of refinement in the building image
5. Demonstration of very high tensile strength as a significant part of the building image
6. A sense of frames or framing as a significant part of the building image
7. Demonstration of steel's low resistance to rust as part of the building image
8. Demonstration of the moderate ease with which the shapes of steel products may be changed as a part of the building image

ANALYSIS

Bavinger House
Norman, Oklahoma; Bruce Goff; 1955

The suspension system visible above the roof expresses the tensile nature of steel (Fig. 10–1). The visual impact of the hangers is aided by their large number. Their convergence to a single point at the top of the mast increases the visual

Figure 10-1 *Bavinger House.* The varied backgrounds of the tensile system and its varied reflections compromise its visibility and therefore its structural statement.

density of hangers as they become more distant from the viewer. The silver-colored hangers tend to blend with the sky, making them difficult to see against that background. The percentage of struts silhouetted against the sky increases with height, but so does the density of struts. The increasing density helps compensate for the increasing loss of a contrasting background.

Generally, the background of the struts is not helpful to their visibility. The roof tone lacks contrast and the trees provide a busy texture. The shiny elements are clearly visible against the dark stone. The nonreflective sections are less so. The combination of reflective and nonreflecting sections of each strut interferes with the visibility of the system. It is difficult to find one that has a clear identity from top to bottom. Changing backgrounds and reflections prevent it.

Regardless of the conditions obscuring the tensile system, it is visible. Its image is that of fine lines. The extreme slenderness of component profile eliminates images of wood, masonry, and concrete from the expression. The linearity of the system contributes further to the image of steel.

The expression of strength makes less of a contribution to a sense of steel in this system than does form. While great spans or loads would contribute to an image of strength, they are not apparent (Fig. 10-2). The spiraling wall system requires a series of joist spans from short to long. The shorter spans are within the capability of the 2 × 6 roof joists used in the structure. The intermediate spans are within the capability of larger wood joists. The largest spans are within the capability of steel joists. The ends of wood joists are visible, thus revealing their size and spacing. Casual observation, however, does not detect their inability to perform the spans with the loads they carry.

The impression of the exterior view is that the tensile system is supplementary or not necessary and therefore carries little load. This impression is not correct because suspended rooms and stairs inside the space add significant load to the tensile system (Fig. 10-3). They fail to contribute directly to the expression of the exterior struts, however, because the steel and the loads are not visible at the same time. Numerous hangers are in the shape of an up-

Figure 10-2 *Bavinger House.* The credibility of the tensile system is suspect in the exterior view, as its support of rooms within the building is not apparent.

Figure 10-3 *Bavinger House.* These stairs as well as several small rooms are supported by the tensile system above the roof.

side-down Y, with two connections to the roof and one to the mast. The joining of two lines near the roof surface reduces the number of lines visible higher up. The two lower segments typically have different reflective qualities, rendering one clearly visible and the other nearly invisible. Many struts therefore seem to bend near the roof, suggesting that they are not taut. The appearance of a sag suggests that no tension is present. The condition is an optical illusion that reduces the sense of serious loading on the system. The sense of load is increased somewhat by the glass skylight strips that border the roof on both edges and physically separate it from the walls. Combined with the widely spaced joists, the roof seems to float between the walls, suggesting that its weight must be distributed to the hangers to some degree.

The fact that the hangers are stainless steel eliminates durability as an issue of expression. The workability of steel is not challenged. The expression of the hanger system can only be that of steel, due to its form. The expression of high strength fails to develop, however, leaving the overall visual image of steel weakened slightly.

Crown Hall
Illinois Institute of Technology, Chicago, Illinois;
Mies van der Rohe: 1956

The expression of steel form in this building is strong as a result of the numerous components exposed to view (Fig. 10–4). An image of linearity is established as the identities of the long, thin, and straight members are made clear by their isolation in a field of glass. The linear image is stronger when closed blinds lighten the tone at the glass, thus increasing the contrast with the steel.

An image of refinement is achieved by the thinness of exposed flanges and neatness of joints. The exposed top ends of the mullions contribute to a sense of sharpness, as they are within the range of vision. The visual effect of the bottom ends is subdued, however, by their closeness to grade. The overlapping connections of the mullions and spandrels, although neatly done, do not maximize the sense of refinement possible in steel. Reduced contact between the members would increase the feeling of both precision and strength.

The great span of the structural system, which reaches across the entire width of the building without intermediate columns, exploits the high strength of steel. The feat is magnified by its rarity in such a low nonindustrial building. Some expression of the accomplishment is achieved in the exterior by the plate girders exposed above the roof. The view from the ground reveals the ends of the girders, thus establishing the probability (for uninformed observers) that they pass across the entire roof. The fact that they do so without assistance from interior supports is not apparent from the outside. This missing piece of information dilutes the expression of strength, at least temporarily.

Figure 10–4 *Crown Hall.* The visibility of the lines on the facade is enhanced by their contrast with the surfaces on either side. Large spans are suggested by the members visible above the roof.

Figure 10–5 *Crown Hall.* The sense of great openness, and therefore great span, is apparent immediately upon entering the building.

The limitation in understanding is less obstructive than in most buildings, however, where the association of inside to outside is less clear. A nearly unobstructed view of the entire ceiling is revealed immediately upon entering (there are no vestibules) (Fig. 10–5). Two chases reaching the ceiling temper the sense of openness somewhat. Unlike most buildings that have numerous interior walls and visual distractions, the nature of the simple open space may be grasped quickly. The speed of understanding facilitates the merging of exterior and interior images. The joint expression is that of great span and great strength.

The durability level of steel is not strongly expressed, as its protection systems are not exaggerated. Attention is not drawn to the finish of the steel as a method of protection, as its dark color is not particularly attention getting. The fact that the steel mullions do not touch the ground is not particularly noticeable, as they end very close to the ground. The visibility of the narrow strip of concrete foundation wall above grade is dependent on the height of the grass and is therefore intermittent. The flashing protecting the top of the wall system is the same color as the steel. Its visibility, which is limited, is the result of a shadow line generated by its loose fit with the fascia.

The workability of steel is not an issue, as no cutting beyond the standard was done. No steel was bent. The expression of the building is in the nature of steel, with form and strength establishing the image. Although the expression of strength is unique for a building of this size, it is not realized by observation of the exterior alone.

United Air Lines Hangar
San Francisco; Skidmore, Owings and Merrill; 1960

The hangar expresses the great strength of steel by virtue of its long span (Fig. 10–6). A series of plate girders cantilever remarkable distances in opposite directions to provide large column-free openings and spaces. Although the span is unlikely in any other material, the failure to clarify certain associated conditions has compromised the strength expression somewhat.

Figure 10–6 *United Air Lines Hangar.* The long cantilevers of the plate girders are apparent in the side elevations but are subdued by their low contrast with the cladding below.

The recognizability of the structural condition is served by the exposure of plate girders in the end walls and the protrusion of others into the fascias. The equally spaced bumps in the sloped fascias indicate the presence of girders throughout the roof system. When the doors are open, the cantilevers of intermediate girders are verified by the absence of columns at the door line. The visibility of the end girders is aided only slightly by their color, which has little contrast with the curtain wall below. A color of strong contrast and/or bright hue would increase the expression of form, strength, and the limited durability of steel.

The clarity of the system is reduced by the curtain walls, which appear to support the exposed girders. The absence of support in the end walls could have been demonstrated by the visual separation of the walls from the girders. A band of glass, a large reveal, or a strip of contrasting color between the two elements could suggest such a separation. A similar detail would be useful at the large doors, which appear to support the roof when closed. Their slender proportions make the structural accomplishment of the cantilevers especially notable and frustrates their simulation in any other material. While exposing all the girders is the obvious way to increase the expression of their form, it would have more significance here than in most buildings. The hangar is seen by airport visitors from a high vantage point on the road to the terminal. Girders above the roof would have had relatively high visibility.

Other issues are secondary to the structural expression of the hangar and will not be analyzed. The building expresses the nature of steel with regard to strength and form. The intensity of the expression falls short of its potential.

Cadet Chapel
United States Air Force Academy, Colorado Springs, Colorado;
Skidmore, Owings and Merrill; 1962

The chapel has a clear sense of triangulation, linearity, and precision (Fig. 10–7). The strong expression of these steel characteristics is especially notable because the structure is not exposed. The image is a result of the configuration of the structure and the detailing of the aluminum cladding.

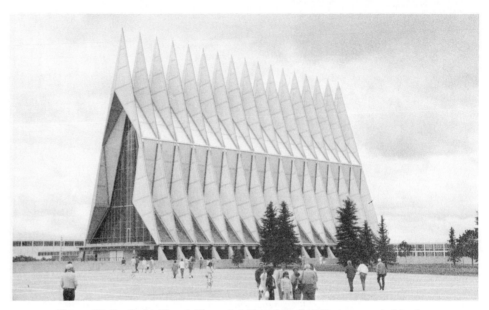

Figure 10-7 *Cadet Chapel.* Characteristics of the building as revealed by the building surface are visually strong because of the significant depth of the surface configuration.

A number of steel characteristics are revealed by the configuration of the cladding, which follows the form of the structure. The undulation of the surface produces a series of long parallel and equally spaced edges, giving both the surface and structure a sense of linearity. A strong image of triangulated structure results from the prismatic building form and the triangles that form all elevations in their entirety. The recessed glass curtain walls in the end elevations reveal the triangulated underside of the end structural elements. The triangulated undulating surface continues throughout the interior of the building.

The strong sense of triangulated structure combines with a degree of linearity to establish a base for an expression that can only be steel. The characteristic that clarifies the separation of the image from wood or concrete is its high degree of refinement. A quality of literal sharpness is established by the tops of the triangular frames (Fig. 10–8). Their cladding as individual points

Figure 10-8 *Cadet Chapel.* The expression of sharpness is maximized at the ridge of the chapel, as its configuration is a series of points.

Figure 10-9 *Cadet Chapel.* The longevity of the aluminum cladding's contribution to the image of precision is assured by the protection its recessed position affords its thin edges.

contributes far more to this image than would a continuous ridge with the same acute angle. The acute angles of the frame edges and the numerous acute angles throughout the triangulated surface continue the sense of sharpness and refinement.

The precise detailing of the aluminum cladding continues the image at the smallest scale. The exposed edges of aluminum sheets express a near knife-like sharpness (Fig. 10-9). Vulnerability to impact damage is avoided by re-cessing the sheets with a surrounding reveal as well as isolating most of the building from sidewalk traffic. Many closely spaced parallel edges and numerous exact connections combine with an overall high level of workmanship to pro-duce uniformity and neatness. The sense of thinness and refinement is well beyond the capabilities of other materials, especially when considering that it has not dulled with age.

While other properties are overshadowed by those of the preceding dis-cussion, it is noted that the level of workability natural to steel and aluminum is not superseded. Although the number of fastenings is large, cuts are rela-tively simple. The durability of steel is served by mounting of the frames on concrete pedestals which hold the structure above grade. The chapel is remark-able in the proportion between steel expression and steel exposed. Many other buildings have exposed more steel but expressed the spirit of steel less.

Meredith Hall
Drake University, Des Moines, Iowa;
Mies van der Rohe; 1965

The classroom building expresses the nature of steel by exposing numerous flanged components. The repetitive mullions give the facade a strong linear quality (Fig. 10-10). From the adjacent sidewalks, the thinness of the flanges is visible. At this range, a high degree of precision is apparent. Where inter-ruption of the mullions by a door reveals the cross section of the flanged mul-lions just above eye level, the sense of refinement is increased (Fig. 10-11). The exposed ends of the mullions at the top and base of the building maintain a level of refinement higher than if they had butted trim. Their distance from

Figure 10-10 *Meredith Hall.* The linearity of the surface is apparent but subdued by the lack of tone contrast between the mullions and glass.

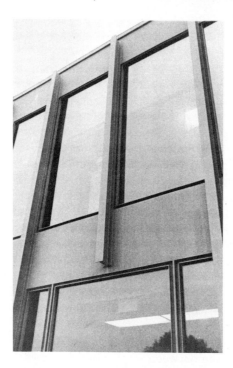

Figure 10-11 *Meredith Hall.* The mullion ends that are near eye level are few but are located over the entries, which maximizes their visibility and thus their contribution to the sense of refinement.

the eye reduces their contribution slightly. The joining of all facade components is extremely neat. The surfaces of the steel are characteristically smooth, which adds to the overall image of refinement.

The fact that the building has two stories eliminates height as a device for expressing the strength of steel. Another option, long span, is not employed. A third option, extreme delicacy of members and connections, is not exploited. The mullions are thin but the spandrels are not. Although the building does not seem massive, neither do its components seem especially small in section. Great strength is therefore not expressed. The workability of steel is not challenged, as the components have standard forms.

The durability of steel is expressed slightly at the base of the building (Fig. 10-12). The steel is raised just above grade by a concrete base. The expression is limited by the low height of the concrete. The protective cap at the top of

Figure 10–12 *Meredith Hall.* The small distance between the steel and grade reflects, to a small degree, steel's durability level. Some sense of refinement is projected by the sharpness of the mullion ends.

the wall is visible mostly because it is not tight to the fascia. Its color matches the facade, thus establishing the intent to prevent its expression. Although its lower edge is revealed, the detail reads more as a loose fit than a purposeful expression of thinness. The color of the finish is nearly neutral, thus reducing attention to the method of corrosion protection. The net effect of the detailing and finish is only a slight expression of the low durability of steel.

The equal spacing of the mullions suggests a framelike configuration, the typical form of steel structure. The absence of diagonal lines leaves the structural image short one common characteristic of steel framing, triangulation. The connections of the mullions to the spandrels, although neat, are overlapping. The overlapping configuration has several advantages that are important to wood but not to steel. It prevents the building from having an even higher sense of thinness and precision than it already has. It obscures the back flange, thus reducing the expression of thinness of each mullion by nearly half. The lengthy contact of the mullion and spandrel yields a less refined appearance than would the reduced contact of butting.

The overall expression of the building is that of steel when viewed from close range. Thinness and precision prevent the expression from being confused with wood, which could produce nearly the same image when viewed from a distance.

United States Pavilion
Expo '67, Montreal, Canada;
R. Buckminster Fuller and Shoji Sadao; 1967

The compatibility of the pavilion with the nature of steel is initially suspect because of its roundness (Fig. 10–13). The difficulty of imagining the same expression in wood, masonry, or concrete, however, indicates that the image of steel is present. The building's large size, somewhat linear texture, and sense of refinement constitute the basis of its expression.

The dome's potential relationship to masonry is prevented by its size and geometry. Unlike a dome that is half a sphere or less, the three-quarter sphere requires resistance to tensile stresses from gravity loads. The potential for tensile stresses from wind load is generated by its large profile. Its great span further removes the structure from the practical realm of masonry.

The dome geometry is not superfluous to steel in this pavilion. The efficiency of the structure, combined with the high strength of steel, allows the

Figure 10-13 *United States Pavilion.* The spherical shape violates the rectilinear image of steel. The fine-lined angular grid on the surface expresses the nature of steel.

members to be slender in comparison to the span. The visual result is a sense of thinness and refinement over the entire surface of the building. These characteristics are significant in maintaining an image separate from the realm of concrete or wood.

Reconciliation between a round form and a straight component is facilitated by the roundness of the members themselves. Although roundness is not mandatory in the struts of geodesic domes, there is at least a philosophical compatibility of some practical consequence. The radial symmetry of a pipe cross section frees it from having a preferred orientation in the structure. This is in contrast to flanged members or rectangular tubes, whose one or two preferred orientations are sometimes difficult to accommodate at both ends. The curved structure is a rare expression of this secondary steel form characteristic.

The pipes appear as straight lines in very large quantity and are expressed three-dimensionally (Fig. 10–14). This combination, which could be expected to yield an exceptionally strong linear expression, is tempered by several condi-

Figure 10-14 *United States Pavilion.* The position of the glazing reveals considerable information about the structure but interferes with the visibility of the steel by its lack of contrast and its visually busy surface.

tions. The pipes are relatively short in comparison to the size of the pavilion. Their lengths are prevented from being exaggerated by the nature of the connections, which punctuate the ends of the pipes. Their silvery surfaces blend somewhat with the reflective acrylic cladding. Upper chords, struts, and lower chords cross each other at an infinite number of angles and points, which obscures individual lines and orderly patterns. A variety of reflections and tones also contribute to the busy surface. While the structure is composed of many linelike components, the impression is a netlike linearity. The lines lack clear individual identities except upon close inspection.

The relatively low durability of steel is not expressed in the galvanized finish of the pipe. The steel-like color does not draw attention to itself as a coating. The level of working required on the components is within the nature of steel. This is made possible by the fact that the structure is not a perfectly smooth sphere but a series of straight lines. The shorter the lines, the higher the level of working (due to an increase in quantity of components). The greater number of worked units is compensated by the repetition of worked characteristics. Steel is more highly prefabricated than the other materials, thus is compatible with conditions that require repetition in the shop preparation of components.

Despite the dome shape, which has a philosophical connection to masonry, the building expresses the nature of steel. This is a common condition in buildings where the steel is exposed to view. The absence of rectangularity is not troublesome in building form or detail, as the components themselves are not rectangular.

West German Pavilion
Expo '67, Montreal, Canada;
Frei Otto and Rolf Gutbrod; 1967

The pavilion expresses the nature of steel in its image of tension and thinness (Fig. 10–15). The cable establishes a base for expressing tension, as it is too thin to resist any other type of stress. The geometry of the structure in certain areas heightens the sense of tension despite the relatively small spans and light load-

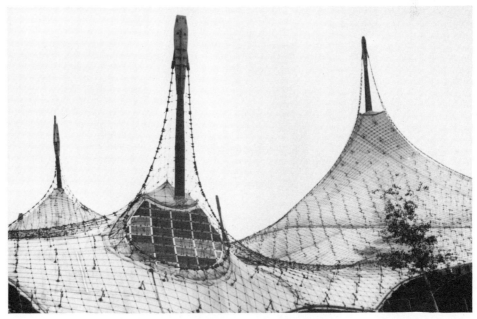

Figure 10–15 *West German Pavilion.* The visibility of the steel is enhanced by the plain, contrasting background provided by the fabric.

ing. Tautness is emphasized where the cable deviates most from a natural-appearing sag. Relatively abrupt turns, from nearly horizontal runs to steep slopes, occur in sufficient quantity to express an overall spirit of high tension. The small diameter of the cable couples with the general sense of high tension to express the great strength of steel.

Although the cable consists of long lines, the prevailing image is that of a net. Linearity is expressed less by lines that cross than by those that do not. The weblike thinness of the net is more noticeable than the linearity expressed. The visibility of the fine net is aided by a plain background provided by the fabric roof below it. The highest level of refinement and precision is not achieved, however, due to the relatively bulky clamps and connectors. Although consistent with the refinement of heavier steel systems, the bolted fastening devices appear as lumps in the otherwise delicate texture of the building.

The finish of the steel does not draw attention to its need for a protective coating. The durability of steel is therefore not expressed. The natural workability of steel is not surpassed even though the structure is nearly free form. The absence of rectangularity or even the regularity of single-radius curves does not tax the workability of the cable. Its ability to turn an infinite variety of angles with a minimum of fuss is an inherent quality of this secondary steel form. This pavilion geometry that would violate the nature of primary forms of steel expresses the nature of cable to a greater extent than would simpler shapes.

Alcoa Building
San Francisco, California;
Skidmore, Owings and Merrill; 1968

The expression of linearity in this building is especially strong even though the lines cross (Fig. 10–16). Several conditions increase the importance of each line beyond that typical of multistory buildings. The pattern of columns and lateral bracing occurs on all facades and controls the aesthetic order of the building.

Figure 10–16 *Alcoa Building.* The lines in the facade are emphasized by the separation of the diagonals and alternate vertical members from the curtain wall.

They are what distinguishes it from other office buildings of similar size. The impact of the pattern is magnified by its structural role. A purely decorative pattern would lack the significance that this one projects. The visual strength of the pattern is also enhanced by its precise relationship to building edges, cap, and base.

Each column and diagonal is emphasized by its significant projection beyond the curtain wall (Fig. 10–17). The diagonals are entirely separated from the glass. Half the verticals are freestanding, with contact to the curtain wall occurring only at each floor. The deep members with their shadows and reflections give the lattice high visibility. Different orientations of the sun give varied emphasis to the various parallel sets of lines. Often, some sets are visually stronger than others, which reduces the tendency of the facades to read as grids. A grid is not as strong a linear expression as the linearity of parallel lines. The linear expression is three-dimensional and of a magnitude rare in tall buildings.

The expression of triangulation is especially strong. Triangles cover nearly all the surface. Their visual strength is also a result of the conditions that enhance the expression of linearity. The structural role of the triangles contributes to their visual significance. The linearity and triangulation combine to express a sense of steel. Other conditions fail to support the image of steel as clearly as these two.

Refinement, the characteristic that typically separates steel from wood and concrete, is below the average for steel. The shapes of the linear members are rectangles, typical of wood and common in concrete. A base for the expression of thinness, established by comparing member thickness to building size, is not supplemented by flange edges or other very thin profiles. Although workmanship is neat, the detailing of the aluminum cladding does not take advantage of the metal to echo the thinness, sharpness, and refinement of the steel behind it.

The connections appear to be those of merging members, a configuration not physically possible in rolled steel (or aluminum). The finish is nearly neutral, which fails to draw attention to the cladding protecting the steel. Working the steel is kept to a minimum that is compatible with its nature.

Figure 10–17 *Alcoa Building.* The contribution to the image of linearity by members not touching the wall surface is doubled by their nearly freestanding shadows.

Despite the absence of supporting expressions in certain categories, the example seems like a steel building. It does so on the strength of its linearity, triangulation, and slenderness of components.

John Hancock Center
Chicago, Illinois; Skidmore, Owings and Merrill; 1969

The similarities of the Hancock Center and the Alcoa Building emphasize their differences with regard to the expression of steel (Fig. 10–18). Since they both expose triangulated lateral bracing covered in dark aluminum, certain conclusions from their analyses are the same.

For example, connections of the Hancock also appear to be the merging type. The finish of its aluminum cladding also contributes little to the expression of durability in steel or aluminum. Like the Hancock, the level of workability expressed in the Alcoa Building is acceptable. Similarly, the detailing of the aluminum cladding fails to exploit its potential for expressing the thinness and refinement possible in metals. The profiles of the linear components have the boxiness of wood or concrete, as do those of the Alcoa Building. Like the Alcoa Building, these characteristics do little to promote a sense of steel in the expression of the Hancock Center.

Like the Alcoa, the characteristics controlling the image with respect to materials expression are linearity and triangulation. Unlike the Alcoa, the Hancock is tapered and extremely tall. Its lateral bracing does not stand free of its surface. There are fewer triangles. Which building has the stronger expression of steel? It is a difficult question, as there are both an increase and a countering decrease in the intensity of steel expression compared to the Alcoa Building.

Figure 10–18 *John Hancock Center.* The linearity and triangularity of the facades are apparent but are subdued by the absence of a contrasting and simple background.

The great height of the Hancock Center suggests steel as a demonstration of strength. The tapered form magnifies the expression of height. The Alcoa Building is not tall enough to be an issue. The tapered form of the Hancock suggests a need for increased stability, a condition that detracts from the strength of steel. Hancock's expression of linearity is weaker. Linear diagonal and vertical members are visible in the surface of the building. They interrupt the curtain wall as they protrude slightly beyond it (Fig. 10–19). Their visibility is obscured somewhat by the presence of horizontal bands of the same cladding material at each floor line. The spandrels provide a partial background of similar color and texture to the vertical structure. The linear elements tend to blend with the spandrels. This was avoided in the Alcoa by the flush surface of the glass curtain wall.

The columns and diagonals are also less visible than in the Alcoa Building because they are not separate from the curtain wall. Their expression is therefore less three-dimensional. Shadows are connected to the elements that cast them, unlike the freestanding shadows possible from freestanding members. Consequently, the shadows are less pronounced than on the Alcoa Building.

The column and lateral bracing pattern is a significant part of the aesthetic system. Although very important, it plays less of a role than does the corresponding pattern in the Alcoa Building. In the Hancock, the building taper and the spandrels compete for attention with a few large triangles (or ×'s) of lateral bracing. In the Alcoa, the numerous triangles had little visual competition. The structural significance of the patterns on both buildings are equal. The structural pattern is less visible on the Hancock.

The Hancock Center expresses the nature of steel by virtue of its linear pattern of triangulation and great height. It does so to a greater degree than do many other steel buildings, which draw attention to neither the form of their elements nor their structural systems. It expresses its material less intensely than the Alcoa Building, however. Its one stronger characteristic, height, loses influence in the image because support from other steel characteristics is not strong.

Figure 10–19 *John Hancock Center.* While visibility of the structural members is strengthened by their shadows, a second set of lines is not produced, as the shadows are not separated from the members.

Kemper Arena
Kansas City, Missouri; C. F. Murphy Associates; 1975

The nature of steel is expressed in the exposed structural system beyond that typical of exposed pipe (Fig. 10–20). The enclosed volume is not as strong in its expression of steel.

The triangular and open nature of the trussed structural system is emphasized by its three-dimensional form. Linearity is also enhanced slightly by the ability to see the pipe members at many angles in one view. Their three-dimensionality is clarified by this condition. The visual strength of the lines is subdued somewhat by the minimal opportunity for shadows on a flat background. The emphasis afforded by the repetition of many parallel members is also missing. The linearity expressed is not remarkably strong but does provide a base to which other expressions of steel may be added. The image of triangularity, for example, is strong. The repetitive triangles contribute to a sense of steel structure. Openness, a characteristic that distinguishes trusses from solid webbed components, is emphasized by the views of components on the far side between the members on the near side.

Steel's great strength is revealed more clearly here than in many long-span structures, as the nature of the system may be grasped from casual observation. The end trusses can be seen passing across the entire roof in views of the north and south facades. Visual comparison of the truss span to the very large vertical supports suggests that additional supports do not occur inside the building. They would consume too much space. A trained eye is not required for the impression.

The nature of steel pipe is expressed in the exploitation of its form. The radial symmetry and simplicity of the round sections minimize the complexity of connections that are not at 90 degrees and are not between members on the *X, Y,* and *Z* axes. The presence of only tension or compression in the members calls for a section with structural properties that are the same on any axis of the section. The round form meets this requirement, which maximizes the efficiency of the structural design.

Figure 10–20 *Kemper Arena.* Because of its strong angular and linear image, the structure expresses, the nature of steel more strongly than does the curtain wall system.

A high sense of precision is expressed in the ends and connections of the members, a significant accomplishment for pipe (Fig. 10–21). The top chord of the truss assumes a prominent position in the facade, as it turns down to a vertical position in the base of each frame. The thinness of the steel in these pipes is expressed by recessing a closure plate into the end, thus leaving the pipe wall exposed to view. The view of the pipe thickness is emphasized by the cutting of the pipe end at an angle rather than perpendicular to its axis. The oval opening produced by the angled cut reveals a greater perimeter of exposed pipe wall than would the circle of a perpendicular cut. The plane of the oval is more nearly perpendicular to typical sight lines than would be the circular plane. A sense of sharpness results from the wedge shape formed by the oval plane and the body of the pipe.

A refined expression is established in the connections by the expression of plate edges. The plates' visual and structural roles are emphasized in the connections where they connect pipes that do not touch each other. These connections have the highest sense of precision as their visual mass is minimized. The ends of the pipes that are held back from the joint by the plate add to the sense of sharpness by exhibiting a 90-degree corner (in elevation) which would not exist if the pipes merged. The refining effect of the plate connectors is especially noticeable compared to the merged pipe connections of the Moscone Center in San Francisco. The detailing of the trussed frames is compatible with the level of workability associated with steel.

The mounting of the triangular trusses on relatively tall slender piers adds to their sense of precision. The pointlike tops of the piers transfer a pointlike quality to the trusses. They also clarify the identity of the horizontal pipe running between the tops of the piers by holding it a significant distance above grade. This gives each truss one more clear, thin, linelike statement that would be lost if too close to the ground. The potential for a similar statement is not fulfilled in the Moscone Center.

The curved walls of the enclosed space generate a softness that is unlike steel. The cantilevers of the upper corners suggest steel rather than wood or masonry. Little is present, however, to suggest that the walls are not concrete. The rectangular grid of lines between panels are reminiscent of concrete form

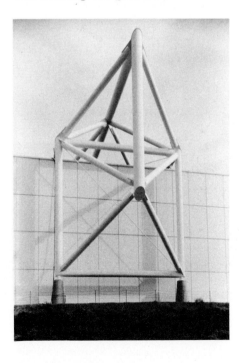

Figure 10–21 *Kemper Arena.* The connections express a very high level of precision and exploit the roundness of the pipe.

lines. The expression of panel durability is more compatible with concrete than with metal, as they seem to merge with the ground. The base detail is especially significant, as it is in contrast with the base detail of the steel trusses. The holding of the truss bases well above grade expresses the relatively low durability of steel.

The finishes on the trusses and wall panels neither violate nor particularly express low durability. The white color is only a slightly stronger expression than would be a neutral gray. The whiteness of the panels both helps and hurts the expression of truss linearity. It is a contrasting background for truss shadows but not for the white trusses themselves. A more intense truss hue superimposed on the white panels would increase the expression of both the low durability and linear character of steel.

The major structural elements of the building express the nature of steel, whereas the enclosed volume does not. A determination as to whether the total building is in the nature of steel depends on which element is judged to govern the visual image. Probably the uniqueness of the trusses gives them the edge despite their low number (only three). If so, the overall expression is slightly expressive of the nature of steel.

Reunion Arena
Dallas, Texas; Harwood K. Smith; 1980

The building expresses the great strength of steel in the limited but efficient expression of its long-spanning space truss system (Fig. 10–22). The edge of the roof structural system acts as the building fascia in a way that reveals the size and nature of the system. In the distant daytime view, a dark band is apparent above the walls that passes uninterrupted across the entire building. The separation from the top of the walls suggests that the band spans between columns. The system is further defined as being more than fascia trim, with an identity separate from the walls in its projection beyond both walls and columns at the corners (Fig. 10–23). The long cantilever expresses the need for significant strength and establishes the projected fascia as a structural entity. This expression is particularly significant, as the main entrance occurs below such a cantilever. Large numbers of people therefore see it at close range from many angles.

Figure 10–22 *Reunion Arena.* At a distance, the fascia (defined by the roof structure) reads as a distinct element with its own identity. This lends importance to the roof structure even before its members come into view.

Figure 10-23 *Reunion Arena.* The strong relationship between the fascia and the roof structure is revealeld by the glazing. The straight structure behind the curve is expressed in the soffit as contrasting lines.

At midrange and closer, the transparency of the fascia glazing reveals a latticework of steel behind the surface. The senses of linearity and triangulation reflect the nature of the actual spanning members. The red color of the steel draws attention, as it has adequate contrast with the darker background. Unlike many partially exposed systems, this one has emphasized visibility at night, when lighting behind the glass shines through the fascia. Attention is drawn even more strongly to the system during evening hours, when the building has extensive use.

The steel is held far above the ground and protected from the weather by the enclosing glazing, thus expressing the low durability level of steel. The bending of steel components is shown to be limited to thin supplementary members by the exposure in the soffits of the straight pieces carrying most of the structural load. The rounded corners of the fascia block soften the image of the steel system. The softened image contrasts with the nature of steel. It is a significant subtraction from the expression of steel, as the fascia block has no other form features to counter the strong statement of the rounded corners.

Generally, the expression of the roof system is in the nature of steel. It controls a major part of the aesthetic system. It is a remarkable condition since so little actual steel is visible.

Crystal Cathedral
Garden Grove, California; Philip Johnson and John Burgee; 1980

During daylight hours the building expresses its steel structure to a limited degree with its overall form (Fig. 10-24). Opposite ends of the plan form acute angles, giving a sense of sharpness to the image (Fig. 10-25). The characteristic is not exploited extensively, as numerous other angles are obtuse and fail to support the same sense. The flatness of the glass surface fails to reveal characteristics of the steel system behind it. The building shape does not express steel with a suggestion of great height or span (although a great span does exist). The horizontal look of the church suggests a stability that is more compatible with masonry.

Figure 10-24 *Crystal Cathedral.* Since only glass is visible in the exterior view, only building form is available for expression of the structural material. The image is slender and sharp, like steel.

Figure 10-25 *Crystal Cathedral.* The sharpness of the building form is strongly revealed in end views.

A sense of steel is clearly expressed in the interior view (Fig. 10–26). The space frame's multitude of thin lines could only be produced in metal. The association of interior steel to exterior image is fairly strong once the observer has been inside. On certain days a large section of the wall opens to reveal the linear network of steel to the outside.

Other aspects of material expression are prevented from being issues by the limited exposure of steel in the exterior. While the expression of steel is limited and abstract, the building seems more likely to be identified as steel than another material.

Figure 10-26 *Crystal Cathedral.* The long span and visually delicate lines of the space frame structure express the high strength and refinement of steel in the interior view.

Moscone Center
San Francisco, California;
Hellmuth, Obata & Kassabaum; 1981

Expression of the spirit of steel is weaker in this building than in the Kemper Arena in all respects but one. Here the triangular trusses over the lobby express the great strength of steel more clearly because their long spans are more apparent (Fig. 10–27). The full spans of the end trusses are visible below the roof and outside the building walls. The exposed ends and partial view of the

Figure 10-27 *Moscone Center.* The high visibility of the triangular trusses emphasizes both their success and failure in expressing the nature of steel. They express strength but not refinement.

other trusses through the glass curtain wall suggest to observers outside the building that they perform the same structural feat. Although their spans are shorter than those of the Kemper Arena, their close proximity to the sidewalk and lobby occupants magnifies their structural achievement.

While the triangular sections emphasize lines and triangles as described for the Kemper Arena, expressions of linearity and triangulation are slightly less here than is typical for exposed structures. The plain surface of the roof soffit could be a visually supportive background but does not contrast with the color of the trusses. The overhangs prevent the lines of the trusses from being duplicated in the form of shadows. The glass curtain wall contributes little to the clarity of truss form, as its varied reflections compete for attention. The nature of steel pipe form is expressed beyond simply its exposure to view in the same way as described for the Kemper building.

A significant difference between this building and the Kemper is the lower expression of refinement in the trusses of the Moscone Center (Fig. 10–28). The merging of the pipe at all connections gives the false impression that a number of the members pass through the intersection and all components become one at this point. Unlike concrete, this is not physically possible with wrought steel pipe. The merged rounded shapes produce a visually soft form that lacks the sharpness associated with steel.

The small contact area of the truss proper to its base triangle fails to fulfill its potential in producing a sense of precision. The merged connection lacks the sense of refinement expected of a point contact. The closeness of the lowest horizontal pipe to the horizontal concrete base obscures its linearity slightly and adds weight to what visual lightness the truss does establish despite its connections. This phenomenon is especially noticeable when the base is compared to the lighter, more precise expression of the Kemper foundation detail.

The expression of steel's durability is a little above neutral. The white color of the paint is slightly more expressive than gray and the steel is held above grade. The workability of steel is challenged to a greater extent than in the Kemper building but is not violated. The structural and form statements are in the nature of steel. The level of refinement is below that possible in steel. The net expression is that of steel. It is not a particularly strong expression of the material.

Figure 10–28 *Moscone Center.* The apparent merging of the pipe neither reveals pipe wall thickness nor suggests that the pipe is hollow. The connection lacks a sense of refinement.

Kuwait Chancery
Washington, D.C.; Skidmore, Owings and Merrill; 1982

The building expresses the great strength of steel with the long cantilever of the upper floors (Fig. 10–29). The size of the building contributes to the strength of the expression, as its scale is notably smaller than that of the truss system and its span. Diagonal members of the upper floors suggest the presence of large trusses. They reveal the fascias and columns actually to be clad truss components. The aesthetic order of the embassy is controlled by the structural expression since it affects such a large percentage of the facade.

The clarity of the structural condition is aided by the thin framed glass wall below the cantilever. The absence of columns is apparent when the curtains are open. The diagonal position of the entry curtain wall leaves the end bays to extend over open space at the corner. This further clarification of the cantilever contributes significantly to the expression because it occurs at the entrance.

The thin diagonals help the thicker verticals and chords read as steel. Without the influence of the diagonals, the chords could be confused with concrete. Other form characteristics do not contribute to the sense of steel. A significant part of the distinction between steel and concrete is carried by the stainless steel cladding. The form of the surface is not helpful as its joint lines are not so different from form lines in concrete. The silvery shine of the surface is unmistakably metal, however. Workability is not an issue. The conflict of steel's durability and its closeness to grade is tempered by this alloy's higher resistance to deterioration.

The expression of the building is in the nature of steel. It is for the most part based on the expression of strength. With the absence of great height as an expressive vehicle, great span was the only option. The smallness of the floor plan made the achieving of a long span difficult. The use of the cantilever magnified the sense of span length. The achievement of expressing great strength is magnified because it is difficult in small buildings.

Figure 10-29 *Kuwait Embassy.* The aesthetic order of the building is based almost entirely on its structural expression, which reflects the high strength of steel.

High Museum of Art
Atlanta, Georgia; Richard Mier and Partners; 1983

The expression of the museum is that of steel acting like stone, concrete, and steel (Fig. 10–30). The massing of the building, although rather blocky, as might be expected of masonry, is frequently tempered with linear elements (Fig. 10–31). These signs of steel are significant, as they are usually missing from blocky steel buildings and could easily have been omitted. Two undulating forms have the softness of concrete and challenge the workability of steel (Fig. 10–32).

Figure 10–30 *High Museum of Art.* The building has a mixture of expressions both in harmony and in discord with the nature of steel. The dark grid at the left is granite. The light grid beyond consists of steel panels. They look nearly the same.

Figure 10–31 *High Museum of Art.* Reference to the linearity of steel is found in several freestanding grids. Otherwise, the building has a sense of thickness and massiveness.

Figure 10-32 *High Museum of Art.* The undulating surface expresses a lack of linearity and straightness that is compatible with concrete. Even the panel joints are reminiscent of formwork joints.

Where the porcelain enamel steel panels resemble blocks, the image of stone prevails. This occurs at some corners and openings where the panels seem to have significant thickness (Fig. 10–33). Where joints between panels occur exactly on a corner, the thinness and precision of steel is expressed (Fig. 10–34). While the panels are generally 2-foot squares and therefore unitlike, their image as stone cannot be taken too seriously. Their use in soffits and nonarched spans is more like concrete or steel than it is like stone.

Figure 10-33 *High Museum of Art.* The absence of joints at the corners suggests that the units have significant thickness. The opening appears to have been made by the omission of a block rather than a panel.

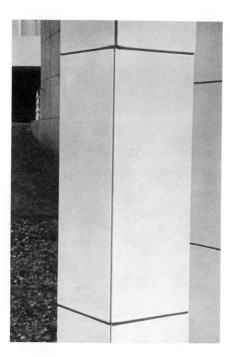

Figure 10–34 *High Museum of Art.* The joint on the corner suggests that the cladding is a thin and precise material, not a monolithic mass.

The sheen of the porcelain enamel is much like that of the granite used in the building. It lacks the toughness expected of steel, however, as a few chipped edges indicate. The durability of steel is addressed in the detailing of the base, where the steel panels are prevented from touching grade. The significance of the detail is verified by its contrast with the granite, which is allowed to touch grade. A more abstract but more apparent reference to durability occurs with the use of stone as a building base, with the steel panels above and far from grade (Fig. 10–35).

The panels lack the highest level of precision, as they are not perfectly flat (Fig. 10–36). The undulating surfaces and consequent sense of lumpiness

Figure 10–35 *High Museum of Art.* As the grade drops, granite (the darker tone) provides a visual base for the steel panels. The detail is compatible with the durability of steel and the component weights of both materials.

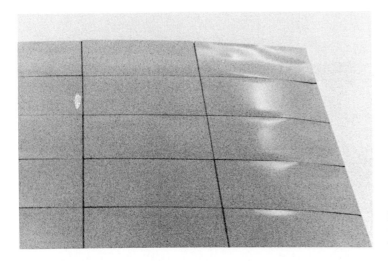

Figure 10-36 *High Museum of Art.* The slightly wavy surface of the cladding is incompatible with the high level of precision expected of steel.

is apparent only in certain light and at certain angles. The building lacks a sense of commitment to the expression or violation of any material. It does not express the nature of steel to a degree that would prevent very nearly the same image from being produced in concrete or even steel-supported stone.

Greyhound Bus Station
Portland, Oregon; Skidmore, Owings and Merrill; 1986

The tensile system supporting the roof expresses the strength of steel as well as its precise and refined form (Fig. 10-37). The intensity of the expression is subdued by the structure's lack of clarity. The visual impact of the masts is emphasized by their use of pairs and their extension well above the connection of the cables. Some of the attention drawn to the compressive part of the system is likely to move to the tensile elements that connect to it.

The tensile system does not have a strong visual image, due to the low number of cables. The roof over the bus loading area appears to hang from the cable system, as close inspection reveals that there are no other supports. Walls surrounding the bus side of the site prevent casual observation of this fact. The hanging nature of the roof over the waiting area on the opposite side is obscured by the curtain wall enclosure and traditionally structured spaces surrounding it. The impaired view of the bus side of the building hinders the mental transfer of its hanging image to the other side.

Figure 10-37 *Greyhound Bus Station.* The absence of columns under the roof on the right is obscured by the brick wall. When the curtain wall is installed under the roof on the left, this fact will be even less apparent than it is now.

Figure 10-38 *Greyhound Bus Station.* The thinness of the cables suggest both the high strength of steel and a sense of precision. These expressions would be stronger if the cables were more noticeable.

These obstacles to seeing and recognizing the tensile system do not eliminate its expression. The use of cables in straight lines from mast to roof gives a sense of tautness. Emphasizing the significance of the load in this way contributes to the impression that the strength of the thin lines must be significant.

The slender masts and lateral bracing are compatible with the level of refinement natural to steel (Fig. 10–38). The reduction in diameter from mast to mast extension projects a sense of delicacy while allowing the thicker pipes below to maintain a more visible profile. The linearity of the mast system is clear but lacks the repetition of lines required to establish linearity as a base for aesthetic order. Because the connections look bulky in comparison to the very thin lines of the cables, they do not contribute to the system's sense of refinement.

Neither durability nor workability are issues in the aesthetic system. Protecting the steel with a neutral coating is balanced with the maintaining of steel well above grade. The cutting of steel is standard in quantity and sophistication. Although the expression of the tensile nature of steel fails to fulfill its potential, it is as strong as most tensile structures. Revealing the reality of tensile systems is always made difficult by the curtain wall enclosures.

Chapter 11

PROPERTIES OF CONCRETE

All concrete considered here is reinforced. Concrete that is poured-in-place is also referred to as site-cast, cast-in-place, or simply concrete. Reinforced concrete that is cast prior to its installation is called precast, factory-cast, or, if appropriate, prestressed. Site-cast can also refer to precast concrete, which is cast on the site. The term "concrete" can refer either to the substance concrete (unreinforced) or a reinforced concrete installation. The shortest terms possible are used to avoid an awkward narrative. Overlaps in the meanings of the terms are tolerated because their context makes them clear.

FORM

Poured-in-Place.　Poured-in-place concrete differs from wood, masonry, and steel in that it is a cast composite material and is not prefabricated (Fig. 11–1). These conditions allow concrete to assume a broad range of shapes, including those similar to the other materials. Consequently, to identify a form that represents the uniqueness of concrete, reasoning different from that for the other materials is required.

The primary form of concrete is less affected by limitations of substance and production than are the primary forms of the other materials. The form of wood is strongly influenced by the limits of tree shape and size. Masonry is largely shaped by strength limitations. The desire to limit cost and weight encourages the production of steel in slender and thin forms. Wood, masonry (except concrete block), and steel have a simplicity of form that is generated to some degree by the economics of sawing, extruding, and rolling. Since concrete (reinforced) approaches the strength of steel without the limitations of wrought manufacturing processes, its potential forms are greater in variety than those of the other materials. This broad range of choices is a boon to the usefulness of concrete but an obstacle to its sense of identity. Although direct imitation

Figure 11-1 Plastic concrete arrives at the sight able to take a wide variety of shapes. The nature of formwork, reinforcing steel, and the casting process define broad but finite limits. The desire to express a form unique among materials narrows the choice to one.

of other materials is less common than it was in historical use, confusion of concrete shapes with those of other materials continues to be an issue (Fig. 11–2).

Linear components—beams and columns—are standard in concrete construction (Fig. 11–3). Since linear forms are typical of wood and steel, they cannot be associated with concrete alone. Consequently, linear forms are not efficient in expressing the uniqueness of concrete. An aesthetic order based on the properties of concrete will lack clarity if linear forms are central to the expression. This does not mean that concrete beams and columns must be omitted. The usefulness of these members assures their continued use. Limiting their use to utilitarian roles or, at most, roles that are incidental to the expressive order will limit the ambiguity they would bring to the composition.

Figure 11-2 This facsimile of stone is one of several material limitations in which concrete is used. By definition, such limitations exclude the expression of properties that are unique to concrete.

Figure 11–3 Square, nearly square, or round concrete columns share a general image with steel tubes, laminated wood, or wood poles. Although the concrete columns may not be mistaken for other materials, they dilute the uniqueness of concrete in the building image.

If concrete is shaped into small block forms, it becomes masonry. If shaped into large boxlike (hollow) forms, it is similar to a form common in certain precast systems. Blocklike forms, then, are not unique to site-cast concrete. Volumetric or blocklike forms are therefore not efficient shapes with which to distinguish concrete from other materials.

Having ruled out the line and the volume as geometries unique to concrete, a third basic geometry, the plane, remains to be examined. Plywood, stone panels, and steel plate form small, thin planes. They are not considered to be planar materials, however, since one piece does not form a complete structural component such as a beam, column, or bearing wall. Concrete can form a plane that acts as a complete structural component. Walls and structural slabs are common concrete forms. Concrete is therefore identified as a planar material (Fig. 11–4). Planar shapes are identified as primary forms of concrete because they are unique to single concrete components. Linear shapes are primary in wood because wood is generally limited to those forms. The reasoning used to

Figure 11–4 The concrete planes differ from masonry, wood, and steel planes in that the concrete forms a plane as a single component. The other materials do not.

determine the primary form of concrete is different from that for the other materials. It is essentially one of elimination. The forms available in the other materials are eliminated from the broad range possible in concrete.

Certain masonry walls may have a planar quality. The characteristic is of the assembly, however, not the unit. The more planar the masonry wall, the less blocklike its expression. Detailing can cause a masonry wall to be less planar and more blocklike, which clarifies its distinction from the image of concrete. The detailing of concrete walls can reduce the ease of their duplication in masonry. While masonry walls have similarities to concrete walls, the uniqueness of the image of concrete as a structural plane can be demonstrated by detailing. Structural slabs do not have a counterpart in masonry. The efficiency of their visual exploitation in expressing concrete is higher than that of walls. Structural slabs are not to be confused with unreinforced concrete paving, which is much like masonry in its compressive role.

Defining concrete as a planar material is not meant to limit it to forms that are flat, as strict use of the term suggests. Here "planar" refers to having two dimensions that are not significantly different from each other but are significantly larger than the third. One major dimension may be several times the other but not so many times larger that the form resembles a line. The third dimension should be sufficiently small as to avoid the appearance of a compact or blocky form. The actual configuration of the plane that is most concretelike is influenced by several factors. Properties of the substance, formwork, the manufacturing process, and the desire to avoid shapes of other materials are among the factors.

Although formwork is influential in defining the configuration of the concrete plane, it is only one element in the production of concrete. Several considerations free concrete from an implied obligation to express only the properties of wood, steel, or fiber-reinforced plastic (typical formwork materials). One major difference between concrete and its formwork is longevity. The temporary nature of the formwork broadens the range of shapes possible beyond those associated with the same material as a building component. This is especially noticeable for wood. Wood formwork need not resist weathering for the life of the building. A certain assembly of wood members may not be able to survive rain and sun for a number of years but may be expected to perform for the duration of a concrete pour and curing.

The bracing that temporarily obstructs circulation below a structural slab or beside a wall during construction reduces the structural demands on the form material compared to those on the same material as a building structure (Fig. 11–5). With wood, even the allowable stresses are greater than for the same wood used in a permanent construction. To differentiate between concrete shapes because of their different formwork materials is possible but is too complicated to be useful.

For example, it may be reasoned that concrete produced in steel forms may have fewer curves than concrete formed with wood. The concept is based on the idea that steel, costing more, must be used on more jobs than wood to pay for itself. Straight sections are more likely than curved sections to have applications on more jobs. This level of sophistication is rejected in lieu of a simpler approach. Generally, the material or combination of materials that provides the greatest design flexibility is assumed to be the choice for the formwork.

Concrete that is sprayed from a hose is not viewed here as a material different from the poured variety. It is considered to offer another option in formwork where the form is on one side of the plane instead of both sides (Fig. 11–6). The flexibility of shape afforded by spraying is in the pool of ideas from which selections may be made to express the essence of concrete. Other issues are used

Figure 11-5 The unacceptability of this form-work as a permanent part of the building illustrates a difference between wood and steel as formwork compared to wood and steel as building materials.

Figure 11-6 Where sprayed concrete forms building components, the resulting planes emphasize concrete's natural aversion to high precision. Its use as a coating or imitation stone, however, is not the standard for analysis of this installation process.

to further refine the definition of primary form for which formwork sets general parameters.

Given the straightness of primary forms in wood and steel, curved planes have greater potential than straight ones to demonstrate the uniqueness of concrete. Since curves demonstrate certain characteristics of masonry, concrete curves must be different from masonry curves if they are to express only concrete. It follows that concrete curves can be different since the limitations and

Figure 11–7 The gentle curves of the canopy could be formed in masonry if the same form was rotated to be a wall on grade. As a horizontal spanning plane, however, a sense of masonry is the most remote of all materials from the image.

potential of reinforced concrete are quite different from those of masonry (Fig. 11–7). These differences occur in strength and configurations of connections, surfaces, and edges. The concept of the curved plane as the primary form for poured-in-place concrete is further refined in the subsequent sections addressing those issues.

The level of refinement natural to concrete is affected by its nature in both the plastic and the cured state. The need for concrete to flow into every part of the formwork is an issue that affects the water/cement ratio, the use of admixtures, aggregate size, reinforcing design, form design, and placing techniques. The mix that has the minimum water needed for hydration will not flow into formwork to an acceptable degree. A limited amount of water is included as lubrication, which reduces the strength of the concrete. The sacrifice of strength is a major concern. This fact is illustrated by the common use of admixtures and vibrators to reduce the extra water for flow.

Considering the magnitude of the flow issue, it follows that very thin, especially sharp, shapes require special effort and attention (Fig. 11–8). This

(a)   (b)

Figure 11–8 The rough edge resulted when the concrete failed to fill the acute-angled corner of the formwork. The example illustrates concrete's incompatibility with sharpness based on the internal nature of the substance.

consideration alone would force the refinement level of concrete to be lower than that of steel. The level of refinement natural to concrete form is identified as medium. It is higher than wood, about the same as masonry, and lower than steel. Justification of this conclusion continues in the discussion of strength.

The primary form of poured-in-place concrete (for purposes of unique expression) is identified as a curved plane. Since standard products are not available in this material, secondary forms are not as well defined as in wood, masonry, and steel. For simplicity, all poured-in-place shapes that are not primary forms may be identified as secondary forms. Certain characteristics can be expressed in the connections, surfaces, and edges of secondary forms that are unique to concrete. If the image of the secondary form is similar to another material, these details can pull the expression toward concrete and away from the other material.

Precast.   A certain category of forms can be identified as primary in precast concrete with reasoning similar to that used for cast-in-place concrete. The process begins with consideration of all the possibilities and eliminates certain forms for various practical and philosophical reasons.

Since precast and site-cast concrete are generally the same substance, they have many characteristics in common. Like poured-in-place concrete, precast can be produced in a wide range of shapes. Some differences occur because of their differing production and handling. Highway restrictions affect the sizes and shapes of factory precast components. The economics of hauling encourages the use of simple forms that stack efficiently (Fig. 11–9). Simplicity of shape is compatible with the need to remove cast products from factory forms without dismantling the forms. Since straight, flat, and rectangular shapes respond to these goals, they are common characteristics of precast components.

The formwork for factory-produced precast components tend to be more sophisticated and durable, thus have higher initial cost than site-assembled formwork (Fig. 11–10). The need to amortize the cost of factory forms over many castings encourages repetitive and generic shapes. Tee sections and floor planks respond to this need. The common use of planks and tees in floor and roof structures yields little opportunity for their architectural expression. Double tees

Figure 11–9 The widths and lengths of the precast planks either match that of the trailer bed or are nearly exact subdivisions of its dimensions.

Figure 11-10 Installation of reinforcing steel and removal of the precast component from the steel form are facilitated by the movable side. Other forms tilt for easy removal. Vibrating forms aid consolidation of plastic concrete.

are particularly efficient, because they can serve as enclosure as well as structure. They lack the flatness (compactness) that maximizes the number that will fit on a trailer but do stack conveniently. Mass production overcomes any loss of stacking efficiency to assure that they are economical products.

The use of double tees as the exterior walls of some buildings seems to establish their eligibility as a precedent for primary precast form. Most of these buildings, however, are not considered to be architecture. Their use in utilitarian structures, never intended to be judged by architectural criteria, reduces the credibility of the component as a definer of primary form. Double tees are therefore identified as secondary precast forms.

The broad flange of a double tee emphasizes a planar quality. The legs have a linear quality. The common orientation of double tees in a wall exposes the ribs on the exterior (Fig. 11–11). Their linear appearance controls the image of a double-tee wall, as the broader flanges tend to lose their identities in the wall surface. A single component has a more planar sense. When installed they have a linear image. As with secondary forms in other materials, expression of all the product characteristics is considered to be the more pure expression. Installations that express both the planar and linear qualities of double tees would accomplish this. Separating the tees in a wall by placing windows between them tends to express all form traits of the product. Cutting openings in the flanges and butting the tees is not as clear an expression of product form.

Figure 11-11 Separating precast double-tee wall components as shown here maintains their individual identities. The planar identity of the flange is subdued and the image of the wall is controlled by the ribs if the sides of the units are butted.

The use of precast columns and beams requires space-enclosing components (Fig. 11–12). Buildings with linear precast components, then, may be expected to have a larger number of pieces than do buildings built with concrete planes or boxes. The increased handling and site work that are associated with a large number of pieces leave an advantage of precasting untapped. Theoretically, the maximizing of component size can minimize truck trips, crane lifts, and site connections. The partial exploitation of precast potential limits the significance of the linear components. Also, since wood and steel are identified as linear, linearity is rejected as the primary form for precast concrete, which has more options.

Small blocklike members in precast concrete are generally identified as masonry and do not contribute to a blocklike image for precast. Room-sized volumetric components make up a small percentage of all the precast produced each year. Their production often involves more than one casting step. Floors, for example, may be cast before walls and roofs. The product of this process may be more accurately called an assembly. These conditions prevent blocklike forms from being primary in precast concrete.

Planar precast forms meet the requirements for efficient factory production and transporting. Since they fall between linear and volumetric components in size they avoid the disadvantages associated with the sizes of the other geometries. Flat rectangular components with dimensions matching the bed of a truck trailer stack most efficiently in a horizontal position. This system is more common for floor planks than for wall sections, however.

Transporting finished panels horizontally could damage the faces of the units and complicates their lifting into a vertical position. The more common method for transporting wall sections stands them in a vertical or slanted position (Fig. 11–13). Some efficiency is lost, as fewer sections can be placed on the trailer in this orientation. In this regard, planar members lose some credibility as the form most compatible with the nature of precasting. The loss is balanced by the increased sense of plane generated by the wider dimension common in sections hauled in the slanted position.

Figure 11–12 The relatively small size of the post-and-beam precast structural system takes only partial advantage of the nature of prefabrication. Small units require more crane lifts and more connections than do larger pieces.

Figure 11–13 The tilted position of the wall panels aids unloading, reduces abrasion, and allows the transport of broader units than does carrying the panels horizontally. It also wastes the space under the panels.

Precast components may be cast on the site and lifted to their final position in a building. Although still qualifying as precast, this process combines characteristics of both in-place and factory casting. The largest component sizes, for example, tend to be larger than those of factory-cast concrete but smaller than the largest cast-in-place concrete (Fig. 11–14). They have the simplicity of form typical of factory cast, but their production lacks the sophistication of factory formwork and quality control. The very large percentage of precasting on the site being in the form of tilt-up wall slabs further encourages the adoption of the plane as the primary form of precast concrete.

Figure 11–14 The site-cast tilt-up slab is larger than typical precast units transported on public roads. The size of this type of component is not limited by highway laws. Architect: Planners Architects Collaborative.

Given the compatibility of a structural plane with the concept of precasting, hauling, and handling, and its uniqueness among primary forms of other materials, it is identified as the primary form of precast concrete. The need for simplicity of form in precasting nearly eliminates curves and angles as options in precast components. Straightness, rectangularity, and limited size distinguish factory-precast planes from cast-in-place planes. Site-cast precast tolerates simple curves because its formwork is less rigid than in a factory, and hauling is not required.

Since the quality of precast concrete is generally higher than that of site-cast, it is possible to cast thinner, sharper, and generally more refined shapes with a higher success rate than with poured-in-place concrete. The advisability of doing so, however, is very low because of the high likelihood of impact during the extensive handling that follows casting. These considerations produce a rating of medium for the refinement level compatible with precast concrete.

Linear forms (precast columns and beams) are considered to be secondary products, as are precast cladding and the other miscellaneous components that are too numerous to identify. As with poured-in-place concrete, the secondary precast forms have characteristics that are unique to concrete (the subject of following sections) and can be exploited to pull their image toward that of concrete.

Concrete's Uniqueness.   Limitations of form in other materials have been a major influence in the identification of concrete as primarily a planar material. This does not mean that linear or blocklike forms must be avoided in concrete as a practical matter. Certainly, linear beams and columns will continue to be useful and necessary in concrete construction. The structural plane is a geometry that is most likely to express concrete as a material with a form potential different from that of wood, masonry, and steel. It represents an image on which an aesthetic order may be based if expressing the uniqueness of concrete is a goal. This goal calls for the limitation of nonplanar forms to supplementary roles in the visual order of concrete architecture.

STRENGTH

Only reinforced concrete is considered in this analysis. It is usually referred to simply as concrete. Concrete has a wide range of strengths, which varies with the amount of reinforcing steel included. In typical applications the strength of reinforced concrete falls above wood and below steel. Maximum reinforcing produces concrete with strength approaching but not matching that of an equal weight or cross-sectional area of structural steel.

Bending stress seems particularly compatible with concrete because it is a composite, as is concrete. Bending produces compression on one side of the component (resisted by concrete) and tension on the other (resisted by steel). Both materials contribute strength and are justified on that basis. The expression of bending is accepted as being compatible with the nature of reinforced concrete. Since wood and steel are commonly used in bending, the demonstration of this ability alone is not enough to express the essence of concrete. Because concrete's bending strength is not at an extreme, expressions of minimal or remarkably great bending ability are not efficient ways to distinguish concrete from the other materials. Spans that are too long or too short may confuse the image of concrete while moderate spans simply go unnoticed. Avoiding the violations, however, may be as sophisticated as one can get when expressing the bending strength of concrete.

Pure compression offers a less philosophically clear potential for expression. The division of compressive load between the steel and concrete lacks the clarity of the division of stresses in bending. Each material's contribution varies with its strength and area. The ability of the other three materials to resist compression prevents justification of its expression in concrete on a basis of uniqueness. It is prudent to recognize some potential for the expression of compression in concert with other properties that can make the image of the component unmistakably concrete. As a practical matter, it is recognized that concrete will always be used in compression. It is important to understand that to question the efficiency of this expression is not to question the utility of compression in concrete.

The resistance of pure tension is easily rejected as an expressive device for concrete. It is, after all, only the steel that resists tension in concrete. The load is not shared as it is in bending and compression. In pure tension, concrete's structural contribution is negative, as it only adds more load to the steel. Theoretically, a concrete beam (precast) could span over supports and accept bending stresses without connecting to its internal steel. The same could be said of columns and their resistance of compression. This is not possible, even on a theoretical basis, for a concrete component in pure tension. The expression of tension is incompatible with the structural reality of reinforced concrete.

The greatest potential for expressing the uniqueness of concrete with regard to strength is identified as being in the area of bending. Compression has less potential. If compression is expressed, detailing must show that the concrete assemblies are different from masonry assemblies to preserve the uniqueness of both materials. The expression of pure tension violates the nature of concrete.

A concrete component has the strength characteristics of reinforced concrete only where steel is present. The structural depth of a beam spanning between two points, for example, is measured from the top of the concrete to the center of the tensile steel (not to the bottom of the concrete). The inch and a half or so of concrete below the steel is ignored as having no significant tensile strength. The concrete outside the steel (in any direction) will perform like unreinforced concrete when stressed. It will resist significant compression, limited shear, and insignificant tension. Accidental impact loads often stress concrete that is outside its reinforcing at edges and corners.

The vulnerability of a corner to impact failure is a function of concrete thickness. Acute-angled corners are more delicate than rounded corners or those with obtuse angles (Fig. 11–15). The extreme edge of a sharp corner has limited concrete thickness to resist impact and is a relatively long distance from the nearest steel. While the intensity of the violation varies somewhat with the location within a site, sharpness is generally incompatible with the expression of concrete. The forming challenge and potential damage during construction secure this conclusion for site-cast concrete.

Lifting, stacking, transporting, and installation of precast concrete introduces stresses in addition to those expected in site-cast concrete. These are generated by both anticipated loads and accidental impact. The higher quality of formwork, concrete, and control of precast makes the production of flawless sharp corners more likely than in site-cast concrete. The advisability of precasting thin, highly refined, and precise elements is very low, however. The extensive handling required of precast makes accidental impact and damage to thin detailing likely (Fig. 11–16). Elements centrally located in a precast plane are subject to damage but to a lesser degree than are edge details. Once installed, vulnerability continues, as the units are subject to the same damage from daily use as cast-in-place concrete.

Figure 11–15 The 30-degree corner of the retaining wall/bench is too sharp to withstand minor impacts, as shown by the broken corners. The failures illustrate concrete's incompatability with sharpness based on its strength properties.

Figure 11–16 The thin (unreinforced) concrete cover over the lifting loop did not come close to having the strength to resist lateral forces generated in moving the precast component.

Although 90-degree corners are easier to form and less vulnerable to damage than acute-angled corners, they are not immune to damage. Recognition of the limited compatibility of site-cast and precast concrete with 90-degree corners is revealed in the common practice of chamfering them (Fig. 11–17). Inserting a triangular strip of wood into the corners of the formwork blunts the concrete corner subsequently cast. Two obtuse angles are formed in place of a 90-degree corner. The blunter corner expresses the nature of concrete (site-cast or precast) more accurately than would the 90-degree corner.

Figure 11–17 Chamfered edges are standard details in both cast-in-place and precast concrete. The blunt image they produce is representative of concrete's incompatibility with thin refined forms.

The nature of site-cast and precast concrete with regard to strength does not justify thin sections or refined detailing. Consequently, a rating of medium is assigned to the level of refinement expected of all concrete. This conclusion (based on strength considerations) confirms the rating assigned to this category of site-cast concrete based on forming difficulties. The rating is higher than wood because of the devastating effect that warpage has on the precision of wood.

DURABILITY

Concrete has a low tendency to corrode chemically, as cement is not extremely remote from the state of its raw materials. Special cements are available that are resistive to the chemicals that to which normal cement is not resistant. Concrete can deteriorate by a physical process. The surface of concrete lacks tensile strength, as the reinforcing steel is positioned some distance from it. If water penetrates and freezes, tensile stresses are created by the expanding ice. Tensile failure of the unreinforced layer is signified by particles of concrete breaking loose from the surface (Fig. 11–18).

The deterioration (spalling) is most common in paving, as water penetration is assisted by gravity. It is the result of human error (finishing in the presence of bleed water or too much water in the surface mix). It is not a natural property of concrete as a substance. The susceptibility of the manufacturing process to human error however is in the nature of poured-in-place concrete. Precast processes are less susceptible because of the more uniform conditions typical of a factory compared to a building site. In any case, the possibility of physical deterioration is considered to be less of a natural condition than is wood's tendency to decay.

The deterioration rarely occurs in beams, columns, and walls, where the vast majority of surface area is vertical and sheds water. Since it is these components rather than paving that affect the image of a building, the occasional spalling of concrete is not considered to be a strong influence on the level of durability at which concrete is identified.

Figure 11-18 The spalled concrete does not signify a low level of durability for concrete in general. It does not occur if standard practices are performed during production of the installation.

Cracking in concrete is common. Hairline cracks are expected from shrinkage during curing. Larger cracks may occur that permit water to corrode the reinforcing steel (Fig. 11–19). Since rust (iron combined with oxygen) has a larger volume than iron alone, the corrosion has a swelling effect. Like the formation of ice, this expansion within the concrete introduces tensile stresses. Failure of the concrete in tension between and around the steel is possible. Particles can break away from the concrete to a depth that eventually exposes the steel.

Figure 11-19 The streaks indicate rusted reinforcing steel from water passing through cracks in the concrete retaining wall. Physical deterioration is likely to follow the visual deterioration. This is harder to prevent than spalling but is also less common.

This type of concrete deterioration is not common in buildings. Surfaces in frequent contact with moisture, such as bridge decks and retaining walls, are most vulnerable. Since these components have little influence on building image, the deterioration has nearly no effect on the durability rating of concrete in this study.

Concrete easily rates as being more durable than wood or steel. Concrete systems have far fewer joints than do masonry systems. Consequently, the ability of a concrete wall to prevent the penetration of water is higher than that of a masonry wall. This characteristic gives concrete a higher durability rating than that of masonry. Concrete is identified as having very high durability. This characteristic may be expressed by designing concrete elements so as to challenge its durability. Bringing it into contact with the earth and other moisture (without protection) can affect the appearance of a building and shows that the material is durable.

WORKABILITY

The term "workability" is used here to describe the ease of changing the form of a component after the concrete has cured. Traditional use of the term refers to the ability of plastic concrete to flow. In a sense the term refers to the same property of concrete both before and after curing. Remembering that the term as used here always refers to the changeability of cured concrete is critical to the reasoning in the analysis that follows. Using the term for hardened concrete may seem inappropriate since it is nearly impossible to change the form of concrete after it cures. This condition is significant in rating the workability of cured concrete.

Comparisons of material properties are most useful if like properties are compared. It is tempting to compare the formability of plastic concrete to the workability of wood or steel. A comparison of formability and workability is not useful at this level of analysis, as the properties represent different aspects of materials. Formability relates to the initial shaping of raw materials into basic product forms. A comparison of formability is a study of primary material forms. A comparison of workability analyzes the ease of changing primary forms after the initial manufacturing processes are complete. The distinction has the effect of minimizing the scope of issues to be analyzed. Clarity of cause and effect is the goal for having such a distinction.

The bending, cutting, and rejoining that are standard in steel and wood construction are absent from traditional concrete processes. The strength of reinforced concrete and the brittleness of the substance are obstacles to these shaping techniques.

Some cutting of cured concrete occurs in the precast industry. One production sequence extrudes 400-foot prestressed planks and saws them into usable lengths after curing. It is one of the most significant changes to form that occurs from a standard practice. It is also about the only example of working where the material on both sides of the cut is usable. It may be argued that this is merely a step in the initial manufacturing process and should not be identified as working the component. Working does clearly include the cutting of notches and holes that are often required in precast planks (Fig. 11–20).

Changing the general form of cast-in-place concrete is usually limited to corrections of errors. The chipping of sections that were cast too large or in the wrong place is tedious and primitive (Fig. 11–21). Even the removal of unreinforced pavement is a challenge. The working in either case is disruptive in nature. In both the precast and site-cast examples, the expressive effect of the

Figure 11-20 The sawing of a notch in the precast plank disrupts the repetitive nature of production and therefore violates a major justification for precasting. Although physically possible, the nonrepetitive cutting is not compatible with the production process.

Figure 11-21 The chipping required to reduce the slab to the correct size was far more tedious and disruptive than would be the sawing required to shorten lumber that was too long. The comparison signifies the relative workability of the two materials.

working is nil. Although the examples demonstrate that general form can be changed slightly in cured concrete, the absence of expressive significance minimizes the importance of the potential.

Expressive effect may be achieved by working the surface of cured concrete. Changing the surface of concrete is difficult, as demonstrated by the challenge of hiding the marks of forms and form ties. Removing the form marks is usually an exercise of covering. Paint is rarely adequate. A cement wash coating which is also painted is often required. Sandblasting can reveal aggregate and produce a slight texture (Fig. 11-22). Sawing is generally limited to the production of paving joints. Although these methods do change the surface, the change is limited.

A slightly greater change is produced by the breaking of ribs cast into the concrete for that purpose (Fig. 11-23). Although a broken ribbed surface is quite different from a smooth surface, the working exercise affects only the texture of the ribs. The breaking of ribs is a long and tedious handwork process. Some skill is required to produce a uniform texture. The motivation for working concrete in this way is largely eliminated by the availability of form liners, which produce textured ribs in the initial casting process. Future use of the breaking method is expected to be minimal.

Figure 11-22 The use of the lifting, spraying, and protective equipment necessary to sandblast these panels represents a significant effort. The reduction of blemishes by the procedure in preparation for painting represents a minimal change in form.

Figure 11-23 The breaking of ribs represents one of the largest ratios among the materials between effort and change in form. The effort is enormous, whereas the change to the form is not.

Comments regarding the difficulty of working concrete and its limited effect have saturated the discussion. It is not difficult to conclude that the workability of concrete rates very low. It rates below masonry. Although working can cause only small changes to the form of masonry, the ease of making them is high compared to concrete. The expression of workability compatible with the level natural to concrete may be achieved by eliminating the working of concrete entirely.

Chapter 12

ASSEMBLIES IN CONCRETE

STRUCTURES

Square and circular columns are standard in concrete structures. They are economical and their directionally balanced resistance to buckling is efficient in most applications. Their linear forms are not, however, the most efficient expressions of concrete's unique potential in structures. Small square and rectangular sections overlap the range of forms available in steel tubes and laminated wood. Round columns are available in both concrete and steel pipe with the same diameters (Fig. 12–1). Their images, thus their contributions to

Figure 12–1 The general form of the round concrete column is not helpful in distinguishing it from a steel pipe column. Color and texture (including spiral marks from the cardboard tube form) alone are carrying this burden.

a building's character, are similar. If a demonstration of material uniqueness is a goal in the aesthetic order, a dependence on simple square or round concrete columns as visual devices is not efficient.

A number of design decisions can be affected by the desire to achieve material clarity in the use of concrete as a compressive material. Simple square and round columns can be limited to uses that do not have prominent visual roles. This can occur in spaces that are utilitarian in nature or where other visual issues are so demanding that a neutral structural statement is desired. They can be used in association with other concrete structural elements whose strong visual statements alone carry the material message.

A more direct approach is to manipulate the linear form of the columns to exploit the unique properties of concrete. The plan section of the column could take a shape that is not common in wood or steel. Triangles or the radial pattern of flower petals have the symmetry that is structurally efficient in many column applications. Parallelograms and ovals are nearly as efficient as squares and rectangles. Free-form shapes have potential for efficiency if it is required. Considerations such as concrete's level of refinement and limitations of formwork will affect the final shapes. Rounded corners can occur on parallelograms and triangles, for example, to reduce their sharpness.

The elevations of the columns can be manipulated as well. Columns can taper upward or downward (Fig. 12–2). They can do so with profiles that are curved, jagged, or wrinkled. The irregularities of the vertical profiles need not be symmetrical. The surfaces themselves can be patterned. Although these manipulations require some effort, they are compatible with the process of casting. They seem less compatible with the production processes of wood and steel components.

Regardless of the detailing that eliminates the uniformity found in steel and wood, a concrete column's linearity is shared with wood and steel. This strong association can be subdued or eliminated by reducing the linelike sense of the concrete compressive component. This can be achieved by widening a symmetrical column enough in one direction so as to reduce the length-to-width ratio. As the width increases, the column becomes less like a line and more like a plane (Fig. 12–3). The planar form has been identified as primary for concrete

Figure 12–2 The taper of the concrete bridge supports helps their linear forms seem less like the linearity of wood or steel columns, where the sides are typically parallel.

Figure 12-3 The concrete columns are more like planes than lines. Their image is, therefore, more like concrete than like wood or steel. Architect: Planners Architects Collaborative.

and does not compete with steel or wood in its structural expression. This form also makes the column stronger in one direction, which has a logical application where loads are not symmetrically applied. Planar columns can have significant impact on building image when located in the facade.

A bearing wall is a compressive form that has great potential for expression of concrete's planar nature. First, the wall is a plane. Second, it has an important role in the building as both a support and definer of space. Finally, at least some of the bearing walls have highly visible positions at the exterior of a building. Unlike the clear identity of a freestanding column, however, the geometry of a bearing wall is often obscured by its detailing. One expressive challenge, then, is in the revealing of its planar characteristics in the finished building (Fig. 12–4). Since walls also exist in other materials, another challenge is to express a plane that is like concrete rather than wood, steel, or masonry. This can be done by exploiting the form, strength, durability, and workability characteristics of concrete.

Figure 12-4 These concrete walls maintained their identity as planes in the completed building because their edges remained exposed above the roof and beyond the facade enclosure wall.

Unlike wood and masonry, moment resistance is standard in concrete connections. This characteristic can be exploited to give concrete walls a structural expression different from that of wood or masonry. Omitting lateral bracing and maintaining a high ratio of height to thickness challenges the ability of the base connection to prevent overturning. A large, thin, freestanding plane seems most compatible with concrete's ability to resist lateral loads throughout the plane, especially at the base. In wood or masonry the same image fails to achieve a sense of stability.

Expressions of extreme strength in the vertical cantilever obscures the structural distinction between concrete and steel. While the planar expression in concrete contrasts with the linearity of steel, competition in the area of strength diminishes the distinction between the two materials. No height or thinness is specified here as the philosophical limit for the concrete plane. A sense of concrete is served if the plane is clearly stronger (as defined by its height/thickness ratio) than wood or masonry of equal dimension but weaker than steel.

A straight plane delivers the greatest challenge to its base connection since no element projects laterally to form a buttress. Straight planes are identified with the nature of precast concrete. Curved or otherwise undulating planes demonstrate site-cast concrete's lack of mandatory association with rectilinearity and right angles (Fig. 12–5). The curved form, however, provides a geometry that is advantageous to the stability of masonry walls and is compatible with masonry units.

Since the limitations of masonry are more clearly defined, it is incumbent on concrete to have characteristics outside the range logical in masonry. The goal is challenging since it requires reconciliation of conflicting characteristics. Gentle curves that provide little bracing to a wall express the strength of concrete. They are also the most logical curves (based on form characteristics) for masonry. Straight masonry units do not produce an accidental texture in large-radii curves. The reverse is true for the deep undulations of small radii. A wall with many undulations of varied radii (large and small) is more in the spirit of poured-in-place concrete than of masonry. The lack of regularity detracts from an image of stability; the small radii are difficult for masonry without special units. The varied radii make special masonry units impractical since so many different shapes would be needed.

The distinction between masonry and concrete bearing wall planes is significantly obscured by the fact that they both resist compression. If a wall plane

Figure 12–5 The curve of the concrete wall plane helps distinguish it from wood or steel framed walls. Additional techniques, however, are necessary to separate its image from that of masonry. Its small radius and sloped unprotected top help in this regard.

Figure 12-6 The separation of the wall from grade at the left of the steps removes its image from the realm of masonry. Angles in its profile further distinguish the plane from block, brick, or stone.

were lifted above grade slightly so that it touched a base only at certain points, the image of masonry would be lost while that of concrete would be strengthened (Fig. 12–6). The wall plane would have lost its compressive sense because it would no longer act as a bearing wall. It would have become a beam resisting both compression and tension. The plane itself could otherwise look exactly the same as before the levitation. Only the hidden reinforcement would have to change. The bearing wall is eliminated but the vertical plane remains.

A wall plane acting as a beam has the potential for clear and strong concrete expression, as the nature of its strength and geometry combine to reduce its compatibility with other materials. The plane is not, however, the common geometry for beams. Minimizing beam depth minimizes building height, which has economical advantages. The result is that beams are typically linear. The economy of linear concrete beams assures their continued use. The linear form, however, shares an image with wood and steel, which prevents it from expressing the uniqueness of concrete.

Surface and connection characteristics can be manipulated to make linear concrete beams less like wood or steel. The linear form need not always be straight or rectangular in cross section (traits of wood and steel). An increase in depth beyond the minimum would help the beam express concrete even if the form was not a plane (Fig. 12–7). The line would become less slender and therefore project a linelike quality less intensely. An increase in depth would have at least one economical benefit. Less reinforcing steel would be required. If the deeper (more planelike) beams were uneconomical or too obtrusive, they could be limited to exterior applications and entrances, while linear beams could occur in the internal structure of a building.

A number of concrete characteristics, unique among building materials, can be demonstrated by a structural slab (Fig. 12–8). The slab is a plane, the primary form of concrete. The identity of the plane, however, is dependent on the expression of thickness supplemented with information about its other two

Figure 12-7 The cantilevered concrete beam has nearly enough depth to project the image of a plane. Achieving the planar image would help distinguish the beam from steel or wood components.

Figure 12-8 The long exposed edges and absence of beams, ribs, and other surface interruptions give each concrete slab a strong planar image. In the finished building the image was lost, as masonry curtain walls concealed these characteristics.

dimensions. A slab edge, visible in a facade and flush with a curtain wall, hints that there might be a slab present. Such a slab can be confused with a beam, even though its thickness is less than that of typical beam depths. Projection of the slab through the curtain wall to a dimension beyond a typical beam width is likely to secure its true identity. Balconies or the need for shading can justify such slab projections. Detailing of the projections can further contribute to the image of concrete. Thinness, curved edges, lack of trim, and absence of lines in the soffit suggest concrete rather than wood or steel.

Span limitations of flat slabs prevent them from serving all structural demands on concrete. The beams and ribs that increase the span capability of concrete slab systems add linearity that obscures the planar image. The rectangular section of the beams is much like that of wood beams. In many cases the sizes are about the same as are typical in laminated timber. Curving the beams would help their image be less like timber and more like concrete (Fig. 12–9). Concrete ribs typically have sloped sides which help distinguish their profiles from those of wood. Sloping the sides of concrete beams or introducing curves in those surfaces would add to the sense of concrete. An undulating or other bottom surface that was not straight would do the same.

Using ribs in more than one direction projects a stronger sense of concrete than of wood or steel. The common example is a two-way ribbed slab (Fig. 12–10).

Figure 12–9 The curves draw the linear image of the concrete beams away from that of wood and steel, which are typically straight.

Figure 12–10 The linearity of the ribs is diluted by their crossing to form a strong visual pattern of squares. The double span of the system is compatible with the notion that concrete is not limited to a single direction in its span as a linear material is.

The crossing ribs divide the lines into a series of visually short segments. Since long lines project a stronger sense of linearity than do short ones, the effect is one of subdued linearity. Although it is possible to see the surface as having twice the number of lines as a one-way system, the square voids are visually dominant. They tend to obscure the linearity that might be produced by doubling the number of lines.

The dual directionality of the system is more in the spirit of a plane than is a one-directional system. As defined for purposes of this study, the plane has two relatively large dimensions compared to the third dimension. Increasing the number of directions that the ribs span approaches the concept of a plane that visually spans in all directions. Spanning in an infinite number of directions is conceptually more planelike than is spanning in one direction, which is more linelike. Although an infinite number of rib directions is not practical, the reasoning suggests that the more directions utilized, the more concretelike the image. Three-way or multiway ribbed slabs have the additional benefit of demonstrating concrete's compatibility, with geometries that are not based on 90 degrees. Three-way ribbed systems have the disadvantage of requiring acute angles that can project a sense of sharpness beyond a comfortable level for concrete. Introducing curves into multidirectional ribbed systems draws them away from images of wood and steel. Curves ribs are more compatible with multidirectional systems than in one-way slabs because the crossing ribs laterally brace each other.

Cantilevers are compatible with concrete. A cantilever requires moment resistance at its base. Moment resistance is a standard characteristic of connections in concrete. Cantilevers of continuous spanning elements have a structural benefit in that they reduce deflection between supports. A cantilever alone, however, is not enough to establish an image of concrete. Used in concert with an expression of primary form, a clear sense of the material can be established (Fig. 12–11). Cantilevered slabs have an expressive advantage over fixed-end slabs in that usually no beam exists at the edge to obscure the thickness of the plane. A clearly defined edge combined with at least partial expression of width and length are characteristics compatible with cantilevered slabs and are strong expressions of a plane.

The curves of umbrella-type hyperbolic paraboloids push this type of cantilevered slab even farther from the realm of wood or steel (Fig. 12–12). While the edge thickness of this form is usually clear, the thickness at the central support is not. This condition reduces the sense of plane that could exist if detailing revealed to some degree the cross section of the structure. It would be

Figure 12–11 The cantilever of the landing gives the slab a strong planar sense, as its edge and smooth surfaces are exposed. The curved edge contributes further to the separation of the image from that of straight components such as wood or steel.

Figure 12-12 The curves of the cantilevered hyperbolic paraboloids project a sense of plasticity that is concretelike. A sense of plane is reduced somewhat by the absence of information about the thickness of the slab at its center.

helpful to the concrete image if the slab thickness were shown to increase toward the central support but remain thin enough to qualify as a slab.

Folded plate slabs have greater span capability than flat slabs but without the linearity that is associated with ribs or beams (Fig. 12–13). The overall sense of plane is stronger than in ribbed slabs. Similarity between the images of wood and concrete folded plate structures is, to a large degree, due to the failure of the wood detailing to reveal the linearity of the wood. It is prudent, nevertheless, to utilize supplementary detailing that would move concrete away from the image of the typical wood installation.

Curves are the likely vehicles to give the concrete slab an identity, unlike straight materials such as wood or steel (Fig. 12–14). The undulating concrete plate can maintain an identity separate from that of vaulted masonry by demonstrating that there is no thrust, spanning parallel to the axes of the vaults and cantilevering in one or both directions. Changes in slab thickness, outward-leaning ends on the vaults, and sloped slab edges also contribute to an image that is remote from masonry.

Figure 12-13 The exposed edges, cantilevers in both directions, absence of linear elements, and absence of thrust establish a strong concrete image for this folded plate structure.

Figure 12–14 The curves, varying thickness, cantilevers, point supports, outward-leaning peaks, sloped edge, relatively smooth surface, absence of linear elements, and absence of thrust give this undulating slab a strong concrete image. Architect: Wright and Selby.

Concrete vaults or domes that have thrust resistance available from the earth, buttresses, or ties share a general image with traditional masonry. In contemporary construction masonry is not the likely choice for large vaults or domes. If thrust resistance is present, large size is therefore a characteristic that draws the image away from masonry and toward concrete. The condition is logical for concrete, as thrust resistance allows an increase in span with a reduction in steel reinforcing. Relative thinness, gradual change in slab thickness, rounded, sloped, and curved edges, outward-leaning vault ends, and openings that are not arched help vaults and domes seem more like concrete than like masonry.

The tapered-leg rigid frame shape common in metal industrial buildings is not an efficient structural form with which to express the unique qualities of concrete (Fig. 12–15). The strong association of the configuration with steel systems is the major obstacle to its expression in concrete. Modifications to the form can make it less compatible with steel, more compatible with the image of concrete, and can increase structural efficiency. Curving the connection between the vertical and horizontal legs would ease the stress concentration at the joint, would provide a better geometry to resist the moment, and is a form that expresses the plasticity of concrete while avoiding the straightness and sharpness of steel. One or both edges of the legs could undulate to match stress distributions more closely or simply to draw the form away from the image of steel.

Figure 12–15 Only the color and absence of flanges distinguish this concrete rigid frame from steel. Its shape and size are the same as steel's would be.

Figure 12–16 The crack caused by tension in the connection suggests that a gap between the vertical and horizontal elements would have been appropriate. The detail would have avoided both the tensile expression of concrete and the tensile failure.

Although pure tension can exist in reinforced concrete, its expression is rare. Pure tension can exist in truss members. The examples are few and the tension is not readily apparent. Pure tension virtually assures failure of the concrete covering the steel reinforcing (Fig. 12–16). Expressed tension encourages disbelief. These conditions keep purely tensile systems in concrete to a minimum. Tension does not express the nature of concrete.

CONNECTIONS

Cast-in-place concrete connections differ from those of other materials in that the components can actually merge (Fig. 12–17). The concrete particles in the intersections of walls, beams, or ribs belong equally to both components. This is in contrast to connections in wood, steel, and precast concrete, where notching or welding can give the appearance of merging but cannot cause a physical blending of the particles in each component. The reinforcing steel in cast connections does not merge but has no visual impact on the connection.

The merged characteristic strengthens a building's concrete identity in proportion to the clarity of the characteristic. The typical connection between walls where two surfaces meet at a corner is a mild demonstration of the merged condition (Fig. 12–18). Only the absence of a joint hints that the walls become one at the intersection. This corner also fails to reveal the planar nature of the

Figure 12–17 The concrete beams physically pass through each other. This is in contrast to wood or steel beams, which may appear to merge but physically remain as separate components.

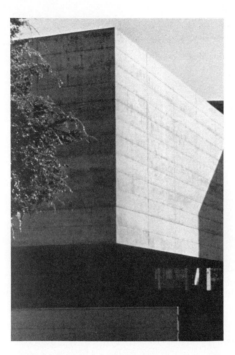

Figure 12-18 A typical concrete corner does not emphasize that the two concrete planes have merged. Only the absence of a joint hints that this has occurred. The absence of the expression of thickness prevents the concrete from appearing as two planes.

concrete, as no thickness is revealed for either wall. The common use of the detail causes it to be neutral in its expression of the nature of concrete.

Corners where one wall passes beyond the intersection to form a fin expresses the planar nature of one wall but obscures the nature of the joint between the two (Fig. 12–19). The fact that one wall seems to stop at the side of the other projects a sense of butting rather than merging. The fact that no joint exists at the apparent butt is not particularly noticeable. If both components extend beyond the intersection, the image of merging is expressed. The thickness of both elements is also expressed, which contributes to the planar image

Figure 12-19 The corner where one wall passes beyond the intersection to form a fin expresses the planar nature of the fin wall by revealing its thickness. A sense of merging is not developed, however, as the absence of a joint between the two walls is obscured.

of each. Large fillets between the intersecting surfaces would reduce sharpness, facilitate form removal, express the absence of joints, and in general separate the image of the connection from its imitators in other materials.

If the angle between connecting surfaces is acute, a sharp image is likely to result. Since the nature of concrete does not encourage sharpness, such a connection fails to contribute to the spirit of the material. This condition is especially misleading when the building is covered entirely with glass (Fig. 12–20). Since casting imperfections do not show, nor is impact damage likely, the physical need for bluntness is negated in this type of building. The philosophical need is magnified, however, as concrete color and texture are not available to express the material. If no concrete is visible, the burden of its expression is carried by the general form of the building. A building form with soft flowing lines seems more like concrete than does a sharply angular one, even when covered with a curtain wall (Fig. 12–21).

Figure 12–20 The sharp-angled image of this glass-clad building does not relect the character of the hidden concrete structure.

Figure 12–21 The soft flowing form of this glass-clad building reflects the character of the hidden concrete structure. Architect: Schipporeit and Heinrich. (Photo Courtesy of Jeffrey Dublin.)

Figure 12-22 The curve is compatible with concrete, but its large radius and compressive nature are also compatible with masonry.

Rounded connections avoid the sharpness of steel but could overlap the image of masonry if certain conditions exist (Fig. 12–22). The sense of concrete can be enhanced if the radii of curves are small and the structural potential of masonry is superseded. Lifting the connection off the ground can avoid a sense of compression common to masonry, for example.

Certain form characteristics shared with wood produce precast connections that are somewhat like wood. Profiles in both materials tend to be rectangular and solid. Both typically incorporate steel to secure their connections. Lapping precast has handling advantages, but its dimensional stability and greater uniformity of size renders exaggerated projections less appropriate than in wood (Fig. 12–23). Small projections of lapping members are helpful in maintaining

Figure 12-23 The projections of the inverted T beams and the gaps between spandrels and T beams help clarify the identity of the various precast pieces.

component identity. The casting process easily produces bearing ledges on columns and beams in precast (Fig. 12–24). Since the haunch or shelf is concrete, its stubby or blunt image is appropriate.

Reasoning for wood encourages the expression of steel in joints to the degree that they depend on the steel. Standard practice rarely exposes the steel in precast connections. One reason for using concrete is its high durability. If steel is expressed (exposed to view and the weather), the durability of the assembly is lowered to that of the steel. This is not an issue in wood, as the material is of lower durability than its steel connectors. This consideration often produces precast connections with no visible support for the member carried.

Haunches and bearing ledges express the method of supporting gravity loads. The steel hidden in these connections acts in a supplemental capacity (i.e., resisting lateral loads). The supplemental nature of the welded connecting plates renders their expression less important than the support system for the gravity loads. The natural form of precast connections can then be identified as overlapping, where the lower element might be a wall, beam, shelf, or haunch.

When the lower member is a shelflike device, the large-scale image of the connection resembles a butt joint. This shared image with steel is reasonable, as concrete owes much of its structural nature to steel. Lapped and butted images are both natural expressions of the characteristics of precast concrete if the butted members express lapping at the small scale (over a bearing shelf). Components that seem to attach only at the butted edges because no provision for bearing is visible reflect a sense of steel rather than concrete (Fig. 12–25).

Handling difficulties encourage significant tolerances in the meeting of precast components. The butting of precast is different than the butting of steel, in that the tolerances useful in precast encourage a significant gap between components. Gaps such as these reflect the nature of precast handling and help define the individual pieces. Component identity is important to the distinction between cast-in-place and precast concrete, as the latter is more unitlike and less continuous (Fig. 12–26). Expressing a merging of material does not re-

Figure 12-24 The haunches are easily produced as part of the column. They express structural reality and have the low level of refinement that is compatible with the nature of concrete.

Figure 12-25 The narrow panel in the center and the spanning panel on the left butt connect to their supports more in the spirit of steel than of concrete. Neither overlaps nor haunches carry the loads. No steel is visible to explain the structural reality.

Figure 12-26 The turning out of the precast members at the midspan joint clarifies component identity. The absence of a visible means of connection is less pure at midspan than in the joints at the columns, due to the greater structural challenge at midspan.

Figure 12-27 The apparent merging of the precast beams at the intersection violates the nature of concrete. The detail expresses the image of cast-in-place concrete. The separation of column and beams is more pure, as it contributes to the clarity of component identity.

flect the reality of precast as it does for cast-in-place concrete (Fig. 12–27). Connections that appear to be merged components violate the nature of precast just like they violate the nature of wood and steel. Merged connections express the nature of cast-in-place concrete only.

SURFACES

When casting concrete that is to be covered or occurs in utilitarian areas, little effort is made to overcome the natural effect of the formwork on the surface. Plywood leaves impressions of wood grain, patches, tie holes, and faint joints on a 4-ft by 8-ft grid. One-way steel pan systems leave bulges and irregular offsets at panel overlaps. These surfaces are straightforward expressions of the production process but are not the standard for architectural expression because of their unfinished quality.

Occasionally, an attempt is made to produce a smooth cast-in-place concrete surface equal in size to part or all of a building facade. To do so, several tendencies natural to concrete must be overcoome. Form joint lines and tie holes must be totally obscured. All form panels must remain in exactly the same plane without deflection. Achieving these conditions is nearly impossible. Cast-in-place concrete can come closer to a smooth jointless facade than can wood, masonry, steel, or precast concrete. This type of surface does, then, provide a clear distinction between concrete and the other materials. The uniqueness of the surface encourages its use as an expression of the unique nature of cast-in-place concrete. The difficulty of perfecting the surface discourages its use.

For all practical purposes, perfectly smooth jointless concrete facades cannot exist. Attempts to achieve them typically result in slightly lumpy planes, faint form lines, or both (Fig. 12–28). The sense of failed attempt (although slight) projected by most of these surfaces prevent their serving as strong expressions of concrete potential. The imperfections can be subdued or eliminated by coating the concrete. Although this approach can be appropriate for certain aesthetic goals, it is not a strategy for concrete expression. After all, masonry can be coated so as to have the same appearance as coated concrete.

Imperfections in cast-in-place concrete surfaces can be reduced and obscured by methods that are related to the nature of concrete and the production process. Form lines and form tie holes can be emphasized rather than hidden, thus eliminating their image as imperfections by making them decorations (Fig. 12–29). Wood strips can be applied to form joints, which leaves uniform grooves

Figure 12–28 The irregularities in the wall surface are typical of large plain concrete surfaces. They are an indication that jointless and perfectly smooth facades are not in the nature of concrete.

Figure 12–29 The grooves give a planned and neat emphasis to the form joint marks. The uniform pattern of holes do the same for the form tie holes. The construction system is expressed while visually obscuring irregularities in the surface.

in the concrete. Cone-shaped plastic collars on form ties that are spaced in a regular pattern leave a series of neat holes that have a planned appearance. A variety of plug materials are available that seal the holes and contribute to the purposeful appearance of the system. The visual interruption of the grooves and holes obscures the effects of forms that deflected or were not exactly in the surface plane. The practice is so common that the resulting appearance is closely associated with cast-in-place concrete and therefore can be considered to be the basic expression of that material.

Numerous variations of this pattern have resulted from the desire for variety. Emphasized form lines with tie holes hidden or the reverse express only half the construction system. The hidden aspects are never perfectly hidden, which produces a mild sense of failed attempt. Another partially successful variation is the pattern of grooves, which does not match the proportions of the forms (Fig. 12–30). The success of these options in expressing the spirit of concrete can be measured by the degree to which hidden aspects are truly hidden and the surface reflects a purposeful pattern. Variety can be achieved without hiding form joints by matching grooves to the edges of forms that are not 4 feet by 8 feet in size. Plywood can be subdivided with wood strips to produce other proportions. While the dimensions of a standard sheet of plywood deserve some recognition, subdividing them is not ignoring them. Creating patterns with larger dimensions might require using materials such as steel plate that come in sizes larger than plywood.

Form lines and tie holes do not occur in precast concrete. The steel formwork can be as large as the precast units, thus eliminating form lines. Panels are cast in a horizontal position, eliminating the need to tie two vertical forms together. Forms can have adequate outside bracing to avoid the need for form ties. The smooth surface of the steel leaves no accidental marks in the precast surface. The surface of precast panels can be perfectly flat and smooth. Handling limitations, even in tilt-up, prevent the dimensions of a precast panel from being the size of an entire building elevation. Consequently, a perfectly smooth jointless concrete facade is not available in precast.

Figure 12-30 The upper horizontal groove did not coincide with the upper horizontal form joint. The faint line parallel to the groove detracts from the planned and neat appearance of the surface.

The joints of the precast panels typically give a facade surface a rectangular pattern. Only vertical joints occur where the panels are equal in height to the building. The joints in precast surfaces are expressions of component form. In cast-in-place concrete, form joints express a system of production. Subdividing a precast panel with decorative grooves has potential for expressing the substance but might obscure the expression of component form (Fig. 12–31). It is possible to avoid the form violation if the decorative lines are not confused with joint lines or do not obscure the joint lines.

Plywood is not the only legitimate form material for cast-in-place surfaces. While lumber was replaced by plywood as the common form material, it remains an option. With its use comes a pattern in the concrete that looks very much

Figure 12-31 The grooves obscure the identity of the precast panels, thus violating the form of the components. They express the formability of the concrete surface, but their ability to obscure irregularities is reduced because they are relatively far apart.

like the boards themselves. Grain texture and knotholes are faithfully reproduced (in a mirrored image). The legitimacy of the woodlike image as an expression of concrete can be questioned. The key to a conclusion lies in the appearance of intent.

If the board image appears to be casual, that is, to occur merely as a result of a production process, the nature of concrete is expressed. If it appears that some effort has been made to imitate wood, the uniqueness of concrete is not expressed. Dedicated imitations of wood are rare. Academic imitations (imitating while knowing the result is not convincing) violate the nature of concrete slightly less than do dedicated facsimiles (Fig. 12–32). Actual intent is not the issue. It is the appearance of intent upon which the expression is judged. The distinction between the expressions of certain surfaces is slight. Categorization of borderline cases will vary with personal judgment. A board texture seems less casual in precast than in cast-in-place concrete. Boards do not have a tradition as formwork in precast, and consequently are likely to produce an appearance of an academic imitation at best.

The inevitability of reflecting formwork texture is a characteristic that can be exploited to express the uniqueness and potential of both cast-in-place and precast concrete. This impressibility is demonstrated each time a sidewalk slab is textured with a broom as part of the normal production sequence. The uniqueness of this potential is not exploited by forming textures that are possible in other materials. The board texture, for example, is available in wood siding. Ribbed surfaces, readily available from form liners, are much like corrugated sheet steel (Fig. 12–33). Ribbed surfaces are less like steel if the ribs are textured or have proportions unlike those of corrugated siding.

Shared images are not inevitable in concrete surfaces. Cast-in-place concrete is not tied to linearity and rectangularity to the high degree as are other materials. Neither are surface patterns of precast, even though panels are typically rectangular. Patterns without long lines or perpendicular lines cannot resemble wood, steel, or brick. Curvilinear patterns are the least like the

Figure 12–32 The board pattern in the concrete fascia is typical of wood-surfaces but not of wood formwork. Although the imitation of wood does not appear to be a serious goal, the expression is too diluted with the image of wood to represent the essence of concrete.

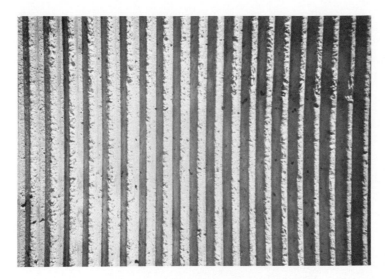

Figure 12-33 Only the color and patina of this surface suggest concrete. The ribbed texture is the standard for corrugated sheet metal.

geometry or other materials, are easily produced in concrete, and therefore are an expression of concrete's uniqueness and potential. Freeform patterns can occur in precast panels. If the pattern is complete within the panel borders, the form of the panel itself will not be obscured (Fig. 12–34). The economic considerations of precasting encourage patterns from permanent molds to be repetitive. Patterns that do not repeat are compatible with one-time use molds such as sand. Each mold material affects the refinement and complexity of surface patterns according to its own material properties. Patterns that continue across several panels obscure panel form (Fig. 12–35).

Upon initial consideration, an exposed aggregate surface would seem to express the nature of concrete by revealing its ingredients. Certain considerations, however, affect the credibility of these surfaces as natural expressions of concrete. Exposed aggregate surfaces require effort beyond that of standard production. While the extra work is not so much greater than that of preparing forms for decorative impressions, it comes after the standard sequence is complete. Although the internal structure of the material might be revealed, the

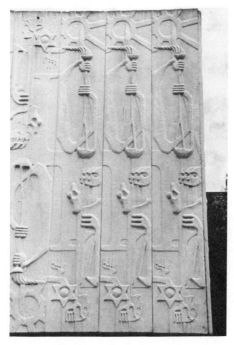

Figure 12-34 The repetitive pattern reflects the reusable nature of the mold. Variety is achieved by turning some panels upside down. The fact that a complete pattern is contained within each panel clarifies panel identity. Artist: John Scott.

Figure 12-35 The nonrepetitive pattern reflects the temporary nature of the sand molds in which these panels were cast. The fact that the pattern continues across panel borders obscures panel identities. Artist: Albert Vrana.

internal nature of a substance has not been established as a characteristic important to its identity.

Exposed aggregate contrasts with the textures of wood, steel, and masonry. Exposed aggregate is not found in limestone, which can otherwise duplicate both the color and texture of concrete. The uniqueness of exposed aggregate nearly balances the extra steps required for production, giving it credibility as an option for expressing concrete.

At times decorative aggregate is applied to the surface of concrete, which is different from the aggregates of the mix. This technique misrepresents the nature of the less attractive and cheaper mix aggregate. The expression is impure to the few designers and workers who are aware that two aggregates exist. It is reasonable to the relatively very large number of viewers who can never be aware of the special condition. The key to the legitimacy of the expression is the degree to which the exposed aggregate appears to be an integral part of the mix. If it looks applied, the expression loses credibility (Fig. 12–36). Exposed aggregate is one of the few material misrepresentations that can actually succeed. In part, this is possible because the aggregate of the surface can perform the same functional tasks as can the internal aggregate. It can be truly part of the mix to its depth in the component.

The need to convince is incumbent upon the exposed aggregate of a homogeneous mix. The concrete, whose exposed aggregates are not immersed deeply in the hardened matrix and therefore have a three-dimensional quality of their own, can appear to be applied when it is not. This aggregate lacks credibility as a mix component and actually misrepresents the process of production. For purposes of expression it is no more pure than the applied stone, which looks applied.

Sandblasting tends to produce exposed aggregate with an integral appearance (Fig. 12–37). While sandblasting can occur in a factory or on the site, it seems slightly more compatible with factory-precast concrete. The effort in-

Figure 12-36 The stones do not seem embedded deeply enough in the hardened paste to be an integral part of the mix. Their applied look fails to establish credibility as an expression of the nature of this concrete.

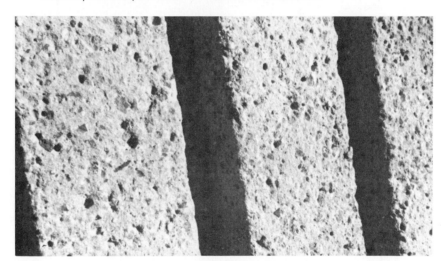

Figure 12-37 The exposed aggregate of this sandblasted precast panel appears to be snugly integrated in the matrix. Regardless of the homogeniality of the mix, the expression of concrete is convincing.

volved can be minimized in a factory, as the equipment need not be moved, the surrounding environment remains constant, and the process can be integrated with a repetitive rhythm of production.

The use of a retarder with the subsequent scrubbing of semiplatic paste from the surface can also produce exposed aggregate with an intergral look. The need for little equipment or concern for the surrounding environment makes this process compatible with site work. A sand-blasted surface will show some signs of abrasion. The difference in expression between sandblasted exposed aggregate and stone exposed by a retarder is not great if the minimum of surface paste has been scrubbed from the latter. Although some conditions encourage the use of one method in a factory and another on the site, a philosophical tie between method and type of concrete is too academic to be useful. The larger issue is the integral versus applied appearance. Exposed aggregate that appears integral with the mix expresses the nature of concrete; aggregate that appears to be applied does not.

EDGES

Unlike wood, masonry, and steel, concrete needs no protective cap on the top edge of a wall. An exposed top edge expresses the high level of concrete's durability compared to assemblies in the other materials. Masonry or other trim appears to be protecting the concrete and therefore violates the nature of concrete (Fig. 12–38).

Straight edges are common in concrete, as they are in the other materials. Because this practical form is commonly seen in all materials, it cannot express the uniqueness of concrete. Although the form is neutral, it is more in the spirit of concrete than is a stepped edge (masonrylike), which is sometimes motivated by stairs (Fig. 12–39). A sloped straight edge is less like masonry and therefore a stronger expression of concrete (Fig. 12–40). An undulating curvilinear edge is compatible with concrete and not typical of other materials. The free-form shape expresses the uniqueness and potential of concrete.

Figure 12–38 The brick trim appears to protect the concrete wall. The expression is backwards, in that the masonry needs protection, not the concrete.

Figure 12–39 The stepped form is more like masonry than like concrete. The use of the top of the wall as a trough for a series of waterfalls is a rare and very strong expression of the high durability of concrete.

Figure 12–40 Each wall beside the ramp expresses the nature of its own material. The top of the brick wall steps. The top of the concrete wall slopes downward, has a rounded edge, and curves in a fairly tight radius. Architect: Taliesin Associated Architects.

A concrete foundation wall in a sloping grade can take a stepped form to conform to the stepped masonry wall it supports. In this case the assumption of the masonry form by the concrete reflects concrete's greater flexibility of form. It is more expressive of both materials' characters than is a curvilinear connection where extensive cutting of the masonry would be required.

Concrete's high level of durability can be reflected by its close proximity to grade. The commonness of grade contact diminishes the expressiveness of typical detailing. Concrete's high resistance to deterioration can be emphasized by increasing the challenge to its durability. Bringing concrete into contact with water, for example, seems to defy the forces of deterioration. This line of reasoning could be the motivation for integrating fountains and pools in the design of a concrete building (Fig. 12–41).

Figure 12–41 Concrete's very high durability is expressed by this demonstration of its compatibility with water.

Figure 12-42 This opening shows that concrete can form curves and span in a horizontal line between the jambs. The combination of achievements is not as easily accomplished in other materials.

The edges of openings can express the uniqueness of concrete in both form and durability. To do so, openings must take shapes other than the arched profiles of masonry or the rectangular forms typical of all materials. Undulating free forms would express concrete, as they are difficult to structure in the other materials. They are difficult to trim in wood and steel. Although it is often omitted, masonry requires protective trim on sills and sloped jambs that can catch water. Concrete's monolithic nature and its high durability make trim unnecessary. Other openings, less unique than free forms, can also express the nature of concrete. An opening with curved jambs and a long straight head challenges the straightness of wood and steel (in the jambs) and the spanning nature of masonry (at the head) (Fig. 12-42).

Circular openings are compatible with concrete but do not show that concrete is different from masonry, with which they are also compatible. Triangular openings suggest sharpness that is more like steel. Polygonal openings could be produced in the linear materials because they have straight sides. Although concrete can form any opening, the free-form shape is less like the other materials and therefore expresses concrete's uniqueness.

Chapter 13

CONCRETE IN ARCHITECTURE

CHECKLIST FOR ANALYSIS

The expression of concrete in historic and contemporary architecture is analyzed in this chapter. The quality of the work is not judged. Its degree of compatibility with the principles of expression discussed previously is determined. Listed below are the major characteristics considered to express the nature of concrete. Refer to Checklist C-4 in Appendix C for this list in a worksheet format with additional notations to assist analysis.

1. Planar quality in the building image
2. (Cast-in-place) Curves in the building image
2a. (Precast) Straightness in the building image
   (Curves accepted in site-precast)
3. (Precast) Contribution to the building image by form characteristics of any secondary products
4. (Cast-in-place) Medium level of refinement in the building image
4a. (Precast) Medium level of refinement in the building image
5. Demonstration of high bending strength in spanning systems as part of the building image
6. Demonstration of high bending strength in walls and columns as part of the building image
7. Demonstration of concrete's very high resistance to deterioration as a part of the building image
8. Demonstration of the very low workability level of cured concrete

ANALYSIS

Fallingwater
Bear Run, Pennsylvania; Frank Lloyd Wright; 1937

The structural roles of the concrete and stone are distinctly different and compatible with the nature of each material (Fig. 13–1). The stone is nearly always

Figure 13–1 *Fallingwater.* Large cantilevers express the structural potential of concrete in bending. The lack of linearity in the spans distinguishes the concrete from wood and steel. (Photo Courtesy of Betsy Johnson.)

expressed in compression. The great majority of concrete is expressed in bending. Several major concrete bearing elements under the cantilevered living room are exceptions. Their low, recessed, and dark location, however, prevents them from having a significant impact on the image of the building. The significant lengths of the cantilevers express concrete's high strength.

Numerous cantilevered roof slabs and canopies express a strong planar image (Fig. 13–2). This sense of spanning plane expresses the essence of concrete by combining the two major characteristics of strength and form. The sense

Figure 13–2 *Fallingwater.* The planar and structural nature of concrete is strongly expressed in the large cantilevered roof slabs.

of multiple planes is enhanced in views from upper levels by the planelike balcony rails.

Some joistlike elements are linear. Their detailing causes them to be as planelike as linear members can appear. They seem to be the positive elements that remained after the plane was pierced with a series of rectangular holes (Fig. 13–3). Their shallow depth and the presence of an edge on all four sides of the series contribute to this sense.

The series of concrete joists that define a canopy over a path to the entry seem partially planelike because they are close to eye level, which, from a distance, obscures the gaps between them. One joist distinguishes itself from the linearity of wood or steel as it deviates from its straight path to form a semicircle around a tree (Fig. 13–4). Although this reminder helps the joists nearby seem more like concrete, it is not enough to carry the image of the whole series.

Figure 13–3 *Fallingwater.* Several sets of linear joists establish implied planes. Repetition of size and spacing subdues the identities of the individual joists. Concrete strips on four sides suggest plane edges. (Photo Courtesy of Wayland W. Bowser.)

Figure 13–4 *Fallingwater.* Concrete's potential to form curves helps separate the image of this joist from that of the linear materials.

Slab, canopy, and rail edges are rounded (Fig. 13–5). The linear footage of these blunt edges is far greater than that of right-angled corners. Consequently, the prevailing character of the concrete is visually soft, a concept compatible with the low level of refinement associated with the material.

The railing of exterior steps on the west exhibits both masonry and concrete characteristics (Fig. 13–6). The stepped form of the upper edge is associated with masonry. The stepped form of the lower edge is more like concrete since the steps are too large for a corbel. The overall sense of the railing is pulled toward concrete by its numerous rounded edges.

The overall expression of concrete in this building is strongly compatible with the properties of that material. Concrete's uniqueness is emphasized by the contrast of its form and structure with that of the masonry elements.

Figure 13–5 *Fallingwater.* Rounded edges express concrete's independence from the rectangularity of wood, steel, and masonry.

Figure 13–6 *Fallingwater.* Only the rounded edges pull the top of the stepped stair rail away from a masonry image. The size of the steps of the lower edge are beyond the corbeling potential of masonry and are therefore structurally like concrete.

Notre Dame du Haut
Ronchamp, France; Le Corbusier; 1955

Except for the concrete frame of the south facade, chapel walls are stone sprayed with a concrete coating (Fig. 13–7). The apparently massive concrete roof seems to rest on the walls, giving them a sense of compression. The fact that the roof is neither as massive as it looks nor is in contact with the walls (it rests on columns protruding above the walls) interferes little with the image. The great thickness of the south wall is more in the spirit of masonry than its concrete frame. This wall and the roof give the entire building a sense of massiveness. The appearance of compression and massiveness, especially in a building this small, suggests masonry.

The masonry walls do not have exaggerated thickness. The curves of the masonry walls increase their stability and therefore express their absence of tensile strength. The narrow windows express masonry. The windows with a long horizontal dimension express concrete. The tall narrow edge of the concrete frame at the building "prow" is too sharp for either concrete or masonry. The texture and continuity of the wall surfaces suggest concrete. The difficulty in identifying the roles of each material adds ambiguity to the visual statement, which includes both pure and impure elements. The vagueness is similar to that of most veneered buildings where the veneers are not expressed as such.

The free form of the roof expresses concrete's lack of a strong tie to rectangularity. Its large smooth and jointless cantilevers eliminate the images of other materials. While few will mistake the depth of the fascia as the thickness of the concrete, the absence of exposed slab edges gives an exaggerated sense of mass. The deep beams between the upper and lower slabs of the roof are not visible. Consequently, the expressive potential of the several large structural planes within the roof cavity is not realized. One vertical side of the roof hints as to the form of the hidden planes but does not have enough of its thickness exposed to influence the image of the roof (Fig. 13–8). The result is a roof which

Figure 13–7 *Notre Dame du Haut.* The apparently massive concrete building actually consists of masonry walls of average thickness and a deep concrete frame in the wall of windows on the left of the illustration.

Figure 13-8 *Notre Dame du Haut.* The apparently massive roof is actually two curved slabs with deep concrete beams between them. The only hint of slab thickness is the exposed edge of a small parapet at the right.

has the combination of structure and geometry that can only be concrete but lacks the planar image that would add clarity to the visual statement.

The sculptural and flowing form of the building is in the spirit of concrete. The sense of massiveness and compression is compatible with masonry. The masonry elements seem like concrete and the concrete-framed wall has a mixture of masonry and concrete expressions. The building expression is ambiguous in regard to its materials.

Chapel of the Holy Cross
Sedona, Arizona; Anshen and Allen; 1956

The deep recessing of the glass curtain walls at both ends of the building reveals the cross, walls, and roof to be broad, flat concrete planes (Fig. 13–9). The

Figure 13-9 *Chapel of the Holy Cross.* The main elevation of the building establishes a strong planar image by the deeply recessed glass curtain wall.

absence of other forms gives the appearance of a single slab "bent" twice to form the enclosure (Fig. 13–10). While the "bends" could be less sharp, the horizontal span of the roof is a stronger expression of concrete than a rounded (vaulted) roof would have been. The inward lean of the wall planes helps pull their image away from masonry.

The sloped surfaces and edges are straight, in contrast to the stepped profile that would be expected of masonry. The exposed aggregate texture justifies the large blank surfaces, where formwork marks would otherwise be expected to show (Fig. 13–11). The high percentage of exposed hardened paste and the apparently deep embedment of the stone suggest that the exposed aggregate is an integral part of the matrix. The lack of protective trim expressed at the tops of the walls is compatible with concrete's high durability but is not a remarkable feature in this desert climate.

Neither concrete's freedom of form nor the formability of concrete's surface is exploited. Despite the absence of these characteristics, which could have moved the expression further from the image of other materials, the building is a strong expression of concrete. The clear sense of a plane with spanning capability secures the image as that of concrete.

Figure 13–10 *Chapel of the Holy Cross.* The entry elevation continues the strong image of a "bent" concrete plane by the deep recess of the curtain wall, which exposes a significant length of the slabs.

Figure 13–11 *Chapel of the Holy Cross.* Sandblasting exposed the aggregate and left it with an embedded appearance. As the stone appears to be an integral part of the mix, the surface expresses the nature of concrete.

Guggenheim Museum
New York, New York; Frank Lloyd Wright; 1959

While the soft flowing lines of the building are compatible with concrete, the radii of the curved forms are large enough to accommodate masonry (Fig. 13–12). The building establishes a sense of concrete without the presence of numerous concrete planes. The forms of the major facade are cantilevered, thus eliminating a sense of masonry. Three of the spiraled elements lean outward at an angle steep enough for corbeling but are not stepped as would be anticipated in masonry. The absence of visible caps or flashing on the top edges of forms throughout the building expresses the high durability of concrete. The painted concrete surfaces do not.

Imperfections in the concrete surfaces are apparent, as the sun's rays are tangent to the curves throughout the afternoon. No emphasized impressions of formwork, form ties, or decorative patterns, textures, or reliefs are present in the main facade to express the nature of concrete surfaces. Such patterns do exist on the northeast corner, where surface impressions play a minor role in the building image (Fig. 13–13). The stepped profile of the patterned surface at this corner is masonrylike, but not the octagon shapes. The individual patterns are small enough to be formable in metal. The straight lines would allow fabrication in wood. The span of the mass over the opening below eliminates it from the realm of masonry. The repetitive nature of the pattern suggests precast concrete. The series of straight-line corbels on the adjacent building form are very much like masonry.

Totaling the effect of individual expressions yields an image that can only be concrete, mostly for structural reasons. A number of opportunities were missed to strengthen the expression of concrete. The planar nature of the concrete could have been emphasized by revealing wall and slab thickness at edges. The plasticity of the concrete surfaces could have been expressed with free-form reliefs. The concrete could have been left unpainted. Few expressions seriously violate the nature of concrete, but many are ambiguous.

Figure 13–12 *Guggenheim Museum.* The structural expression of the concrete helps separate its image from masonry, while the curved forms and smooth surfaces render wood and steel unlikely materials for the visual statement.

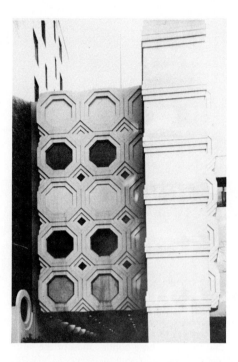

Figure 13-13 *Guggenheim Museum.* The form-ability of concrete surfaces is expressed, but not their independence from uniform geometries. The octagonal pattern might be pressed steel panels. The corbeled lines might be masonry or wood.

Terminal Building, Dulles International Airport
Chantilly, Virginia; Eero Saarinen; 1962

The numerous concrete components of the terminal encourage its analysis as a concrete building despite its catenary steel cable roof system (Fig. 13–14). The smoothness and continuity of the ceiling does not express the shape or location of the equally spaced pairs of supporting cables, the concrete sections poured around each pair for stiffness, nor the precast planks spanning between them to form a roof surface (Fig. 13–15). The end connections of the cables are not expressed. The concrete soffits appear to flow into the ceiling surface, suggesting no change of material or system. The expression of the roof, as a result of these conditions, is that of a concrete slab in every aspect except strength. The

Figure 13-14 *Dulles Airport.* The detailing of the building expresses the roof as a hanging concrete slab. The expression violates the nature of concrete and misrepresents structural reality.

Figure 13–15 *Dulles Airport.* The image of a hanging plane is supplemented by the smooth suspended ceiling, which denies the existence of the cables and seems to be a continuation of the smooth soffit slab.

structural expression is opposed to the nature of concrete, as it is a purely tensile statement.

The tilted concrete beams spanning between the columns and supporting the cables express several characteristics of concrete (Fig. 13–16). A sense of plane is established by revealing the thickness of these beams at the overhangs. Approximate thickness is revealed at the ends of the building and at the openings around the columns. The curved soffit and the rounded and tapered shape of the openings through which the columns pass express the compatibility of concrete with nonrectilinear form. The lack of applied trim around the openings indicates a homogeneous mass that needs no protective covers or caps.

Figure 13–16 *Dulles Airport.* The curved planes of the soffit slabs strongly express the nature of concrete. Given that the columns are linear, their curves, tapers, and soft image clearly distinguish them from steel.

Except for their linearity, the columns are strongly expressive of concrete. The tapers in both elevation and plan and the curves at the top and botoom remove the linearity from the straightness and uniformity associated with steel. The outward lean and increased mass at the bottom of each column gives a sense of resistance to overturning or bending at the base. This structural condition, which is clearly more than simple compression, further removes the columns from the realm of masonry.

The concrete elements of the building strongly express that material. The major feature of the building, the roof, fails to express the linearity and refinement of steel, the discontinuity and repetition of precast, or the bending and compression natural to concrete. The roof system is at best an ambiguous expression and at worst a violation of the nature of concrete which it seems to be.

The Carpenter Center for the Visual Arts
Harvard University, Cambridge, Massachusetts; Le Corbusier; 1963

A strong planar sense is established by the numerous sun screens and slabs revealed by the recessing of the glazing between them (Fig. 13–17). The thinness of the sun screens helps distinguish them from masonry. An exterior stair has a strong planar expression in its cantilevered steps and the central support, which has both vertical edges exposed as well as its sloping top. Several curved masses soften the building image and separate themselves from the image of masonry by their cantilevers. Long curved ramps have strong planar expressions as a result of extensive exposure of one or both edges. Their cantilevers and continuous spans further secure the strength of their concrete statements.

A large rectangular mass is less in the spirit of concrete (Fig. 13–18). Its sense of compression and rectangularity could as well be masonry. The spans over the glass block do not reflect the spirit of masonry but could be wood or steel. Its surface (as do other large blank surfaces on the building) reveals the imperfections that are inevitable when areas too large and too smooth are at-

Figure 13–17 *Carpenter Center.* The exposure of planar characteristics accomplished by recessing the glass is magnified by slanting the planes that act as sun screens. This reveals more of the broad dimension of each plane than does the recess alone.

Figure 13-18 *Carpenter Center.* The long curved cantilevered ramp combines structural and form characteristics that are uniquely concrete in nature. The compressiveness and bulk of the adjacent multistory block are compatible with masonry.

tempted in concrete. At an upper level, freestanding beams and columns express linearity, as do the freestanding columns supporting many cantilevered forms. The visual impact of the linear components is minimal due to their positions either high above eye level or recessed in reduced light.

The building is strongly expressive of its material, having combined both structural and form characteristics which demonstrate the uniqueness and potential of concrete.

Bell Tower, St. John's Abbey Church
Collegeville, Minnesota; Marcel Breuer; 1963

The planar nature of the upper mass and the curves of the base combine to separate the image of the tower from the rectilinear materials, wood and steel (Fig. 13-19). Structurally, the plane is distinguished from masonry by its large vertical cantilever, the two horizontal cantilevers on either side of its base, the long horizontal span in the opening below the cross, and the cantilever of the bell platform. The smooth surfaces of the outward-leaning edges of the large plane contrast with the stepped edge that would be expected of masonry. The lack of protective trim around openings or top of the plane is a concrete characteristic, unlike the other three materials.

The horizontal lines in the plane express the formability of a concrete surface but do not fulfill the potential of this characteristic because they are straight. Only their wide spacing contrasts with the lines typical of wood and steel surfaces. The absence of other joints between the lines contrasts with a masonry surface in which the horizontal grooves also could be produced.

The expression of the base is not as clearly concrete as is the plane above. Since the span and gravity loading of the arches are within the capability of masonry, the distinction of the base from a masonry image can only be partial. The challenge of the wind load to the connection between plane and base does make masonry an unlikely material for this configuration. The base's thinness,

Figure 13-19 *St. John's Bell Tower.* The essence of concrete is captured in the double-cantilevered plane. Simplicity and size enhance these and other concrete charactetistics.

its graceful lines, and the rarity of parabolic forms in masonry add a sense of concrete. The sloped surfaces are more compatible with concrete than masonry, as water penetration is less likely in the former. The slopes are smooth, unlike masonry, which could be expected to step back with a texture relating to the size of the masonry units.

The curvilinear potential of concrete is not exploited in the large plane, and there is a hint of masonry in the base. On the whole, however, the tower strongly expresses the uniqueness of concrete, due to the clearly expressed plane and its structural nature.

Habitat
Montreal, Canada; Moshe Safdie; 1967

The overall image of the site-cast, precast box housing complex is one of stacked units and therefore has a general feeling of compression (Fig. 13–20). The stepping back of the buildinjg form in all elevations gives a sense of stability to the mass that, with the compressive expression and the blocklike forms, is compatible with masonry. A real sense of masonry does not result, however, because of the numerous large cantilevers and other horizontal spans. Because of the building structure, images of wood and masonry are eliminated from the experience of the complex.

The box shape is a secondary form of precast concrete. In the overall sense the complex seems boxlike and clearly derives the essence of its spirit from that unit. The repetitive nature of precast is captured in the similar dimensions that are apparent throughout, especially in the end proportions of the boxes.

The variety of orientations, overlaps, and apparent merging of boxes makes identification of individual units difficult (Fig. 13–21). The individual components are extensively expressed but do not seem to be so from any but an aerial view. The apparent merging of units is a result of the alignment of floor and roof planes, which causes the parapets and concrete balcony rails to overlap with other units. The merged image is in the nature of cast-in-place concrete but not of precast.

The lines visible at the meetings of walls and floors are not part of a planned pattern. Their appearance suggests an attempt to produce a blank surface which

Figure 13-20 *Habitat.* The expression of bending resistance by the box cantilevers excludes the spirit of masonry from the visual statement.

Figure 13-21 *Habitat.* A boxlike character prevails without the complete identity of individual boxes being clear.

was incompatible with the casting system. The otherwise-uninterrupted surfaces do not exploit the formability of concrete. They are, however, reasonably compatible with the nature of precast boxes, where the walls are poured in the vertical position in forms that are not dismantled and must be reused. This process is not particularly compatible with the production of impressions and protrusions. The absence of protective trim on the sills and parapets expresses concrete's high level of durability.

The net expression of the building is clearly within the nature of precast concrete. The structure and the repetitive three-dimensional exhibition of similar box shapes secures the compatibility of the complex with its material.

Des Moines Art Center Addition
Des Moines, Iowa; I. M. Pei and Partners; 1968

The south facade expresses the planar nature of concrete with unique clarity (Fig. 13–22). The key to the expression rests with the deeply recessed glazing, which exposes the edges and widths of several large slabs. The planar characteristics thus revealed are magnified by the vertical, horizontal, and sloped orientations of the components. The variety of positions and angles gives the

Figure 13-22 *Des Moines Art Center.* Deeply recessed glazing and slabs in a variety of orientations establish a strong planar sense of the facade.

illusion, from a fixed observation point, of seeing a plane from many viewing positions. A sense of circling a plane is nearly achieved without the observer having to move. This illusion emphasizes the planar nature of the concrete, as would actual inspection of the planes, by moving around them.

Several exterior slabs stop at the glazing rather than passing through it to become an interior wall or floor. This gives them an emphasized three-dimensional quality because two edges are visible (one from outside and one from inside the building). In the case of the sloped plane, two edges and two sides are visible. The emphasized three-dimensional sense increases the stength of the planar image. A sense of masonry is avoided by the long straight horizontal spans of several planes. Most vertical planes are less distinct from masonry because they are rectangular and compressive. Their relative thinness and visual similarity to the horizontal planes help but do not completely remove them from the realm of masonry. A small vertical plane on the west facade is structurally distinct from the potential of masonry because of its cantilever (Fig. 13-23).

Figure 13-23 *Des Moines Art Center.* Extensive working of the surface has failed to hide joints resulting from the forming process. The cantilevered wall at the left is an example of a beamlike component with adequate depth to read as a plane.

The hammered texture of the surface represents a working beyond the nature of concrete. The failure of the extensively worked texture to obscure form-work joint lines magnifies the contrast of large effort to limited accomplishment. The high durability of concrete is expressed beyond the usual contact with grade and unprotected parapet tops. The absence of an apparent protective cover on the large sloped slab (which is over an interior space) is an unusually strong indication of concrete's high resistance to weather and weathering. A pool of water abuts the north facade, thus expressing further the very high durability of concrete.

The net impression of the building is a strong expression of the nature of its material. The unique clarity of the planar forms mixed with a significant demonstration of bending resistance carries the image well into the realm of concrete.

Goddard Library
Clark University, Worcester, Massachusetts; John Johansen; 1970

The library expresses a fairly clear separation between the structural roles of concrete and masonry (Fig. 13–24). The brick has a simple stacked and compressive appearance throughout. The concrete is assigned the more sophisticated task of spanning, which it does in the forms of both beams and slabs. Among the concrete spans are numerous cantilevers, which emphasize the greater structural potential of concrete over masonry. This image is also reflected by the fact that much of the masonry is carried by the concrete.

Concrete is also expressed in compression but in the form of columns which are less like masonry than bearing walls would be. The linearity of the columns is not particularly expressive of concrete. Their straight-sloped bases are, however, more like concrete than like the other materials.

The expression of compression is not concrete's major contribution to the building image. It is secondary to the expression of bending, which has the greater contrast with masonry's potential.

Figure 13–24 *Goddard Library.* Concrete is assigned the spanning tasks as well as compression in the form of columns. Brick takes the structurally more elementary role of compression in the form of walls.

Figure 13-25 *Goddard Library.* Concrete forms the sloped planes and nonrectangular components. For the most part, brick forms the simpler rectangular vertical components.

While a number of the masonry walls are more planar than the concrete forms, the concrete shapes are more sophisticated (Fig. 13-25). The brick walls are nearly always simple rectangles. Concrete takes numerous sloped and angled forms which exploit the formability and in some cases the structural potential of the material. The use of concrete for the sloped surfaces expresses concrete's structural nature and the contribution that the lack of joints makes to its high level of durability.

Concrete is expressed within its nature in this building, especially in the horizontal systems, where its bending potential and planar nature are realized. The characteristics of concrete are clarified by the nearly complete separation of tasks assigned to the concrete and masonry.

Kimbell Art Museum
Fort Worth, Texas; Louis I. Kahn; 1972

The building does not express concrete as a planar material. The strong association of roof system with the image of vaulting obscures its more accurate identity as curved planes (Fig. 13-26). The structural reality of the roof system is in the nature of concrete while its expression is less so. It is not apparent to the casual observer that the roof forms are vaults in shape only. The structural condition of the roof vaults is that of two postentioned beams which curve toward each other and span parallel to the long axis of each vault. The pairs of curved beams are separated by a continuous skylight at the peak of each vault, except in the canopies. In the facade, the interior vaults could be masonry since their spans are not large and resistance to thrust is available at each side.

The absence of support along the edges of the vaults is apparent in the facade only at the canopy vaults. These vaults do not express thrust and their correct span is more apparent than in the other vaults (Fig. 13-27). The influence of the canopy bays on the structural identities of the other vaults is limited. The exposure of space-enclosing vaults and columns in the end facades reveals that they are similar to the canopy vaults. The visual information is there to

Figure 13-26 *Kimbell Art Museum.* The repetition of the enclosed bays establishes an image of structural vaulting. They subdue the more structurally clear message of the open bay at the end of the series.

Figure 13-27 *Kimbell Art Museum.* The absence of thrust resistance and the lack of support along the outer edge indicates that the curved canopy is not a structural vault.

conclude that all the space-enclosing vaults are structurally like the canopies. It is probable that, for most viewers, the reverse occurs because of the greater number of space-enclosing vaults.

Importance is given to concrete surfaces by their exposure between travertine-clad areas. The concrete surface reflects the production process by emphasizing form lines and tie holes to an elevated degree. The tie holes are covered with recessed lead plugs, the dark color of which is more visible than that of cementitious or plastic fillers. V-shaped ridges protrude from the wall, suggesting form lines. The uniqueness of the ridged grid compared to common grooved patterns brings additional attention to this aspect of concrete production. The sharp profile of the ridge, however, is not compatible with the medium level of refinement consistent with concrete. A number of ridged segments have broken off.

The expression of concrete durability is neutral, with a major demonstration on its behalf and an expression that detracts. The use of concrete in the lower level of the building and the restriction of travertine to the upper half is a positive expression of concrete's high durability. The use of a protective cladding on the canopy roofs (under which no valuable goods are stored) demonstrates little faith in the durability of concrete.

The form and structural use of the material are more in the nature of concrete than they appear to be. Appearance is, however, the essence of expression. The overall expression of concrete is at best ambiguous.

Colonnade Building, Christian Science Church Center
Boston, Massachusetts; I. M. Pei and Partners; 1973

The south facade of the building clearly expresses the primary form of concrete in its long colonnade of planes (Fig. 13–28). The angled orientation obscures the planar nature of the columns slightly in that one broad side is emphasized at the expense of the other. The freestanding nature of the columns helps emphasize the form in that all sides and edges can be viewed by moving around them. The plan of each column plane is a thin parallelogram with the two acute angles blunted by 90-degree corners. These tapered ends are much in the spirit of concrete in that the obtuse corners are straight vertical lines. The same effect in masonry would require special units or extensive cutting. The absence of sharp angles at any corner respects concrete's medium level of refinement. The surface of the edge is wider than the thickness of the planes, making them look thicker than they are. The planes depend somewhat on their thinness to contrast with masonry walls. Some contrast is lost in the illusion of greater thickness. The arched openings in the planes contribute to a sense of masonry due to the significant mass on either side that is available to resist thrust.

The large fascia (several narrow flat strips approximate a curve) seems massive, especially at its west end (Fig. 13–29). From this view, the nature of

Figure 13–28 *Colonnade Building.* The planar nature of concrete is strongly demonstrated by the freestanding very broad and relatively thin columns. The forms demonstrate that concrete columns need not be linear.

Figure 13-29 *Colonnade Building.* The closed end of the curved fascia obscures its planar nature and gives a sense of mass that is greater than exists. Its projection beyond the columns eliminates masonry as a likely material for its construction.

its form is misrepresented. The overhang of the mass prevents it from seeming like masonry, however. The mass is actually hollow, making the fascia, more or less, a curved cantilevered plane. This combination of structure and form represents the essence of concrete. Opening the west end of the form or recessing the enclosure panel would have revealed this strong concrete characteristic. A scupper would have, at least, provided a hint to the reality of the form.

An indication of the actual form occurs at the east end (Fig. 13–30). The small gap that separates the fascia from the adjacent wall reveals the thickness of the concrete by its shadow. This information is available even on cloudy days when reflected light casts a faint shadow. It has great impact on the image of the concrete. At once it clarifies the form and structure of the fascia. The small detail is emphasized by the intensity of expression produced when the very long concrete fascia stops a few inches from a likely destination.

The surface of the concrete has some emphasized joint lines, faint closely spaced parallel lines suggesting board formwork and form tie holes. Nothing further expresses the formability of concrete surfaces. High durability is expressed in the absence of protective trim on top edges.

Figure 13-30 *Colonnade Building.* The shadow of the fascia reveals its planar form. Attention is drawn to the shadow by the visual tension created in the gap.

The expression of the facade is structurally and geometrically compatible with concrete. The slight overlap with masonry expression in the colonnade is not a serious dilution of the strong feeling of concrete planes. The nearly maximum expression of the nature of concrete, easily accessible in the fascia, is not realized.

Arcosanti
Cordes Junction, Arizona; Paolo Soleri; under construction

Forms and details of several buildings constructed between 1970 and 1975 will be examined to identify a collective image of concrete. Both on-site precast and cast-in-place concrete are included.

The cast-in-place shells of the foundry and ceramic apses express the freedom of concrete from rectangular geometry (Fig. 13–31). This is further demonstrated in the upper and lower surfaces. Ceiling ribs taper in pattern and profile, as do decorative protrusions and impressions. The upper surface of the ceramic apse bulges slightly at each of a series of colored circles, giving it an appearance of gentle undulation. These surface patterns and shapes partially remove the half domes from the realm of masonry, with which they share a structural image (Fig. 13–32).

Figure 13-31 *Ceramic Apse.* The undulating surface of the apse expresses the nature of concrete rather than masonry. The precast at the steps has a strong planar image. The curved edge of the plane is more like concrete than like masonry.

Figure 13-32 *Foundry Apse.* The surface of the ceiling has nonrectangular protrusions and impressions. They express the ability to manipulate the surface of concrete and are distinctly unlike masonry, wood, or steel.

Figure 13-33 *Ceramic Apse.* The identity of each curved precast plane is expressed to some degree by the clear joint lines and strongly by the decorative shapes at certain joints. The cantilevered elements move the image away from the realm of masonry.

The precast fascias of the two apses strongly express the planar nature of concrete, due to extensive exposure of edges and both faces of the slabs (Fig. 13-33). The cantilevering decorative shapes that are integral with the precast help distinguish the arched concrete from the image of masonry. The curved top edges of the arches (which double as stair rails on the ceramic apse) are more like concrete than are the stepped edges typical of masonry. The curved lines also distinguish the concrete from the straight materials. The identity of the precast components is assured by joints that are always visible and in some cases celebrated with decorative detailing.

The arched trim of the north and south vaults echo the characteristics expressed in the precast of the apses (Fig. 13-34). The curved precast planes of the vaults are not unlike masonry in their structural achievement. Adequate buttressing is available to resist the thrust of a purely compressive vaulted structure. Large circular holes in the curved slabs reveal them to be too thin to be

Figure 13-34 *South Vault.* The vault and segmental arched openings in the adjacent housing are structurally like masonry. Concrete characteristics are found in the sloped edges and openings of the vault roofs, which show the concrete to be relatively thin.

masonry, considering the span of the system. The underside of the vaults are covered with murals, the curved lines of which do not suggest the rectangularity of a masonry surface. The murals do not violate the durability of concrete, as they occur under the vault, where protection from the weather is not an issue. The sloped edges along the stairs over the housing on either side of the south vault reflects the option for concrete to be independent from rectangular form.

The visitor's center (restaurant building) has the compactness and rectangularity of masonry but separates itself from the image of compression in the expression of numerous cantilevers and other horizontal spans (Fig. 13–35). The planar nature of the precast concrete is not as clear as in the previous buildings. Significantly fewer panels have both faces exposed on either side of an expressed edge. A planar image is supported by a number of unglazed openings which do reveal thickness and both broad surfaces (Fig. 13–36).

Figure 13–35 *Visitor's Center.* The blocklike spirit of the building is reminiscent of masonry. Numerous projections and the openness at the base keep the building image within the realm of concrete.

Figure 13–36 *Visitor's Center.* The circular openings reveal the planar form of the precast panels and render the image unlike wood or steel. The structural conditions eliminate the element from the spirit of masonry.

Spiral impressions occur in the precast at the top of the foundry apse (Fig. 13–37). They are a rare exterior expression in this complex of the formability of concrete surfaces. The surfaces exhibit a relatively high percentage of honeycombing, pour lines, discoloration, and other flaws. By traditional standards, the flawed surfaces violate the medium level of refinement logical in concrete. The construction is the product of the well-known workshops at Arcosanti, utilizing semiskilled and unskilled participants and relatively unsophisticated technologies. It can be argued that because the surfaces are the natural result of a particular production method, they express both the system and the substance. The credibility of the argument is enhanced by the fact that the surfaces have an air of acceptance. Repairs are not apparent, apologies are not offered, and the system of production continues to be used.

The durability of concrete, not a serious issue in the desert, is expressed by the numerous exposed upper edges and surfaces. Numerous circular openings help separate the concrete from the image of wood or steel. A number of semicircular openings with straight lintels and curved sills distinguish the material from masonry (Fig. 13–38).

Figure 13–37 *Foundry Apse.* The spiral impressions in the precast express the formability of the surface and the independence of concrete from rectangularity.

Figure 13–38 *West Housing.* The semicircular windows are uniquely concrete in their curved bottoms and straight horizontal lintels.

The spirit of the concrete construction is a mixture of visually soft, molded, and planar forms (not combined in the same components). While some structural expressions overlap with those of masonry, a relatively strong sense of concrete prevails in the complex.

River City
Chicago, Illinois; Bertrand Goldberg Associates; 1985

The undulation of the building facade (the footprint is S-shaped) demonstrates the affinity of concrete for nonrectangular geometry (Fig. 13–39). The visual softness of the rounded elements in the facade expresses concrete's incompatibility with sharp and delicate forms. The potential of an image shared with masonry is eliminated by the structural expression of the material. The upper two-thirds of the facade cantilevers over the lower third. A number of balconies are also cantilevered. Long segmental arches curve outward as they arch upward, thus rendering masonry less appropriate for these components than concrete. The openings for the smaller windows are uniquely compatible with the form and structural potential of concrete. The short-radius curves, straight-leaning jambs, and straight horizontal lintels combine to eliminate wood, steel, or masonry as likely wall materials.

The broadness of the columns pulls their otherwise linear shapes toward more planar forms. Their apparent merging with the adjacent spandrels reflects the cast nature of the material. The smooth transitions of the column edges into the curved cantilevers at their tops reflect both form and structure compatible with the nature of the material.

Thin vertical ribs have been cast with the surface of the concrete to diminish the effects of weathering (Fig. 13–40). They also tend to obscure irregularities that might have occurred in the forming process. The ribs express the formability of the surface of concrete. The linear texture does not exploit the compatibility of concrete with free forms and other patterns that are not uniform. While the thinness of the ridges makes them somewhat vulnerable

Figure 13-39 *River City.* The nonrectangular geometry, visual softness, and structural spirit of the indulating facade express the nature of concrete. (Courtesy of Jeffrey Dubin.)

Figure 13-40 *River City.* The window openings are uniquely concrete. The curves eliminate the images of wood and steel, while the long straight lintels exclude masonry from the structural image. Photograph by David Belle. (Printed with permission of the architect: Bertrand Goldberg Associates, Inc.)

to impact, the majority are above the level where damage is likely to occur. The surface also expresses form tie holes, thus reflecting the cast-in-place nature of the concrete.

While the absence of protective trim on the window sills express the high durability of concrete, the exposed tops of the parapets are too high to contribute to this visual statement. The expression of durability is maximized where the columns of the marina area stand in water.

While the building does not have a clear planar image, a number of other strongly expressed characteristics combine to produce an overall spirit of concrete. It is difficult to imagine the building in any other material.

Chapter 14

CONCLUSION

A QUIZ

Each building material has a set of characteristics that, taken as a group, produce a unique image. The images of buildings that express the properties of their materials should therefore differ if the materials of each are different. Frank Lloyd Wright believed that even the floor plan was subject to the imprint of its materials. "A wood plan is slender: light in texture, narrower spacing," he wrote. "A stone or brick plan is heavy: black in masses, wider in spacing."[1]

Paul Rudolph once said: "In any building that's worth anything, one does not have to be told what material it is. One can tell by its innate form." If Rudolph is correct, the material of a building could be identified from a cardboard model or line drawing. This thesis is the basis for the following exercise, which is a quiz only in the sense that it begins with questions. It is not a measure of theories or knowledge. Answers to the numbered questions are not as important as the additional questions generated in the analysis of the drawings. They will reveal the features important to material image.

Line drawings of simple structures are shown. Utilitarian structures have been selected in an attempt to observe reasonably straightforward use of materials with aesthetic goals having a secondary role. For each structure identify the material or materials from the categories of wood, masonry, steel, or concrete. Identify the key conditions for identifying a material by considering questions such as those that follow and as many others as can be developed. Is the overall shape informative? Is the meeting of the structure with the ground helpful? Do the surfaces and edges show useful information? Are the connections between materials revealing? Photographs of the structures are presented in Appendix A.

---

[1]Frank Lloyd Wright, "In the Cause of Architecture: The Logic of the Plan," *Architectural Record*, 63 (January 1928), 49–57.

263

1. Identify the major materials of the bicycle racks (Fig. 14–1A and B). Two different materials are used.

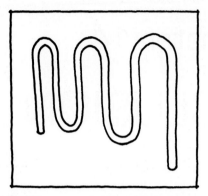

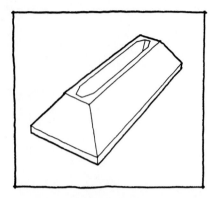

Figure 14–1A *Bicycle Rack.* Note the thinness and the resulting image of strength. Note the sense of strength projected by the minimal amount of material connecting to the ground. Note the linearity.

Figure 14–1B *Bicycle Rack.* Note the thicker image compared to the other rack. Note the extensive contact with the paving. Note the nonrectangular aspects, the straight line corners that are obtuse angles, and the blunted acute angle around the base.

2. Identify the major materials of the water tanks (Fig. 14–2A and B). Two different materials are used.

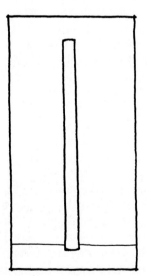

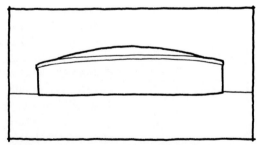

Figure 14–2A *Water Tank.* Note the thinness of mass and great height compared to the other tank. Note the thinness suggested in the tank wall. (A thick wall would leave little room for water in the slender form.)

Figure 14–2B *Water Tank.* Note the greater visual mass compared to the other tank. Note the nonrectangular aspects. Note the absence of joints in the surface. Note the earth-bound image.

3. Identify the major materials of the water towers (Fig. 14–3A and B). Two different materials are used.

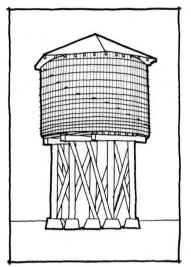

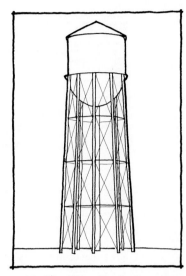

Figure 14–3A *Water Tower.* Note the bulky image compared to the other tower. Note the linearity established by the vertical joints in the tank surface. Note the linearity and bulk of the supporting structure.

Figure 14–3B *Water Tower.* Note the great height compared to the other tank. Note the thinner supporting structure. Note the linearity of the supports.

4. Identify the major materials of the signs (Fig. 14–4A and B). Three different materials are used.

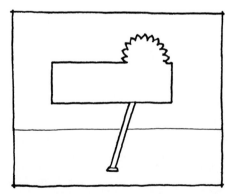

Figure 14–4A *Sign.* Note the sharpness of the pointed elements. Note the strength suggested by the cantilever and the thinness of the support.

Figure 14–4B *Sign.* Note the earth-bound image and broad contact of the base with grade. Note the linearity of the elements in the sign face and their worked edges. Note the blocky forms of the base material.

5. Identify the major materials of the benches (Fig. 14–5A and B). Four different materials are used.

Figure 14–5A *Bench.* Note the absence of joints in the bench, which suggests a single piece. Note the cantilever of the apparently bent plane. Note the taper of the profile and the blunted edges. Note the compact shapes in the wall that supports the bench.

Figure 14–5B *Bench.* Note the linearity of the bench surfaces. Note the thinner supports. Note the strength suggested by the minimum of material at the connection to the ground.

6. Identify the major materials of the light poles (Fig. 14–6A and B). Ignore the arms that hold the light fixtures. These identifications are not as straightforward as the previous ones. Two different materials are used.

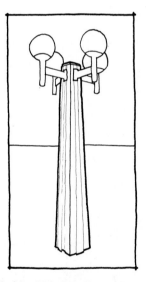

Figure 14–6A *Light Pole.* Reconcile the taper of the pole (nonrectangular elevation) with the linear expression of the surfaces.

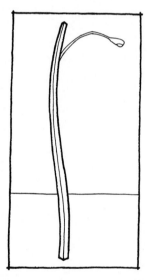

Figure 14–6B *Light Pole.* Reconcile the taper and curve of the pole with the rectangular plan revealed by the perspective at the top and bottom of the pole.

HONESTY

Simply because honesty in human behavior is held in high esteem, it does not necessarily follow that honesty is important in architectural expression. While the popularity of honesty in architecture fluctuates, it is never entirely rejected or embraced by everyone. Typically, little justification is offered, with criticism of architectural dishonesty beyond the "self-evident" variety associated with human behavior. Honesty in building materials is encouraged in this study for reasons unrelated to moral issues. John Burchard associated truth with visual credibility.

Figure 14-7 The repetition of two shadow patterns lacks the randomness of the infinite variety of textures found in rough stone surfaces. The regularity suggests a manufactured product.

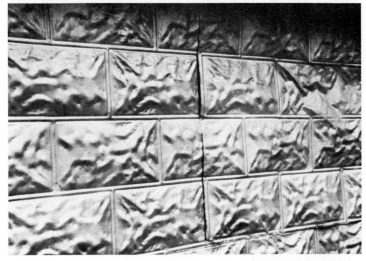

Figure 14-8 The thinness of the metal is revealed in the lapping joints of the sheets. Patterns on the sheets have greater uniformity than in the concrete block's imitation of stone when greater variety could exist.

> The truth of architecture has to be that it serves people well. If illusion is needed there is nothing wrong with illusion. The component of architectural truth which has to do with a sense of visible credibility is that the appearance shall *seem* reasonable?[2]

The call for visible credibility has direct application to the issue of material honesty. Building material imitations are rarely convincing. Consequently, they rarely *seem* reasonable.

The concrete block of recent history that was often cast on the site and always meant to imitate stone lacks the natural randomness of stone (Fig. 14–7). Since every block face has exactly the same lumpy form, only the upside-down variation is available to break the repetitive image. The two alternating patterns do not have enough variety to capture the sense of broken or found stone.

The pressed metal sheets that imitate stone can be no more than amusing (Fig. 14–8). The thinness of the metal is revealed in the joints of the sheets. Although all the shapes on a sheet could have different textural patterns, typical-

[2]John Burchard, *Bernini Is Dead? Architecture and the Social Purpose* (New York: McGraw-Hill, Inc., 1976), p. 31.

ly they are the same. The sheen of the metal has little resemblance to the patina of rough stone. The fasteners holding the metal sheets in place are foreign to masonry. Sheet metal with brick shapes pressed in it has similar problems (Fig. 14–9). Often, installations such as these receive little maintenance. Rust is common, which gives the imitation away if the joints, fasteners, dents, wrinkles, and surface texture do not.

Vinyl and metal siding pressed with a deep wood grain pattern do not look like painted wood clapboard siding for a number of reasons. Painted wood clapboards generally do not have a deep grain pattern visible in their surfaces. The face of wood siding does not have the gentle curve typical of the thinner imitations. The thinness of vinyl and metal is revealed in the lapping of sections and at the corners, where the folded but still thin edge of the vertical trim is visible. Strips that have the shape of two imitation clapboards have a joint pattern showing pairs of "boards" butting throughout the siding. The pattern is not typical of clapboard siding.

Colored concrete paving into which a grid pattern has been pressed is in several respects not exactly like the quarry tile it imitates. The pressing and lifting of the patternmaking tools can roughen the concrete along the grooves. The edges of the concrete squares are often more ragged than those of quarry tiles. The concrete coloring is usually lighter, darker, more intense, or not as rich as the color of clay quarry tile. The concrete color loses additional credibility as it fades. The texture of the concrete is more coarse than the clay it imitates. Its detailing rarely reflects the nature of quarry tile in every respect (Fig. 14–10). Edges curves or bends in the surface express the nature of concrete, not that of tile.

Asphalt shingles colored to look like wood shakes simply do not (Fig. 14–11). The dark bands on the lower edges of the shingles fail to give a sense of thickness. The shingle surfaces are smooth and granular. Shakes have a random linear roughness visible in their surfaces, especially along the butt edge.

Generally, substances applied to plywood do not look like the material they are intended to imitate. The plywood is often too thin and spans too far in the pursuit of economy. Warpage that can result from these conditions reveals the

Figure 14–9 Sheet joints, wrinkles, rust, bolts, and the sliding door suggest steel. Only the small rectangles of the pattern are like brick.

Figure 14–10 The ragged joints are not like quarry tile. The bends in the surface express concrete.

Figure 14–11 The dark edges do not make the composition shingles look thick. Shakes do not curve around corners. No aspect of the shingles can be mistaken for the wood that they imitate.

joints between panels under textured paint (imitating stucco) and suggests thinness behind applied aggregate (imitating concrete). Lack of maintenance destroys any credibility this type of imitation initially had, as deterioration of joints and surfaces reveals the true nature of the products. Typically, the imitations that need the most maintenance get the least.

Not all imitations lack visual credibility. Cast stone is often indistinguishable from limestone. With its long history of excellent performance, however, cast stone has become a product in its own right as much as an imitation of limestone.

The qualities of concrete block, sheet metal, vinyl, patterned concrete paving or asphalt shingles are not being criticized. These materials, as others, have their own properties and corresponding expressions which can contribute to an aesthetic system. Patterns in concrete, for example, express a surface potential of that material. Nothing is gained in the unsuccessful imitation of quarry tile or any other product (Fig. 14–12). Unlike other paving materials, a pattern could still give relief to an otherwise bland concrete surface if it were larger than tile or included curved lines and graphics. Even the humble asphalt shingled surface has a tautness and potential colorfulness that could be exploited in an expressive order.

Burchard's tolerance for illusion is applauded, as is his call for credibility. It is the credibility that is lacking in most material illusions. Imitations are

Figure 14-12 This concrete bridge in Holland has the form of logs, complete with the texture of bark. The imitation does not enhance the aesthetic quality of wood or concrete.

often meant to elevate the image of quality. They nearly always do the opposite. This, alone, is ample reason to avoid imitation. Philosophical or moral judgments are not necessary to reach this conclusion.

OPEN ISSUES

In an attempt to develop a basic and simple approach to the expression of materials in design, a number of complex issues were addressed only briefly. They are the types of issues that are likely to draw different conclusions from different designers. Some are identified here. Their further study is encouraged.

Frequently, the expression of one property violates another property. Workability seems opposed to primary form, for example. Is to demonstrate the workability of wood to obscure its primary form? This is the case with much of the wood in Victorian and other decorative styles. It is possible to shape the ends of lumber while maintaining its rectilinearity. It is possible to produce curved wood components while maintaining their linearity and rectangular section (Fig. 14–13). Do these compromises dilute the expression of wood or strengthen it?

In many climates the issue of durability opposes the expression of masonry form. Stepped wall surfaces and protrusions of masonry units collect water. The increased expression of unit form makes water penetration and damage from the freeze–thaw cycle more likely. Does the increased vulnerability nullify the expressive advantage of projected units? Can different conclusions be drawn for climates that differ in precipitation and temperature?

A number of newer but common material technologies have not been addressed in their own right. Reinforced masonry, chemically treated wood, and composite materials are a few.

Guidelines for any material reinforced with steel can be developed in the spirit of reinforced concrete. Reinforced masonry, unfortunately for clarity's sake, looks exactly like ordinary masonry except with regard to strength expression

Figure 14–13 Linearity and rectangular solid profiles reflect aspects of the form of wood. The curves express wood's workability.

(Fig. 14–14). The fact that reinforced concrete looks like concrete without steel is not a problem since the latter is now virtually restricted to paving. Some might simply reject the use of reinforced masonry. Others might devise ways to express it differently than through traditional masonry detailing. Soldier units in a stack bond facilitate the use of hidden steel. Could this pattern become associated only with reinforced brick? Perhaps a new type of unit is in order, one that more easily receives steel than traditional units. Couldn't they be larger than traditional units, thus expressing the nature of factory handling and assembly?

Figure 14–14 The center opening of this prefabricated brick component reveals its reinforcing steel. The extensive information revealed in this display unit is an expression of significantly higher purity than is typical of installed versions.

Unless reinforced materials are expressed differently than the nonreinforced versions, the distinctions between them will be limited. The reinforcing of materials brings them closer to the structural expression of steel, as concrete is already. It is conceivable that, one day, there will no longer be a distinction between the structural potential of many materials.

A similar clouding of properties occurs when a material of low durability such as wood is made to have high durability with the injection of chemicals. As in the case of reinforcing, no visual confusion occurs if the added element merely increases a safety factor. If treated wood is painted, for example, the chemicals do not interfere with the expression of the component. Leaving chemically treated wood without further protection is convenient and leaves the appearance of the wood largely intact. The advantages of this approach, which violates the nature of wood according to the reasoning set forth, are hard to ignore.

If clarity of materials expression is a goal, one would be more productive in developing new expressions than in denying the existence of the new technologies. It is common for innovations in any industry to have the visual characteristics of traditional products. The first automobiles, for example, looked much like the carriages that preceded them. They eventually evolved into something different. All the possibilities cannot be suggested here. Their derivation is another challenge for the individual designer.

In drawing conclusions for unit masonry, the load-bearing variety has been treated in the same way as veneers. The fact that veneer masonry does carry its own weight makes the distinction one of degree. Masonry carrying building loads could be shown to be thicker than masonry supporting only itself. Occasionally, a veneer is expressed as such by revealing its thickness at an edge, which also shows the material to be clearly superimposed on another component. It can also be argued that the structural material of a veneered building warrants expression (Fig. 14–15). This is sometimes accomplished by exposing a concrete frame which shows that the brick between the structural members is not load bearing. More subtle approaches include the revealing of structural

Figure 14–15 Which materials warrant expression? The studs and plywood have a structural role. The dark sheathing insulates. The wood siding and brick veneer that eventually covered it all are weather barriers.

bays with window grouping or changes in the cladding. Some experiments with the partial omission of cladding and sheathing to show the nature of the construction have occurred. The issue overlaps into the larger design question of what a building should be. These and similar dichotomies fall into the realm of the designer's prerogative. Intuitive judgment derived from the assimilation of many goals and inspirations must eventually be the basis for numerous design decisions. Otherwise, the design process would be one of routine rather than of creativity.

A CAUTION

Many demonstrations of buildings in harmony with their materials can be found in historical architecture. In part, this occurred because designers were once closely associated with the building process. The medium of the designer was the medium of the builder, the materials themselves. Forrest Wilson has noted the growing separation of the designer from the construction process.

> Much of the ability of the individual craftsman to make decisions is removed and given to a new class of workmen who do not work with their hands, but, instead, make decisions concerning the work as a whole. Designing as a separate task comes into being.
>
> The designer manipulates the design and makes changes using ruler and compass on paper, rather than altering the actual material.
>
> Designers are removed from direct contact with the work and must rely on memory, experience, schooling, and imagination to decide what will or will not fit and what can or cannot be made.[3]

If expression of a material's properties is natural for craftspersons handling the material, it follows that designers might be influenced by the characteristics of the media in which they work. Instruments can produce drawings representing a refinement greater than is natural to certain materials (Fig. 14–16). The potential for scaled representation of structural capabilities with

Figure 14–16 Failure of the paving (caused by a failure in the base) demonstrates that the detail has a level of refinement more compatible with drawing tools than with the concrete system.

[3]Forrest Wilson, *The Joy of Building: Restoring the Connection between Architect and Builder* (New York: Litton Educational Publishing, Inc., 1979), pp. 27–28.

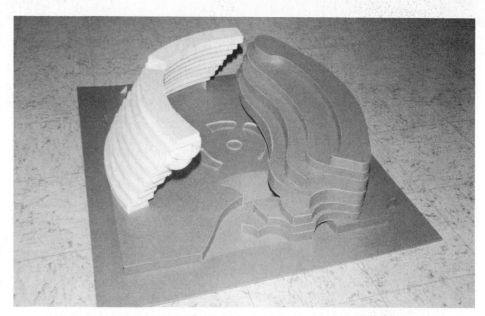

Figure 14-17 The model of the concrete complex was begun in cardboard but finished in polystyrene when the cardboard proved inadequate to express concrete. The exercise demonstrates a struggle to express the building material instead of the model material.

glue and cardboard surpasses the actual abilities of the strongest building materials. On the other hand, the designer's media have limitations that building materials do not have. The two-dimensional nature of drawing can restrict one's thinking in the third dimension. Producing shapes other than the straight and rectangular is difficult with typical model materials (Fig. 14–17).

A challenge in the design process, then, is to think beyond one's tools and supplies to the actual materials of building: their potential, limitations, and uniqueness.

RULES IGNORED

Following guidelines or rules does not guarantee the production of great architecture. Neither does ignoring them necessarily yield poor architecture. Numerous highly regarded buildings have achieved their status despite violating certain generally accepted design principles.

Philip Johnson's glass house in New Canaan, Connecticut, falls short of most standards for privacy or energy conservation. Certain spaces in Le Corbusier' d'Habitation in Marseille, France are too tall, too narrow, and too long. Wright's Price Tower in Bartlesville, Oklahoma has stairs with treads at an angle to the path of travel (Fig. 14–18). Toilets and kitchens are very tight. Certain bedrooms are extremely small. Some spaces are awkward. The elevators are tiny and some have very small foyers. The structural expressions of the Dulles Airport terminal and the Kimbell Art Museum are misleading. Wright's concrete block houses and his entry vault at the Morris Gift Shop are structurally impure. The materials statement of Notre Dame du Haut misrepresents reality.

These buildings and others are, nevertheless, considered to be landmarks of recent architectural history. Their so-called violations undermine the rigidity of design principles in general and should be enlightening to those who follow rules too closely.

Figure 14-18 The Price Tower has achieved an important place in architectural history despite violations in certain floor planning principles.

Professor of philosophy Paul Weiss's remarks on the relationship of wood's properties to design in wood could apply to any material.

> The object of the artist is not to do justice to wood—but to make something beautiful. Maybe he will do this best by paying attention to what wood can or cannot do, but that's not his main question. He is trying to make a masterwork; that is, to produce a work which shows mastery. There is no condition to which an artist must submit, but there are many that bind the craftsman.[4]

Weiss saw architecture as both an art and a craft. If architecture is both, there is merit in doing justice to building materials until their violation yields a greater beauty.

[4]Paul Weiss, "Wood in Aesthetics and Art," in *Design and Aesthetics in Wood*, ed. Eric A. Anderson and George F. Earle (Syracuse, N.Y.: State University of New York, College of Environmental Science and Forestry, 1972), p. 24.

Appendix A

ANSWERS TO THE QUIZ IN CHAPTER 14

This appendix includes photographs of the structures that are the subject of the quiz in Chapter 14. The quiz requires identification of the major materials in the structure from an examination of line drawings. The answers to the quiz are as follows:

1. A. Steel [Fig. A-1A].
   B. Concrete [Fig. A-1B].

Figure A–1A Steel bicycle rack.

Figure A–1B Concrete bicycle rack.

2. A. Steel [Fig. A-2A].
   B. Concrete [Fig. A-2B].

Figure A–2A Steel water tank.

Figure A–2B Concrete water tank.

3. A. Wood [Fig. A-3A].
    B. Steel [Fig. A-3B].

Figure A–3A Wood water tower.

Figure A–3B Steel water tower.

4. A. Steel [Fig. A-4A].
   B. Wood and stone [Fig. A-4B].

Figure A–4A Steel sign.

Figure A–4B Wood and stone sign.

5. A. Concrete and stone [Fig. A-5A].
   B. Wood and steel [Fig. A-5B].

Figure A–5A Concrete bench, stone wall.

Figure A–5B Wood and steel bench.

6. A. Concrete [Fig. A-6A].
   B. Laminated wood [Fig. A-6B].

Figure A–6A Concrete light pole.

Figure A–6B Laminated wood light pole.

Appendix B

SUMMARY
OF
PROPERTY EXPRESSIONS

The properties that have been identified in the text as being compatible with and representing the uniqueness of the limitations or potential of each material are summarized in the following table. The entries identify the property or magnitude of a property that may be expressed to emphasize each material's uniqueness. In some cases the material's limitations govern the listing. In other cases the material's potential is the criterion. Footnotes identify the criteria for the ratings. The intervals between the levels of very high, high, medium, low, and very low are not necessarily uniform within or between categories. Reasoning for each rating can be found in the text.

	WOOD	MASONRY	STEEL	CONCRETE
Form				
Geometry	Linear[a]	Blocklike[a]	Linear[a]	Planar[b]
Attitude	Straight[a]	Curved[b]	Straight[a]	Curved[b]
Refinement	Low[c]	Medium[c]	Very high[c]	Medium[c]
Strength				
Tension	Medium[c]	Very low[c]	Very high[c]	Very low[d]
Compression	Medium[c]	Very high[e]	Medium[d]	Medium[d]
Bending	Medium[c]	Low[c]	Very high[c]	High[c]
Durability	Very low[c]	High[c]	Low[c]	Very high[c]
Workability	Very high[c]	Low[c]	Medium[c]	Very low[c]

[a]Absence of other options.
[b]Most unique of several options.
[c]Highest limit.
[d]Below highest limit but necessary for philosophical reasons.
[e]Higher than actual capability relative to other materials but necessary for philosophical reasons.

Appendix C

CHECKLISTS FOR ANALYZING MATERIAL EXPRESSION

Checklists C-1 through C-4 are aids for the analysis of architecture with respect to the expression of wood, masonry, steel, and concrete. They may be used to analyze a finished building or a design in progress. A checklist is included for each material. Use of more than one list may be necessary to analyze a building that expresses more than one material. In these cases every line item on every list may not apply.

The checklists consist of assemblies subdivided into properties. The intensity of each property expression is to be judged. A three-level rating system is recommended, as follows:

1. (+) = Clear expression of the property

   Clear expression occurs where all the elements of the assembly express the property. It also occurs when the positive expressions are greater than violations of the property in both significance and number.

2. (0) = Neutral expression of the property

   Neutral expression occurs where the elements of the assembly neither violate nor draw attention to the property. This is typical of standard construction practices that are in harmony with the property but are so common as to have little visual impact. It also occurs where clear expressions and violations of the property are nearly equal in significance and number.

3. (−) = Violation of the property

   A violation occurs where the appearance of the assembly suggests that the material has a property different from that it actually has. Often, this condition allows the substitution of another material with relative ease and little visual change. It also occurs where both positive expressions and misrepresentations coexist, with the latter being greater in significance and number.

A more refined rating system may be used by identifying degrees of expressive intensity between the extremes and neutral. Rating systems of more than five levels suggest a greater sense of accuracy than is likely. Assigning points to ratings and totaling also has an air of accuracy that might not exist. If points are totaled, line items must be weighted, as the contributions to the building image of some are more significant than others. Although the final relative weight is left to the user, it is suggested that form and strength be considered highly significant.

It is also possible to subdivide each line item to reduce the scope of each rating. *Durability*, for example, is listed for one rating but may be subdivided into categories of structure and cladding. These may be divided into surfaces, tops, and bottoms. An increase in line items simplifies the identification of each rating but complicates the entire process. A workable compromise may be to subdivide selected characteristics only if it is convenient for a particular design.

A major value of the checklist is the dialogue it generates. It is recommended that the designer justify all forms and details that rate (0) and (−). These ratings do not necessarily indicate a poor architectural design. A significant number of (0) ratings suggest that the materials are not contributing to the visual impact of the building. A significant number of (−) ratings indicates that the spirit of the building is not in harmony with the nature of its materials. Purposeful violations intended to achieve certain visual goals will show as (−) ratings just like accidental violations. This is why their justification is useful. It helps the designer clarify goals and evaluate progress toward them. A design with all (+) ratings is harmonious with the properties of its materials. It is also a design in which the materials are making a significant contribution to the visual image. The quality of the visual image must be judged independently of the material analysis.

On the checklists, conditions are listed that support a rating of (+), (0), or (−). Determining the significance of these conditions is necessary to judge their expressive contribution. The following comparisons identify relative significance of certain characteristics. Comparisons are valid only within each line item. The order of the listing from "a" to "i" does not indicate relative significance between the line items. Characteristics in "a" are not necessarily more significant than those of "b," for example.

Relative Significance of Characteristics

a. Structural > decorative
b. More > less (unless identity is obscured by too many)
c. Parallel > nonparallel
d. Pattern > random
e. Equal spacing > unequal spacing
f. Three-dimensional > two-dimensional (freestanding > attached > recessed > graphic)
g. Contrasting > blending
h. Close > distant
i. High traffic proximity > low traffic proximity

CHECKLIST C-1: Analysis of Expression in Architecture

WOOD

Form

_____ **1.** Linearity in the building image.
   (+) An aesthetic order based on lines.
   (−) Absence of lines in the building image. An aesthetic order based on blocks or planes.

_____ **2.** Straightness in the building image.
   (+) An aesthetic order based on straight forms and segments. Absence of curves and approximated curves.
   (−) An aesthetic order based on curved or approximately curved forms and segments.

_____ **3.** Contribution to the building image by form characteristics of secondary products (if any).
   (+) Aspects of the building beyond the members themselves visibly affected by the forms of the secondary products.
   (−) Other materials could be substituted for the secondary products without a significant effect on the building image.

_____ **4.** Low level of refinement (rustic spirit) in the building image.
   (+) Connections lapped. Members have moderate visual mass. Frequent bracing against warpage.
   (−) Connections butted without significant steel expressed or "merged." Members appear to be delicate or have great visual mass.

Strength

_____ **5.** Demonstration of moderate strength as a significant part of the building image.
   (+) Moderate spans. Numerous members sharing the loads. Members of moderate section. Expression of steel in connections equal to its structural contribution.
   (−) Heroic spans. Few members of minimal section carrying large loads. Tiny spans. Many members of massive section carrying light loads. Hidden steel plates in connections.

_____ **6.** A sense of frames or framing as a significant part of the building image.
   (+) Balanced demonstration of resistance to bending, compression, and tension. Significant visual role of systems to resist lateral loads such as triangulation. A sense of repetitive and equally spaced frames.
   (−) Demonstration of great capability to resist compression, tension, or bending. Visual focus on resistance to compression or tension. Absence of visible systems to resist lateral forces.

Durability

_____ **7.** Demonstration of wood's very low resistance to deterioration as a part of the building image.
   (+) Significant visual role of methods to protect wood from decay

and termites, such as coatings, end-grain protection, separation from the earth, and sheltering.

(−) Image that wood will not deteriorate by the exposure of its bare surface and end grain to contact with moisture, the earth, and other deteriorating forces.

Workability

_____ 8. Demonstration of the relative ease with which the shapes of wood products may be changed as part of the building image.

(+) Significant visual roles of sawn, bent, lathed, drilled, and carved wood forms that require minimal skill and minimal sophistication of tools.

(−) Presence of wood that, by virtue of its reshaping, imitates other materials.

CHECKLIST C-2: Analysis of Expression in Architecture

MASONRY

Form

_____ 1. Blocklike characteristics in the building image.

(+) An aesthetic order based on blocklike shapes. Unit forms emphasized in surfaces, corners, and edges. A sense of rectangularity at the small scale.

(−) Absence of blocklike shapes in the building image. An aesthetic order based on lines or planes. An absence of rectangularity at the small scale.

_____ 2. Characteristics of the building image derived from the opportunities in form afforded by relatively small building units.

(+) Absence of long flat surfaces and long straight corners and edges. Curved walls with large radii.

(−) Excessive flatness and straightness in surfaces, corners, and edges. Curved walls with accidental textures.

_____ 3. Contribution to the building image by form characteristics of secondary products (if any).

(+) Aspects of the building beyond the members themselves visibly affected by the forms of the secondary products.

(−) Other materials could be substituted for the secondary products without a significant effect on the building image.

_____ 4. Medium level of refinement in the building image.

(+) Medium-to-high visual mass. Absence of delicate forms near high traffic.

(−) A sense of delicacy, especially in high-traffic areas.

Strength

_____ 5. Clarity of masonry's nearly complete limitation to compression resistance in the span systems contributing to the building image.
  (+) Absence of masonry spanning in any way or masonry spans limited to very short stone lintels and moderately sized arched forms. Arched spans have significant expression of thrust resistance.
  (−) Unit masonry spans apparently resisting bending action. Very large arched spans. Absence of expressed thrust resistance for arches. Apparent resistance to pure tension.

_____ 6. Extensive demonstration of compressive strength in walls and columns.
  (+) Overall sense of stacking. Air of stability conveyed by spread base, compact form, significant mass, and curved geometry.
  (−) Apparent instability under lateral loading such as suggested by tall slender forms without buttresses or buttressing from the geometry of the plan.

Durability

_____ 7. Demonstration of masonry's imperfect resistance to water penetration but high resistance to deterioration as a part of the building image. (Includes joints.)
  (+) Absence of paint. Expressed protection of joints in surfaces that are not vertical. Contact with the earth of masonry that does not enclose space. Separation from the earth of masonry that does.
  (−) Painted surfaces. Absence of visible protection for joints in horizontal surfaces.

Workability

_____ 8. Absence of the sense that cut or broken masonry contributes to the building image.
  (+) Cut or broken masonry eliminated or limited to an extent less than the standard needed for arches.
  (−) Use of cut masonry beyond the standard extent needed for arches, especially in slender or delicate shapes.

CHECKLIST C-3: Analysis of Expression in Architecture

STEEL

Form

_____ 1. Linearity in the building image.
  (+) An aesthetic order based on lines.
  (−) Absence of lines in the building image. An aesthetic order based on blocks or planes.

_____ 2. Straightness in the building image.
  (+) An aesthetic order based on straight forms and segments. Absence of curves and approximated curves.
  (−) An aesthetic order based on curved or approximately curved forms and segments.

____ **3.** Contribution to the building image by form characteristics of secondary products (if any).

   (+) Aspects of the building beyond the members themselves visibly affected by the forms of the secondary products.

   (−) Other materials could be substituted for the secondary products without a significant effect on the building image.

____ **4.** Very high level of refinement in the building image.

   (+) Connections butted. Members have low visual mass. Relative thinness and high precision apparent.

   (−) Connections lapped. Members have high visual mass. Detailing emphasizing mass with blocky and thick proportions.

Strength

____ **5.** Demonstration of very high tensile strength as a significant part of the building image.

   (+) Extensive use in pure tension and bending. Very large spans, especially cantilevers. Few members of moderate section or numerous members of small section carrying large loads.

   (−) Absence of apparent pure tension and bending resistance. Small spans. Many members of massive section carrying light loads.

____ **6.** A sense of frames or framing as a significant part of the building image.

   (+) A sense of repetitive and equally spaced frames. Significant visual role of systems to resist lateral loads such as triangulation or moment resistance in the connections.

   (−) Excessive focus on compressive resistance in the absence of framelike assemblies. Absence of visible systems to resist lateral forces.

Durability

____ **7.** Demonstration of steel's low resistance to rust as part of the building image. (Excluding stainless and weathering steels.)

   (+) Significant visual role of methods to protect steel from deterioration such as paint and separation from the earth.

   (−) Protective coatings that are not apparent. Protective coatings or coverings that eliminate the visual contribution of steel to the building image. Contact with the earth.

Workability

____ **8.** Demonstration of the moderate ease with which the shapes of steel products may be changed as a part of the building image.

   (+) Cut and bent steel limited to relatively thin sections. Clarity that large bent components are assembled from smaller bent sections.

   (−) Presence of steel that, by virtue of its reshaping, imitates other materials.

CHECKLIST C-4: Analysis of Expression in Architecture

CONCRETE

Form

_____ 1. Planar quality in the building image.
   (+) An aesthetic order based on planes.
   (−) Absence of planes in the building image. An aesthetic order based on blocks or lines.

_____ 2. (Cast-in-place) Curves in the building image.
   (+) An aesthetic order based on curved forms, especially of small radius and varied radii.
   (−) An aesthetic order based on straightness.

_____ 2a. (Precast) Straightness in the building image.*
   (+) An aesthetic order based on straight forms and segments. Absence of curves and approximated curves.
   (−) An aesthetic order based on curved or approximately curved forms and segments.
   *   Curves accepted in site-precast.

_____ 3. (Precast) Contribution to the building image by form characteristics of any secondary products.
   (+) Aspects of the building beyond the members themselves visibly affected by the forms of the secondary products.
   (−) Other materials could be substituted for the secondary products without a significant effect on the building image.

_____ 4. (Cast-in-place) Medium level of refinement in the building image.
   (+) Connections merged. Members have medium visual mass. Absence of sharpness.
   (−) Connections butted or lapped. Members appear to be delicate or have great visual mass. Presence of sharpness.

_____ 4a. (Precast) Medium level of refinement in the building image.
   (+) Lapped or ledge-supported butt connections. Members have medium visual mass. Absence of sharpness.
   (−) Connections merged or butted without a supporting ledge. Members appear to be delicate or have great visual mass. Presence of sharpness.

Strength

_____ 5. Demonstration of high bending strength in spanning systems as part of the building image.
   (+) Long spans, especially cantilevers. Members of moderate section. Absence of apparent pure tension.
   (−) Small spans. Moderate-span arches with thrust resistance expressed. Apparent pure tension.

_____ 6. Demonstration of high bending strength in walls and columns as part of the building image.
   (+) Clear need for moment resistance in vertical components (especially at the bases of cast-in-place components) such as achieved by great height with moderate thickness or a position that is leaning.
   (−) Exaggerated sense of stability in vertical components causing a focus on compression only.

Durability

_____ **7.** Demonstration of concrete's very high resistance to deterioration as a part of the building image.

(+) Exaggerated challenges to concrete from deteriorating elements. Absence of coatings or coverings. Exposure to moisture and the earth.

(−) Apparent lack of confidence in concrete's deterioration resistance. Protective coatings and coverings. Separation from the earth. Sheltering from weather.

Workability

_____ **8.** Demonstration of the very low workability level of cured concrete.

(+) Absence of cutting, chipping, rubbing, or other attempts to change the shape or texture of cured concrete.

(−) Apparent cutting, chipping, rubbing, or other attempts to change the shape or texture of cured concrete, especially when results that could have been cast initially are achieved. Imitation of another material as a result of shaping processes applied after curing.

Appendix D

TEXTURES OF CURVED MASONRY WALLS (running bond)

It is necessary to cut units to achieve curves of radii which are small relative to the thickness of the unit measured on the radius.

LENGTH OF UNIT MEASURED TANGENT TO CIRCUMFERENCE[a]	RADIUS TO CENTER OF OUTSIDE FACE OF UNIT	PROJECTION OF UNIT CORNERS[b]
2 in.[c]	1 ft 3-31/32 in.	1/32 in.
(such as a *Roman* brick in	7-15/16 in.	1/16 in.
a soldier position)	3-7/8 in.	1/8 in.
	1-3/4 in.	1/4 in.
2-2/3 in.[c]	2 ft 4-13/32 in.	1/32 in.
(such as *standard modular*	1 ft 2-5/32 in.	1/16 in.
brick in a soldier position)	7 in.	1/8 in.
	3-5/16 in.	1/4 in.
3-1/5 in.[c]	3 ft 4-15/16 in.	1/32 in.
(such as an *engineer* brick	1 ft 8-13/32 in.	1/16 in.
in a soldier position)	10-1/8 in.	1/8 in.
	4-7/8 in.	1/4 in.
4 in.	5 ft 3-31/32 in.	1/32 in.
(such as a *standard*	2 ft 7-15/16 in.	1/16 in.
modular brick in a header	1 ft 3-7/8 in.	1/8 in.
position)	7-3/4 in.	1/4 in.
5 1/3 in.[c]	9 ft 5-25/32 in.	1/32 in.
(such as a *double* brick	4 ft 8-7/8 in.	1/16 in.
in a soldier position)	2 ft 4-5/16 in.	1/8 in.
	1 ft 2-7/32 in.	1/4 in.
6 in.	11 ft 11-31/32 in.	1/32 in.
(such as an *SCR* brick in a	5 ft 11-15/16 in.	1/16 in.
header position)	2 ft 11-7/8 in.	1/8 in.
	1 ft 5-3/4 in.	1/4 in.
8 in.	21 ft 3-31/32 in.	1/32 in.
(such as a *standard modular*	10 ft 7-15/16 in.	1/16 in.
brick in a stretcher	5 ft 3-7/8 in.	1/8 in.
position)	2 ft 7-3/4 in.	1/4 in.

LENGTH OF UNIT MEASURED TANGENT TO CIRCUMFERENCE[a]	RADIUS TO CENTER OF OUTSIDE FACE OF UNIT	PROJECTION OF UNIT CORNERS[b]
10 in.	33 ft 3-31/32 in.	1/32 in.
(such as a *king-size* brick	16 ft 7-15/16 in.	1/16 in.
in a stretcher	8 ft 3-7/8 in.	1/8 in.
position)	4 ft 1-3/4 in.	1/4 in.
12 in.	47 ft 11-31/32 in.	1/32 in.
(such as a *Roman* brick in	23 ft 11-15/16 in.	1/16 in.
a stretcher position)	11 ft 11-7/8 in.	1/8 in.
	5 ft 11-3/4 in.	1/4 in.
16 in.	85 ft 3-31/32 in.	1/32 in.
(such as a *standard*	42 ft 7-15/16 in.	1/16 in.
concrete block in a	21 ft 3-7/8 in.	1/8 in.
stretcher position)	10 ft 7-3/4 in.	1/4 in.

[a]Nominal dimensions.

[b]Nominal dimensions. The dimension represents the projection of a unit's corners beyond the faces of units above and below if the unit faces continued to the center of the head joints. Actual corner projections are slightly less than these dimensions.

[c]The soldier dimensions are provided for general information, as soldier units are rarely set in running bond. They are almost always set in stack bond, where the faces of all units in a stack are flush (corners do not project beyond the units above and below).

Appendix E

SPAN/DEPTH RATIOS FOR SELECTED SYSTEMS

SPANNING SYSTEM	USUAL MATERIALS AND TYPES	USUAL SPAN RANGE (M)	TYPICAL SPAN/ DEPTH RATIO	TYPICAL SPAN/ THICKNESS RATIO
Cable	Steel with joist or concrete panel deck	30–150	DNA	300+
Arch	Timber, glued laminated	20–40	DNA	35
	Timber truss	30–70	DNA	40
	Steel truss	40–100	DNA	40
	Reinforced concrete, convoluted or ribbed	20–70	DNA	30
Flat deck, floor	Wood Joist with plywood subfloor	2–6	20	DNA
	Beam with planks	4–9	18	DNA
	Steel Beam w/steel subfloor or concrete slab	5–15	22	DNA
	Bar joist with steel subfloor	4–20	22	DNA
	Reinf. concrete Flat plate w/ or w/o drop panels	3–6	30	DNA
	Beam with flat slab	5–10	15	DNA
	Pan joist	5–10	20	DNA
	Waffle pan	7–14	22	DNA
	Precast plank	6–12	38	DNA
Truss	Timber members	7–30	5–12	DNA
	Steel members	20–60	5–15	DNA

SPANNING SYSTEM	USUAL MATERIALS AND TYPES	USUAL SPAN RANGE (M)	TYPICAL SPAN/ DEPTH RATIO	TYPICAL SPAN/ THICKNESS RATIO
Dome	Reinforced concrete thin shell	15–50	DNA	200
	Reinforced concrete (convoluted or ribbed)	30–100	DNA	40
	Steel truss	40–150	DNA	60
Vault	Reinforced concrete thin shell	20–60	DNA	175
Barrel vault and folded plate	Reinforced concrete thin shell	20–40	12	200
Space frame	Steel members	20–80	30	DNA
Warped surface	Reinforced concrete thin shell	20–60	DNA	200
Cable net	Steel	30–100	DNA	600+
Air	Fabric-supported	40–200	DNA	1000+
	Fabric-inflated	20–60	DNA	30

Source: Printed with permission from Prentice Hall, R. E. Shaeffer, *Building Structures: Elementary Analysis and Design* (Englewood Cliffs, N.J.: Prentice Hall, 1980) pp. 8–9.

GLOSSARY

ACADEMIC REFERENCE: A detail that refers to a concept or real element that is not apparent. The image of a lintel painted on brick which passes over the top of an opening in a straight horizontal running bond is an academic reference to the hidden steel lintel.

BATTERED SURFACE: A nearly vertical sloped surface which leans away from the observer. The surface may be stepped or smooth.

BLOCKLIKE: The characteristic describing a form that is compact and has 90-degree corners. The longest dimension is not significantly longer than short-est dimension. To be blocklike, a form does not have to have three equal dimensions.

BUTT CONNECTION: A connection in which the end of one member meets the face or end of another.

CURVILINEAR: Having curves.

DURABILITY: The ability to resist deterioration from such forces as decay, corrosion, insects, and fire.

EXPRESSION: A visual statement or image that draws attention. A construc-tion that is visible but does not draw attention is not expressive. Expression or positive expression usually refers to the exhibition of characteristics that are within the nature of a material. A negative expression usually refers to an exhibition that violates the nature of a material. A two-dimensional expression is graphic or has an insignificant third dimension. A three-dimensional expres-sion exhibits length, width, and depth.

FORM: A primary form is identified as the one that best represents the basic spirit of its material. Typically, it is the form of a common one-piece structural product from the first manufacturing process. Secondary forms are all other standard products.

FREESTANDING: Nearly or completely detached from other constructions. A freestanding column does not touch the building except at certain points, such as where building loads are applied or at lateral bracing. The expression of a freestanding component is three-dimensional.

LINEAR: The characteristic describing a form that has one dimension which is many times longer than the other two. A linear form is more like a line than it is like a plane or a block.

MERGED CONNECTION: A connection in which the members share particles at the intersection. The molecules of a beam are actually the molecules of a column, and vice versa, in the zone where they cross.

MOMENT: The tendency to rotate, bend, or change angle due to an applied force. Wind creates a moment in a freestanding wall which is greatest at the base. The tendency of the wall is to bend or lean, which causes tensile stresses on the windward side and compressive stresses on the leeward side.

NATURE: Spirit, essence, or personality. Manifested in materials by their properties and assembly characteristics.

OVERLAPPING CONNECTION: A connection in which the members pass beside and project beyond each other.

PLANAR: The characteristic describing a form (having a structural identity in its own right) which has two dimensions that are not significantly different from each other but are many times greater than the third dimension, which is, itself, significant.

RECTANGULAR: Having 90-degree angles or having the form of a rectangle. Rectangular is a two-dimensional characteristic, in contrast to *planar*, which requires a significant third dimension. Plywood, steel plate, and stone panel cladding are rectangular but not planar.

RECTILINEAR: A straight line, or having straight lines.

REFINEMENT: A measure of precision and thinness and the relative (a comparison between materials) permanence of these qualities. Visually delicate without being physically delicate.

ROTATION: The tendency to change angle due to an applied force. A loaded beam tends to change the 90-degree angle it forms with a column. Although the change will be very small, the beam is tending to rotate.

TRIANGULATION: Providing rigidity to a structure by incorporating triangles in the framing.

VIOLATION: Usually refers to detailing that is not compatible with the nature of a material.

VISUAL MASS: Bulk. Does not refer to weight. A material of high visual mass may weigh less than a material of low visual mass.

WORKABILITY: The ease with which a material's final manufactured form can be changed. Workability is inversely proportional to skill level and sophistication of equipment required. This use of the word is not to be confused with its traditional use in the concrete industry, where "workability" refers to the ability of plastic concrete to flow. "Workability" here refers to the ease of reshaping cured concrete and finished products of other materials.

Index